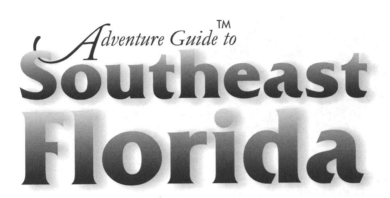

Adventure Guide to ™

Southeast Florida

Sharon Lloyd Spence & Warren Lieb

HUNTER

Hunter Publishing, Inc.
130 Campus Drive, Edison, NJ 08818
732 225 1900 / 800 255 0343 / Fax 732 417 1744
hunterpub@emi.net

In Canada:
1220 Nicholson Road, Newmarket, Ontario
Canada L3Y 7V1
800 399 6858 / Fax 800 363 2665

ISBN 1-55650-811-5

For complete information about the hundreds of other
travel guides offered by Hunter Publishing, visit our Web site at
www.hunterpublishing.com

Cover photo: *Great Egret (Casmerodius albus)*
© Daniel J. Cox, Natural Exposures, Inc.

Back cover: *Kayaking on the Loxahatchee River,* © Warren Lieb

Page 170, *Jupiter Lighthouse,* Barry E. Parker,
courtesy JTJB Chamber of Commerce.

All other photos © Warren Lieb, except as noted.

Maps by Lissa K. Dailey, © 1998 Hunter Publishing, Inc.

2 3 4 5

Contents

Introduction   1
  History   3
  Geography & Climate   11
  Flora & Fauna   14
  How to Use This Book   18
  Information Sources   24

Miami & Surrounding Areas   29
  Getting Here   29
  Getting Around   29
  South Dade   33
    Getting Here   33
    Adventures   33
      On Foot   33
      On Wheels   34
      On Water   35
      In the Air   38
      Other Adventures   40
    Sightseeing   40
    Festivals & Events   42
    Where to Stay   43
      Camping   43
    Where to Eat   45
  Coral Gables & Coconut Grove   47
    Getting Here   47
    Adventures   47
      On Foot   47
      On Wheels   50
      On Water   50
      Other Adventures   52
    Sightseeing   52
      Coral Gables   52
      Coconut Grove   54
    Festivals & Events   57
    Where to Stay   60
      Coral Gables   60
      Coconut Grove   61
    Where to Eat   62

Key Biscayne 65
  Getting Here 65
  Adventures 65
    On Foot 65
    On Wheels 67
    On Water 68
    Other Adventures 70
  Sightseeing 71
  Festivals & Events 72
  Where to Stay 73
  Where to Eat 74
Downtown & Greater Miami 75
  Adventures 76
    On Foot 76
    On Wheels 78
    On Water 79
    Other Adventures 81
  Sightseeing 82
  Entertainment 83
  Festivals & Events 84
  Where to Stay 86
  Camping 88
  Where to Eat 88
Miami Beach 89
  Getting Here 90
  Adventures 91
    On Foot 91
    On Wheels 92
    On Water 94
    In the Air 96
  Sightseeing 98
  Museums 99
  Festivals & Events 100
  Where to Stay 102
  Where to Eat 104
North Miami Beach 105
  Adventures 106
    On Foot 106
    On Wheels 106
    On Water 107
  Sightseeing 109
  Shopping 109

Where to Stay 109
Where to Eat 112

Greater Fort Lauderdale 113
Getting Here 113
Getting Around 113
Hollywood 114
Adventures 114
On Foot 114
On Wheels 116
On Water 116
In the Air 118
Other Adventures 120
Davie 120
Adventures 120
On Foot 120
On Wheels 121
On Water 121
On Horseback 124
Fort Lauderdale 124
Adventures 124
On Foot 124
On Water 125
Sightseeing 130
Festivals & Events 132
Where to Stay 134
Camping 135
Where to Eat 137
Pompano Beach to Deerfield Beach 140
Adventures 141
On Foot 141
On Wheels 142
On Water 143
On Horseback 145
Other Adventures 145
Sightseeing 145
Festivals & Events 146
Where to Stay 147
Where to Eat 148

The Palm Beaches 151
Getting Here 151
Getting Around 151

Boca Raton	152
Adventures	153
On Foot	153
On Water	156
On Horseback	158
Sightseeing	158
Museums & Culture	158
Festivals & Events	161
Where to Stay	162
Camping	163
Where to Eat	163
Palm Beach to Jupiter	165
Adventures	165
On Foot	165
On Wheels	174
On Water	176
In the Air	181
On Horseback	181
Other Adventures	183
Sightseeing	184
Festivals & Events	187
Where to Stay	189
Camping	192
Where to Eat	193
The Treasure Coast	197
Hobe Sound to Ft. Pierce	197
Adventures	197
On Foot	197
On & In the Water	206
In the Air	219
Other Adventures	221
Sightseeing	221
Festivals & Events	223
Where to Stay	225
Camping	227
Where to Eat	227
Vero Beach & Sebastian	231
Adventures	231
On Foot	231
On Water	233
In the Air	237
Other Adventures	238

Sightseeing	238
Museums & Culture	238
Where to Stay	239
Camping	240
Where to Eat	241
Index	**243**

Maps

Areas covered in this guide	x
Miami & Surrounding Areas	28
South Dade	32
Coral Gables	49
Coconut Grove	55
Key Biscayne	64
Downtown Miami	77
Miami Beach & South Beach	90
North Miami Beach, Surfside, Bay Harbor	111
Ft. Lauderdale	115
The Palm Beaches	150
Boca Raton, Delray Beach	153
West Palm Beach, Palm Beach	166
North Palm Beach, Palm Beach Gardens, Juno Beach & Jupiter	168
The Treasure Coast	196
Hobe Sound, Stuart, Jensen Beach	198
Jonathan Dickinson State Park	200
Hutchinson Island & Ft. Pierce	202
Vero Beach & Sebastian	230

☘ ☘ ☘

Acknowledgments

We gratefully thank our sponsors, Continental Airlines and Alamo Rental Cars. Others whose helpful assistance is most appreciated are: Ginny Gutierrez, Miami Convention & Visitors Bureau; Stacy Faulds, Greater Fort Lauderdale Convention & Visitors Bureau; Rebecca Widness, Silver Associates Inc.; Kerry Jennings, Boca Raton Chamber of Commerce; Donna Nottoli, Palm Beach County Convention and Visitors Bureau; Christine Nolan, Stuart/Martin County Chamber of Commerce; Lori D. Burns, Vero Beach-Indian River County Tourist Council, Lana Wilken and Robin Knight, Florida Tourism Corporation. Thanks to our editor, Lissa Dailey, for her encouragement and expertise, and to the adventurers, hotel managers, tour guides, restaurant managers and chefs for their generosity and enthusiasm.

Last, but not least, we thank our friend and neighbor, Gail Green, for her computer expertise.

❦ ❦ ❦

About the Author & Photographer

Sharon Lloyd Spence

Sharon Lloyd Spence is the author of guidebooks on Seoul, Grand Cayman Island, Florida, Chicago, and Santa Fe. She became a traveler late in life, and now explores the world seeking new adventures.

She lives in Los Alamos, New Mexico with her husband, photographer Warren Lieb, and their cat, Roscoe.

Warren H. Lieb

Filmmaker, video producer, and travel photographer Warren Lieb has shot motion pictures and still photos in Vietnam, Korea, Nigeria, Chile, Brazil, Israel, Jordan, Morocco, Burma, Japan, Thailand and throughout Europe. His goal is to continue creating travel books and having adventures.

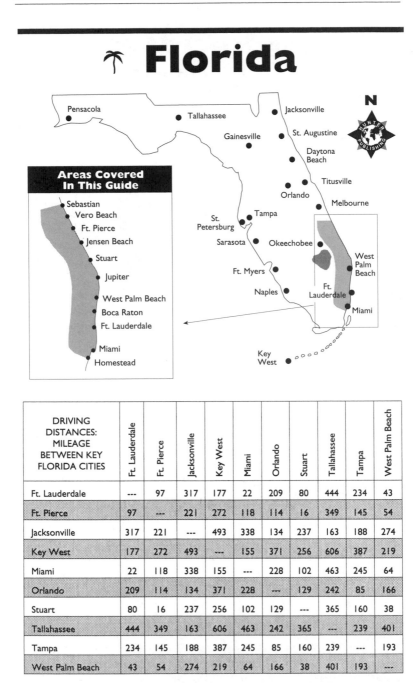

DRIVING DISTANCES: MILEAGE BETWEEN KEY FLORIDA CITIES	Ft. Lauderdale	Ft. Pierce	Jacksonville	Key West	Miami	Orlando	Stuart	Tallahassee	Tampa	West Palm Beach
Ft. Lauderdale	---	97	317	177	22	209	80	444	234	43
Ft. Pierce	97	---	221	272	118	114	16	349	145	54
Jacksonville	317	221	---	493	338	134	237	163	188	274
Key West	177	272	493	---	155	371	256	606	387	219
Miami	22	118	338	155	---	228	102	463	245	64
Orlando	209	114	134	371	228	---	129	242	85	166
Stuart	80	16	237	256	102	129	---	365	160	38
Tallahassee	444	349	163	606	463	242	365	---	239	401
Tampa	234	145	188	387	245	85	160	239	---	193
West Palm Beach	43	54	274	219	64	166	38	401	193	---

Introduction

I looked for adventure in Southeast Florida and almost missed it. With bumper-to-bumper traffic on six-lane highways, the scene was dizzying: Publix grocery stores, Eckerd Drugs, Barnett Banks, Radio Shacks, Burger Kings, McDonald's, Pizza Huts, Kentucky Fried Chickens, and Wal-Marts. Mirrored high-rises, gated neighborhoods, country clubs, trailer parks, and strip malls hawking T-shirts, bikinis and ball caps. Could I find adventure in Southeast Florida?

While researching this book, I came across a quaint tourism promotion published in a 1925 issue of *The Miamian:* "Go to Florida where enterprise is enthroned – where you sit and watch at twilight the fronds of the graceful palm, latticed against the fading gold of the sun-kissed sky."

Does this dreamlike paradise still exist? Is there a "sun-kissed" Florida sky not silhouetted with condos, telephone wires, and neon signs? Are there adventures beyond trendy restaurants, luxury hotels, hip nightclubs, and designer boutiques?

Fortunately, friends and contacts put me in touch with a group of adventurous Floridians. Scuba divers, skydivers, helicopter pilots, deep-sea fishermen, polo players, kayakers, bikers, surfers, balloonists, and park rangers. Outdoor lovers who appreciate Florida's parks, birds, beaches, oceans, rivers, and nature preserves. Thrill-seekers willing to share Florida's adventurous side with visitors like me and you.

When the student is ready the teacher appears. I was ready to dive deeply, soar high above the clouds, venture by foot into forests, by boat into rivers. "Get wet, get dirty, get involved," my teachers encouraged. So I did.

Some of Southeast Florida's adventurers who inspired me:

Ed Bailey, who loves every bend in the Loxahatchee River he's spent a lifetime canoeing; **Terry O'Toole,** who knows the area's best surfing beach and where great horned owls nest; **Alice Butler,** who teaches people to fly a helicopter in one amazing hour; **Vesna Galesic,** who shares the joys of in-line skating in South Miami Beach; **Jeff Bingham,** who has discovered most of

Florida by kayak; and **Todd Carter,** who reveals the Zen of wall climbing in just one lesson.

Along the way I discovered that adventure can be deeply personal, sometimes grabbing you by surprise. Some of my own unexpected adventures:

- Immersing myself in Florida's color palette: relishing a sapphire sky, an emerald ocean, and a crimson sunset, while snuggling into a yellow lounge chair under a poppy-red umbrella.

- Getting soaked while striding through crashing waves at twilight.

- Canoeing alongside mangroves hoping to see a manatee, and having an entire family surface next to my canoe.

- Paddling a kayak near a 1,500-passenger luxury cruise ship and feeling happily small.

- Reeling in a six-foot sailfish, then setting it free.

- Envying the gracefulness of a pink flamingo balanced on one leg.

- Discovering there are 2,700 varieties of palms, 700 of which thrive at Fairchild Tropical Garden.

- Being awed by a great blue heron flying gracefully across my kayak.

- Climbing 109 circular stairs to the balcony of the Bill Baggs Cape Florida Lighthouse and feeling exhilarated.

- Looking into the eyes of a living conch and putting it back into the ocean.

- Gazing into a river and seeing fish staring back.

- Realizing a great white heron is an angel with a beak.

- Learning it's adventurous to daydream and just *be*, instead of *do*.

Finding adventure in Southeast Florida isn't always easy, but it's there if you make the effort. Don't just laze away your vacation. Grab an adventure: it may change your life.

History

Geological Beginnings

Florida's emergence from the ocean as a 4,298-square-mile, finger-shaped peninsula of streams and springs, rivers and lakes, lagoons and swamps goes back hundreds of millions of years. South Florida began life as an arc of volcanic mountains buried 13,000 feet beneath the sea. Limestone sediment was deposited on the underwater plain, caused by erosion of the mountains, whose weight made the land sink even deeper. Over one hundred million years, thousands of feet of limestone were formed, composed mostly of the skeletons of microscopic sea animals. Centuries later, fine sand and clay washed down from the northern mountains, settling over Florida's plateau. The limestone layers arched, and sections of Florida rose 150 feet above sea level. Wind and waves extended Florida's peninsula along the emerging coral reefs, forming marshes and lagoons. This was during the Late Tertiary period.

During the Pleistocene era, an ice sheet covered much of Canada and the northern United States. At this period of development Florida became cool and rainy. Because so much of the earth's water supply was stored in these ice glaciers, the world's sea level was lowered, leaving much of the Continental Shelf exposed. Florida became twice the size it is today.

Herbivorous animals seeking to escape the great ice sheet trudged southward seeking green pastures in warmer territories. Three-toed horses, giant pigs, rhinoceroses, camels, mammoths, sloths, armadillos, and peccaries found a home in Florida.

These docile vegetarians soon became meals for carnivorous beasts of prey: sabre-toothed tigers, four-tusked mastodons, wolves, and lions, who devoured the leaf eaters.

During the Pleistocene and Holocene periods, the northern ice sheet melted and reformed. Sea levels rose and fell, carving bluffs and terraces into the land. The climate became drier, and winds scattered sand dunes onto the newly formed terraces.

Today Florida's landscape is still sculpted by rain, rivers, waves, and wind, continuing to change geographically as the east coast builds up and the west coast gradually sinks.

Signs of Humanity: The First Adventurers

Florida's first human inhabitants arrived about 8000 B.C. There are few clues to the history and lifestyle of these early Floridians except tools and other household artifacts unearthed by modern archaeologists. Written records about life in Florida began with the arrival of Spanish explorer and adventurer Juan Ponce de León in 1513.

The Search for the Fountain of Youth

Juan Ponce de León, whom Spain had made Governor of Puerto Rico, was enthralled with tales told by Puerto Rican Indians. They spoke of a land called Bimini to the northwest, where land was abundant with gold and a magical fountain flowed with water, restoring youth to the aged and health to the sick.

Although drawings of the time show Ponce de León as a robust 50-year-old, the adventurous and capitalistic entrepreneur was eager to see these miracles for himself. On March 5, 1512, he set sail with the *Santa Maria de la Consolacion* and the *Santiago.* After three weeks of journeying through the Bahamas, he sighted Florida's coast at a point just north of where St. Augustine is today, and on April 2 he landed to claim the country in the name of King Ferdinand V of Spain. He never found Bimini, but was delighted with the tropical paradise he did discover.

Ponce and his crew had celebrated "Pascua Florida" (the Feast of Flowers, or Easter) aboard ship before sighting land. So, when he arrived in Florida, he prayed, "Thanks be to Thee, O Lord, Who hast permitted me to see something new." Then he christened the land in honor of the holiday season – "La Florida." The name stuck.

Although he sailed southeast down to the Keys, and up the west coast to Pensacola during a six-month search, Ponce de León never found gold or the fountain of youth. But he returned in 1521 with two shiploads of colonists, horses, cattle, farm tools and seeds to settle the land he would now govern.

Ponce de León and his settlers never found peace in paradise. Florida's Indian natives resented their intrusion and defended their homeland, attacking the Spaniards with stones and arrows. Illness and wounds from Indian battles forced Ponce de León and his entire colony to flee for Cuba after just five months, where the Spanish explorer soon died. His quest had been in vain.

Other Spanish adventurers had heard of "La Florida" and were eager to colonize it, despite stories of Indian battles. In 1539, Hernando de Soto landed between Fort Myers and Tampa. He traveled north, discovering the Mississippi and fighting with Indian tribes, which eventually led to his death as well.

During his travels, de Soto met Juan Ortiz, a Spanish soldier who had accompanied an earlier explorer named Panfilo de Narvaez into the Panhandle area. Ortiz' reports of his experience with the Indians were detailed, and have provided historians most of what is known about early Florida natives.

Although Spanish explorers discovered neither gold nor fountains of youth, their tales of adventure and discovery spread throughout Europe.

Florida's reputation as a land of riches attracted other nations who wanted their slice of the pie. In 1562, the French dispatched Jean Ribault to establish a colony for religious freedom. Two years later, fellow Frenchman René de Goulaine de Laudonnière established Fort Caroline at the mouth of the St. Johns River, which is near present-day Jacksonville.

The Spanish were furious at this French intrusion, and King Philip promptly commanded Pedro Menendez de Aviles, captain general of the armed fleet, to destroy the French colony. In August 1565, Menendez arrived at a harbor he called San Augustin, and the following month established the first permanent European settlement in what is now the United States.

Menendez and his troops massacred the French, renamed Fort Caroline to San Mateo, and converted it into a Spanish outpost. Spanish missionaries, Jesuit and Franciscan friars, then set about converting the Indians to Christianity, trying to save their "heathen souls," amidst all the murder committed by their Spanish leaders in God's name.

Meanwhile, in Europe, the French made plans to avenge the loss of Fort Caroline. Dominique de Gourgues launched an expedition, captured San Mateo and hanged the Spaniards. Triumphant, he returned to France.

England was eager to make her own conquests. In 1586, Captain Sir Francis Drake sacked and burned St. Augustine. This did little to diminish Spanish control of Florida, as more forts and missions were built throughout the state and into southern Virginia. This prompted the English to colonize farther up the east coast in Jamestown and Plymouth. They wanted more and more New World resources for themselves, and gradually pushed the northern border of Spanish Florida southward to its present border.

The English also colonized South Carolina. In 1701, the Carolinians and their Indian allies laid siege to Spanish Florida, capturing the town of St. Augustine, although they were unsuccessful and had to withdraw. Two years later they destroyed the missions of the interior area between Pensacola and St. Augustine, killing and enslaving many Indians.

The French continued their harassment of the Spanish, with their capture of Pensacola in 1719. But the English threat soon united Spain and France, and the colony was given back to the Spanish. The French returned to their settlements along the Gulf Coast, west of Pensacola.

Spanish & English Play Tug of War

Spanish dominance in Florida began to weaken. In 1740, British General James Oglethorpe seized outlying Spanish forts and bombarded Fort Castillo de San Marcos in St. Augustine. After almost a month of bloodshed, he unsuccessfully withdrew. The English persevered, using other strategies. During the Seven Years' War, 1756-1763, England captured Havana, Cuba from the Spanish. To get it back, Spain relinquished Florida. The Spanish evacuated Florida, leaving it virtually empty.

England split Florida into two parts: East Florida, with its capital at St. Augustine, and West Florida, with its capital at Pensacola. They offered export subsidies and land grants to attract new settlers, and mapped out inhabited areas of the state. Peaceful relationships were developed with the Creek Indians, who had moved into Florida from Alabama and Georgia and

BUSINESS REPLY MAIL

FIRST-CLASS MAIL   PERMIT NO 3132   LONG BEACH CA

POSTAGE WILL BE PAID BY ADDRESSEE

AARP MEMBERSHIP CENTER
PO BOX 93156
LONG BEACH CA 90809-9893

FREE Gift with Membership

Give this card to a friend or relative to sign up for an AARP membership, *and* they'll get a FREE insulated travel bag just for joining.

Prefer the insulated travel bag for yourself? You can use this card to renew your own AARP membership, and we'll send *you* the FREE gift!

☐ 1 year/$16
☐ 3 years/$43
☐ 5 years/$63

☐ Check or money order enclosed, payable to AARP. (No cash please.)
☐ Please bill me later.

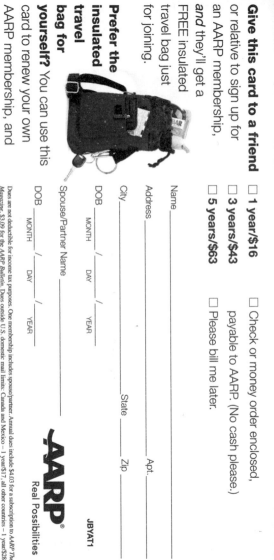

Name _____

Address _____

City _____ State _____ Zip _____

DOB ___/___/___
    MONTH DAY YEAR

Spouse/Partner Name _____

DOB ___/___/___
    MONTH DAY YEAR

AARP Real Possibilities

JBYAT1

changed their triba name to Seminole. Plantations of indigo, rice and citrus sprang up, worked by slaves brought to Florida from Africa and the West Indies.

British ownership was not to last. In 1783, Spain took revenge for losing Florida by capturing the British-owned Bahamas. To regain the islands, England returned Florida to Spain. Once again, the tables were turned as the Spanish flag flew over Florida yet a second time.

Florida's Americanization 1800-1865

Spain's second attempt to develop Florida was a failure from the start. British plantation owners left, and Spanish and American colonists poured in. Many were plantation slaves trying to escape. Instead of becoming more Spanish, Florida became more American, although most of the territory still belonged to the Indians.

Florida's provisional governor, Andrew Jackson, decided in 1818 to move the Seminole Indians to the central part of the peninsula, causing the First Seminole War.

In 1819, Spain and the United States began negotiations to transfer the Spanish colony to the United States of America. Two years later, the Stars and Stripes became the fourth national flag to fly over Florida, with Andrew Jackson the first Governor of Florida Territory. By 1824, Florida's capital was established in Tallahassee, where immigrants from Georgia, Virginia, and North Carolina began their new lives as Americans. By 1830, Florida's population had grown from 15,000 to 34,000.

Indians vs. the White Man

Hostilities between whites and Indians increased as more settlers moved in. A government movement was started to send the Indians to reservations west of the Mississippi.

In 1832, a delegation of chiefs refused to sign a treaty committing them to move after inspecting the land specified in the treaty. Their resistance was led by a young warrior named Osceola, stepson of white trader William Powell, and son of an Indian woman from the Red Stick tribe, a branch of the Creek. His grandfather was Scotch.

Although Osceola was not a chief and had no voice in the councils of his tribe, his leadership skills soon gained him the respect of his chiefs.

When the Seminoles refused to abandon their homes, white settlers tried to move the Indians by force, even seizing Osceola's wife Che-cho-ter as a fugitive slave. The Second Seminole War (1835-42) took a terrible toll on Indian and white lives. Indian war parties attacked Fort King near Ocala, and ambushed two companies of US troops near Bushnell in The Dade Massacre.

Refusing to surrender, Osceola and his warriors sent a message to US troops: "Your men will fight and so will ours, until the last drop of Seminole blood has moistened the dust of hunting ground."

Losses were severe for both sides. The US Government spent $40,000,000 on the war, and lost 2500 soldiers. Osceola, who eventually entered the American camp under a truce flag, was captured and imprisoned; he died in a military jail. And 3,824 Seminole Indians and blacks were sent to Arkansas. Only 300 remained in Florida, some on desolate reservations, others escaping to the Everglades.

Preparing for Statehood and Another War

With the war over, Florida prepared for statehood. Economic progress was everywhere: steamboats chugged the Apalachicola and St. Johns Rivers; cotton and tobacco plantations spread in every direction; and the Tallahassee to St. Marks and St. Joseph-Lake Wimico railroads were completed.

In 1845, Florida became the 27th member of the United States, and William D. Moseley was elected Governor. Five years later, the population had grown to 87,445, which included about 39,000 slaves and 1,000 free blacks. In 1855, the General Assembly passed the first Internal Improvement Act, which enabled swamp and other land ceded to the state by the federal government to become part of an intrastate system of canals and railroads. Despite a period of peace and prosperity, the slavery issue began to dominate Florida's affairs. Most voters did not object to slavery and were angry over the challenge to what they felt was a normal aspect of life. Southerners moved into the Democratic camp, leaving the strength of the newly organized Republican party to the northern states. With the election of Republican Abraham Lincoln as President in 1860, the Florida Legislature rushed into a constitutional convention, appropriating $100,000 for state troops. In 1861, Florida withdrew from the Union as the War Between the States began. During the next four years, Florida furnished 15,000 troops for the Confederate Army, a Florida militia, plus salt, beef, bacon and cotton. During the final months of the war, home guards saved Tallahassee from capture by turning back invading Union forces at the Battle of Natural Bridge. Tallahassee was the only Confederate capital east of the Mississippi River to escape occupation.

As the war came to a close, Federal troops entered Tallahassee on May 10, 1865. Ten days later, the American flag flew over the Florida Capitol once again. A Florida constitutional convention convened Oct. 25, 1865, annulling the Ordinance of Secession. Slavery was finally abolished. However, freedom was still severely restricted, as the right to vote was granted only to "free white male persons of 21 years or more, but none others."

Post-War Changes

Lives and fortunes of Floridians changed significantly after the war. Slaves were now free, and were paid to raise and pick cotton. But many slaves were eager to leave the plantations that had owned them, and so land began to be cultivated by tenant farmers and sharecroppers, who were both black and white.

The last years of the century brought intensive development throughout Florida. St. Augustine was a peaceful fishing village that began to attract tourists. Key West, with 18,000 people, was the largest city, and was both a prosperous naval base and the center of the sponge and cigar industries. Jacksonville owed its prosperity to lumber resources and naval ports. Pensacola was an important Gulf port, and Tampa took off when cigar manufacturers moved from Key West to Ybor City.

Plantations in the north and west produced cotton, corn, and tobacco, orange groves in the northeastern area were growing in commercial importance, and vast phosphate deposits had been discovered in the center of the State. Railroads and tourist hotels built in the 1880's by Henry M. Flagler and H.B. Plant drew thousands of tourists eager to visit Florida's glorious east and west coasts.

The citrus industry spread throughout the state, but cold freezes in 1894 and 1895 ruined most of the groves, forcing many north Florida growers to find other less weather-dependent livelihoods. Farmers who survived developed improved strains of citrus that were hardier and bloomed later in the season, enabling Florida to become the nation's top citrus producer. World War I put a hold on much of Florida's commercial business, but tourism prospered as "snowbirds" came south for sunshine, beaches and adventure.

After the war, real estate deals lured thousands of speculators to buy land and re-sell it for huge profits, turning some risk-takers into overnight millionaires. Between 1920 and 1925, the population increased four times as fast as any other state.

In spring of 1926, the bubble burst – banks failed and millionaires became paupers. That fall, a hurricane killed hundreds of Floridians and left thousands homeless. Two years later another hurricane hit, causing even worse devastation.

The stock market crashed in 1929, plunging the US into the Great Depression. More bad news came when the Mediterranean fruit fly invaded Florida, destroying 60% of the citrus groves. To recover from these years of crisis, Florida entrepreneurs turned to the development of tangible resources, such as paper mills, cooperative farms, port improvements, and commercial real estate.

A Boost from World War II

During World War II (1941-1945), Florida became a training center for troops, sailors, and airmen of the US and her allies at Camp Blanding and Camp Gordon Johnston. Tourist hotels and restaurants in Miami Beach, Daytona Beach, and St. Petersburg became manufacturing centers, where vessels and tools were forged. Highway and airport construction was accelerated, and by the war's end Florida had an up-to-date transportation network, ready for local citizens and the stream of tourists, which by 1973 had grown to 25.5 million per year.

Florida, Present & Future

Since the war, Florida's development has continued beyond tourism, cattle, citrus and phosphate. New industries have created opportunities in commercial space exploration, biomedical and biotechnology industries, electronics, plastics, public utilities, forest products, construction, printing and publishing, TV and movie production, real estate, international banking and international trade.

The postwar era brought desegregation and population growth. Florida has witnessed a massive influx of immigrants from around the world, many contributing to Florida's social, political, economic and cultural growth.

Other trends have contributed to Florida's success: major American corporations relocating to the state in ever-increasing numbers, completion of the interstate highway system throughout the state, construction of major international airports, expansion of the state's universities and community colleges, the proliferation of high technology, and historic accomplishments by the NASA space program.

Although Southeast Florida's population boom has created its share of urban problems, there are still places where people live in harmony with the outdoors. Nature lovers campaign to protect endangered manatees and sea turtles, work at rehab centers caring for injured birds, and maintain their beloved parks, beaches, and wildlife refuges. For adventurers, Southeast Florida offers excitement for all ages, from skydiving to surfing; scuba diving to canoeing; helicopter piloting to deep-sea fishing. Historically, Florida has always attracted adventurers, and they're still arriving.

Geography & Climate

Geographic Beginnings

Florida's geography has greatly contributed to her success as America's favorite playground. Throughout the state's 58,560-square-mile peninsula, no area is more than 60 miles from saltwater. In Southeast Florida you're never more than a short drive away from alabaster sand, crashing waves, and cooling Atlantic Ocean breezes. Florida has 1,197 miles of coastline, more than any state except Alaska. The Atlantic coast has 399 miles, and the Gulf coast has 798 miles. Some 800 miles of Florida's coastline are beaches, and inland are more than 30,000 lakes, including the 730-square-mile Lake Okeechobee, the fourth largest lake in the United States. In fact, 4,424 of Florida's 58,560 square miles are water, adding to the delight of fishing and boating enthusiasts.

Wetlands

A large part of Florida is covered by wetlands – cypress ponds, prairies, flood plains, river swamps, hammocks, freshwater marshes, salt marshes and mangrove swamps. There is a delicate ecological balance between the wetlands and the plant and animal life living within them.

To acquaint you with some of the areas you'll find in Southeast Florida, here's a brief explanation of their characteristics:

- **Hammock** is an Indian word meaning jungle. You'll recognize one by the thick tangle of vegetation in fertile soil. Trees growing in hammocks include cypress, live oak, hickory, and magnolia.

- **Cypress strands** are found in the Fakahatchee Strand and Corkscrew Swamp in South Florida. You'll see canopies soaring over 100 feet high, intertwined with vines, ferns, and brilliantly hued orchids.

- **Freshwater marsh** makes up the state's Everglades. Grasses are wet or dry, depending on rainfall. Keep a lookout here for alligators, as well as dozens of different bird species.

- **Mangrove swamps** have saltwater plants, which serve as breeding areas for birds, fish and shellfish. You'll see them all along Florida's southeast coast.

- **Estuaries** are a combination of freshwater and saltwater. As water flows toward the Atlantic Ocean or Gulf of Mexico, it gets saltier, forming different habitats for a variety of animal life. Frogs and water insects prefer a freshwater environment, whereas jellyfish, flounder, and barnacles thrive in saltwater. The water in between is "brackish" – half salt and half fresh – and home to crabs, turtles, and birds.

Hurricane Categories

Atlantic hurricanes are ranked by the Saffir-Simpson hurricane intensity scale to give an estimate of the potential flooding and damage. Category Three and above is considered intense.

Category	Min. Sustained Winds	Damage
One	74-95	*Minimal:* Damage primarily to shrubbery, trees and foliage
Two	96-110	*Moderate:* Considerable damage to shrubbery and foliage; some trees blown down. Some damage to roofing materials.
Three	111-130	*Extensive:* Foliage torn from trees; large trees blown down. Some structural damage to small buildings. Mobile homes destroyed. Flooding along the coastline.
Four	131-155	*Extreme:* Shrubs and trees blown down. Complete failure of roofs on small residences. Major beach erosion. Massive evacuation of all homes within 500 yards of shore possibly required. Hurricane Andrew, which smashed into South Florida in 1992, is an example of a Category Four.
Five	155+	*Catastrophic:* Some complete building failures. Small buildings overturned or blown away. Low-lying escape routes inland cut by rising water three to five hours before the hurricane's center arrives. Hurricane Camille, a Category Five, struck Mississippi and Louisiana in 1969.

Weather

Besides geography, **climate** is one of Florida's most valuable natural resources. The state's year-round mild temperatures and nearly constant sunshine are a powerful lure for US families weary of winter-gray skies and indoor living in the northeast and midwest. Come discover why Florida is called "The Sunshine State"!

The **Gulf of Mexico** and the **Atlantic Ocean** alternately provide cool breezes in summer, and warm ones in winter. The **Gulf Stream,** flowing near the coast, also contributes its share of warm winds.

Florida does have chilly months. In January, night temperatures can plummet to as low as 41°F, and afternoons often don't get much warmer than 76°.

June through September days are hot and humid, with temperatures soaring to 91°F or more, and nights still warm at 75-80°.

Summer months are also the rainiest, and thunderstorms occur pretty much at the same time every day. South Florida can get rain every day in June and July.

Hurricane season spans June through November, with most hurricanes occurring in September or October. Check TV and newspaper weather services a few days before your arrival for current temperatures and conditions.

Most likely you'll have good weather in Southeast Florida, so enjoy the sunshine, surf, and sapphire skies.

Flora & Fauna

Florida's variety of natural habitats are home to diverse animal species, some found nowhere else in the United States. Here are some you may be privileged to see, either in the wild or in captivity.

Black bears are the largest of all living mammals in Florida, but the smallest of all American bear species. Only 1,000-1,500 of these animals remain in the wild. Loss of natural habitat, poaching, hunting and roadkills threaten the bears' existence. Living on a diet of berries, roots, honey and grass, black bears mostly live near Big Cypress Swamp and Okefenokee Swamp. Shy and nocturnal, they are not a threat to humans. Unfortunately, black bear hunting is still legal in northern Florida, where some 50 are killed each season.

Bobcats, feline hunters weighing 40-50 lbs., prowl mostly at night for rabbits, mice, and squirrels in unpopulated areas, but occasionally raid farms for livestock and poultry. Bobcats are found only in North America.

Coyotes are canines that eat rodents, rabbits, and sometimes sheep and calves. Females bear 5-10 pups per year.

Mink live in freshwater marshes and eat fish, frogs, turtles, snakes, birds and mice. In the Everglades, they are protected by law against hunters.

Opossums, which are marsupials, live in the woodlands, eating berries, eggs and insects. Females may bear up to 14 babies once or twice yearly.

Endangered **West Indian manatees** have affectionately been called "mermaids" in folktales. Fewer than 1,500 of these mammals now remain. Weighing in at 1,200-3,500 lbs., the slow-moving "sea cows" consume a hefty 100 lbs. of river grass daily. The Florida Manatee Sanctuary Act of 1978 established many refuges for the manatees, and public awareness has helped protect them against speedboats and hunters. Join the "Save the Manatee Club" by writing 500 N. Maitland Avenue, Maitland, FL 32751; ☎ 800-432-JOIN.

Changing little in 200 million years, **alligators** are egg-laying reptiles that can grow to 14 feet in length. They mainly survive on a diet of fish, frogs, birds and snakes. Alligators usually bask in the sun or lie submerged just under the water's surface. Alligators are a "Species of Special Concern," almost becoming extinct during the 1960s. Only about 20% of their eggs hatch; hunting for wild alligators is highly regulated and requires a special permit. Alligators are raised commercially on farms for their meat and skins.

Gopher tortoises are also listed as a Species of Special Concern. Many of their habitats have been destroyed by the construction of high-rises and boat docks. Measures are now being taken to protect these tortoises.

Five species of **sea turtles** live in Florida's coastal waters: leatherback, green turtle, loggerhead, Kemp's Ridley, and hawksbill. Weighing from 80 to 1,400 lbs., they subsist on jellyfish, sea grasses, crustaceans, and other sea life. Every year they migrate thousands of miles through open ocean to beach nesting sites, many along the Southeast Florida coast. During June, July, and August, you may participate in beach walks to observe turtles laying their eggs in the moonlight. Local environmental groups and park rangers sponsor lectures and slide presentations, so check area newspapers. Sea turtles are an Endangered Species.

Most of Florida's **snakes** are harmless, eating worms, lizards and frogs. However, keep an eye out for poisonous ones that can be dangerous, and seek medical treatment immediately if you're bitten. Venomous snakes include the **diamondback rattlesnake,** which has diamond-shaped body markings bordered in yellow and a tail rattle; the **canebrake rattlesnake,** gray-brown or pink-beige in color with dark bands across the body and an orange stripe down the back; the **pygmy rattlesnake,** gray with round reddish-orange spots and a buzzing rattle; and the **cottonmouth water moccasin,** olive brown or black with a dark band from the eye to the jaw. **Copperheads** and **coral snakes** are also poisonous. Snakes are basically shy, rarely attacking unless frightened or provoked.

Ways You Can Help Protect Sea Turtles

■ Never disturb or harass nesting turtles by making noise, shining lights, or trying to ride them. Join one of the many state-permitted turtle walks conducted by experienced guides during nesting season.

■ Watch out for hatchlings that may become disoriented by lights and lured onto the road. Be aware of local government ordinances to decrease the impact of beach lighting on sea turtles.

■ Use caution while boating to avoid collisions with turtles.

■ Do not throw trash into the water. Pick up litter on the beach.

■ Never buy products made from sea turtles or other endangered species. It is illegal to bring these products into the United States.

■ If you find an injured or dead turtle, or see someone bothering a nesting turtle, notify the Florida Marine Patrol, ☎ 800/ DIAL FMP.

Birds

Florida's **bird population** is unique in the world. Many are so comfortable around people that they will walk across your path or alight in a tree next to where you're standing. Florida bird-watching provides rare opportunities to get really close. **Pelicans** expertly catch and store fish in their swinging pouches as they dive into the sea along the coast. Many waddle along fishing docks, begging for bait and fish scraps. Pelicans are a Species of Special Concern, their numbers declining in recent years due to insecticides that ruin the walls of their eggs before they can hatch. Near the town of Sebastian along the Indian River is Pelican Island, a wildlife sanctuary where pelicans have lived safely on 7,000 acres since 1905. **Cranes** are graceful, four-foot-tall creatures with six-foot wingspans. Females lay two buff-colored eggs in grassy marshland nests. Cranes are a Threatened Species.

Thanks to environmentalists and **American bald eagle** lovers, the population of the United States' regal national bird is increasing in number. They have a wingspan of almost seven feet and thrive on fish and waterfowl.

Florida has several species of **herons,** including the great blue heron, great white heron, and the delightful pink flamingo. They live mostly in shallow bays and mangrove islands on a diet of fish and frogs.

Ospreys have a dark band across the face, a white breast, and a five- to six-foot wingspan. This "sea eagle" flies over its prey and plunges feet first. They frequently build nests in trees, channel markers, or tops of telephone poles. They are a Species of Special Concern in Florida. The 1972 ban of DDT helped the osprey make a recovery.

Nocturnal **owls** live in field holes or trees, and eat snakes, roaches, grasshoppers and rodents. Florida's owls include the great horned, barred, barn, and burrowing owl, which has beautiful yellow eyes.

This is just a brief list. Other Florida birds include egrets, kites, scrubjays, songbirds, vultures, wild turkeys, wood storks, woodpeckers, and many others. Birdwatching in Florida is a favorite activity, so bring your field book and binoculars.

How to Use This Book

The book is divided into three regions. Our southernmost region, **Miami and Surrounding Areas,** begins in South Dade, which includes Homestead, Kendall, and South Miami. We then move north, covering Coral Gables, Coconut Grove, Key Biscayne, Downtown Miami, Miami Beach, and the North Miami Beach towns of Surfside, Bal Harbour and Bay Harbor, Sunny Isles Beach and Aventura.

Our second region covers **Greater Fort Lauderdale:** the towns of Hollywood, Davie, Dania, Fort Lauderdale, Pompano Beach, Hillsboro Beach, Deerfield Beach, and Coconut Creek.

Our third region covers **The Palm Beaches and the Treasure Coast:** Palm Beach, West Palm Beach, North Palm Beach, Juno Beach, Jupiter, Hobe Sound, Stuart, Hutchinson Island, Port St. Lucie, Vero Beach and Sebastian.

Each section presents adventures *On Foot, On Wheels, On Water,* and *In the Air.* We also share adventures outside these categories, such as horse shows, sea turtle watching, and rodeos. We've included spectator sports like jai alai, horse and motor car racing, and baseball spring training, as well as golf courses and tennis courts. Adventures are followed by *Sightseeing,* which includes zoos, Indian Villages, amusement parks, orange groves, historic districts, ranches, historic homes, memorials, and environmental research centers. Then there are cultural activities: museums, art galleries, and performing arts. Following these descriptions you'll find information on *Festivals & Events, Where to Stay, Camping* and *Where to Eat.* We close each chapter with addresses and phone numbers for convention and visitors bureaus or tourism offices, which offer free brochures and maps.

Where to Stay / Where to Eat

 In our *Where to Stay* and *Where to Eat* sections, highly recommended entries are indicated with a star. These are hotels and restaurants we especially enjoyed, and hope you will too.

Key to Hotel & Restaurant Prices

Hotels:

$ = a double room under $100 per night.

$$ = a double room $100-$150 per night.

$$$ = a double room $150 per night and over.

Rates change often, so check when you call for reservations.

Restaurant prices:

$ = the price of a dinner entrée for one person is $15 or less.

$$ = the price of a dinner entrée for one person is $15-$30.

$$$ = the price of a dinner entrée for one person is $30 or more.

As with hotels, prices change frequently, so ask about costs when you make reservations or check the menu when arriving at the restaurant.

On Foot

This category presents walking and hiking adventures in Southeast Florida. Beachcombing, unusual walking tours, hiking in forests, wildlife preserves, state and county parks, and unusual gardens are featured. Some hikes are on boardwalks, others meander through wildlife refuges. One unusual walk is a guided "photo safari" with a professional photographer who teaches wildlife photo techniques.

Safety Tips for Walking and Hiking

■ Wear comfortable sneakers or hiking boots with socks that wick moisture away from your skin. To avoid blisters, always wear socks. Even beach walking is more comfortable in a waterproof shoe or sandal: sand can be rough on bare skin and you may encounter black sticky tar or broken glass. Pack band-aids, moleskin, and baby powder for injured feet.

■ Always wear a hat with a wide brim to keep the sun off your head and face. Carry water and snacks, preferably in a fanny pack or back pack so your hands are free. Use the trail maps found at most parks and refuges. If the park rangers ask you to sign a log sheet before hiking, please do so. It may be the only way to find you or a family member in the event of emergency.

■ Be careful what you touch: never feed or pet wild animals, even the ones that look friendly, like raccoons. Many animals carry dangerous viruses and diseases.

■ The best policy is one we all know: take only photographs, leave only footprints.

On Wheels

This category features biking or in-line skating adventures. Florida has a diversity of bike paths: within parks, along golf courses and beaches, through city neighborhoods. We enjoyed several terrific **bike tours:** Miami Beach's *Art Deco by Bike* and *Palm Beach by Bike* are just two of them. They are delightful ways to sightsee, exercise, and learn history all at the same time. We also list bike and skate shops, local bike clubs, and bike trail maps you can order.

Bike Safety Tips

■ Begin cycling early in the day to avoid heat and traffic. Never bike at night without headlights and always wear reflecting safety vests.

■ Obey all traffic laws. Bicycles are considered vehicles by law in Florida, and have all the rights and responsibilities of other vehicles.

■ Wear a helmet, preferably ANSI or SNELL approved, while riding.

■ Wear bright colors so other motorists will see you.

- Carry plenty of water and snacks, as well as repair tools. Wear sunscreen, sunglasses and a hat.
- Carry everything in saddlebags on the bike rather than on your back, which can shift your center of gravity and make cycling more difficult.

For more information about cycling in Southeast Florida, contact the following:

Florida Cycling Federation Race Information, ☎ 305/437-8688. BC Wheelers, 600 NW 183rd Street, Miami 33169.

Bike Tech Cycling Club, 14230 SW 62nd Street, Miami, ☎ 305/382-9291.

Miami International Cycling, 9541 Bird Rd., Miami 33165.

Miami Mountain Bikers, 9400 SW 170th St., Unit #1, Miami, 33157. ☎ 305/232-9286.

Niagara Bicycle Club, 3237 NW 7th St., Miami 33125.

South Florida Bicycle Polo League, 15800 Palmetto Club Drive, Miami 33157.

On Water

 This category includes swimming, snorkeling, scuba diving, boating, fishing, cruising, canoeing, kayaking, windsurfing, waterskiing, and sailing. We also list names of fishing guides, boat charters, fishing clubs, and bait shops.

 Fishing licenses are required for both freshwater and saltwater anglers in Florida, with exceptions for youths under age 16 and adults 65 or older. Most tackle shops sell fishing licenses and have free brochures listing the basic rules for both freshwater and saltwater fishing. They may also offer information on guides or charter boats.

Southeast Florida's rivers, Intracoastal Waterway, and Atlantic Ocean are the main reasons millions come to play here each season. The beauty of Florida's watersports is in its diversity: you can paddle alone in a kayak quietly watching birds in the mangroves, or enter a sailing competition. Windsurf with friends at sunset, or dive 150 feet into the ocean to explore an ancient wreck. Swim laps in an Olympic-size pool or bodysurf Atlantic Ocean waves; take a dinner cruise to nowhere or waterski along the coast.

 Always wear sunscreen and a wide-brimmed hat. Pack a long-sleeved shirt to protect against the sun, and a waterproof jacket in case the weather changes. Always have snacks and bottled water on hand. And wear your life jacket; it may not look fashionable, but it could save your life.

In the Air

 This category introduces you to skydiving, hot air ballooning, and helicopter touring/flying lessons.

Obviously these sports might not be suitable for those with acrophobia, but one hot air balloon pilot assured us no one has ever regretted soaring over Florida's beautiful coastline!

You'll receive expert instruction and safety tips before skydiving, ballooning, or helicopter piloting, so just relax and enjoy the scenery.

A Special Feature of This Book

We've interviewed a unique group of adventurers. These **snapshots** are casual conversations with people you might want to contact. Many are instructors in kayaking, scuba diving, fishing etc., and will be happy to teach the fundamentals of their sport.

Adventurers we met:

- **Reed Robbings,** Instructor, SkyDive Miami, Homestead.

- **Robert Rose,** Director of Training, Miami Seaquarium, Key Biscayne.

- **Vesna Galesic,** rollerblade "queen" and Front Desk Manager, Indian Creek Hotel, Miami Beach.
- **Todd Carter,** Wall Climbing Instructor, Eden Roc, North Miami Beach.
- **Jeffrey Bingham,** Instructor, Waterways Kayak, Hollywood.
- **Alice Butler,** President/Helicopter Instructor, Rotors in Motion, Hollywood.
- **Captain Dan Coltrane,** airboat captain at Everglades Holiday Park, Davie.
- **Captain Carolyn Williams** and **Captain Nadine Nack,** Southeast Yachting School & Charters, Ft. Lauderdale.
- **Rusty Harr,** Animal Curator, Lion Country Safari, West Palm Beach.
- **Calixto Garcia-Velez,** Director of Polo Operations, Palm Beach Polo Club & Resort.
- **Eric Bailey,** owner, Canoe Outfitters, West Palm Beach.
- **Bernie DeHart,** owner/instructor, Cove Kayak Center, Stuart.
- **Captain Barry Ross,** owner/instructor, Blue Dolphin Dive Charters, Stuart.
- **Mark Chapdelain,** owner/pilot, Balloons Over Florida, Stuart.
- **Terry O'Toole,** Park Ranger, Sebastian Inlet State Recreation Area, Sebastian.

Sprinkled throughout the book are first-person adventure essays to give you vivid ideas of adventures awaiting you in Southeast Florida.

Please let us know about your experiences. We read all letters and will use your suggestions and recommendations in future editions.

Information Sources

These organizations provide free information and maps to help you plan your Florida adventures.

State Agencies

Florida Department of Commerce, Division of Tourism, Visitor Inquiry, 126 W. Van Buren Street, Tallahassee, FL 32399-2000. ☎ 904/487-1462. Call or write for complimentary copies of the *Florida Vacation Guide, Planning Guide for Travelers with Disabilities, Florida Events Calendar, Florida Trails: A Guide to Florida's Natural Habitats,* or *Florida Value Activities Guide.*

Historical Sites: Call or write **Department of State Bureau of Historic Preservation,** R.A. Gray Bldg., 500 S. Bronough Street, Tallahassee, FL 32399-0250. ☎ 904/487-2333.

US Forest Service, 227 N. Bronough Street, Suite 4061, Tallahassee, FL 32301. ☎ 904/681-7265. Call or write for information on national forests in Florida.

Department of Agriculture and Consumer Services, Division of Forestry, 3125 Conner Blvd., Tallahassee, FL 32399-1650. ☎ 904/488-6611. Call or write for state forest information.

Department of Environmental Protection, Office of Recreation & Parks, Mail Station 535, 3900 Commonwealth Blvd., Tallahassee, FL 32399-3000. ☎ 904/488-9872. Call or write for information on state parks.

Convention & Visitors Bureaus

Greater Miami & The Beaches Hotel Association, 407 Lincoln Rd., Suite 10G, Miami Beach, FL 33139. ☎ 800/SEE-MIAMI.

Greater Miami Convention & Visitors Bureau, 701 Brickell Avenue, Suite 2700, Miami, FL 33131. ☎ 800/283-2707, 305/539-3084; fax 305/539-3113. Web site www.miamiandbeaches.com.

Sunny Isles Beach Resort Association, 17100 Collins Avenue, Suite 208, Miami, FL 33160. ☎ 305/956-9527.

Greater Fort Lauderdale Convention & Visitor Bureau, 1850 Eller Drive, Suite 303, Fort Lauderdale, FL 33316. ☎ 800/22SUNNY.

Palm Beach County Convention & Visitors Bureau, 1555 Palm Beach Lakes Blvd., Suite 204, West Palm Beach, FL 33401. ☎ 800/544-7256.

Chambers of Commerce

These will send you free brochures, maps, calendars of events, and information on sightseeing, hotels, restaurants:

■ Miami Area

Greater South Dade/South Miami Chamber of Commerce, 6410 SW 80th St., Miami, FL 33143. ☎ 305/238-7192.

Greater Miami Chamber of Commerce, 1601 Biscayne Blvd., Miami, FL 33132. ☎ 305/350-7700.

Greater Homestead-Florida City Chamber of Commerce, 43 N. Krome Avenue, Homestead, FL 33030. ☎ 305/247-2332.

Miami Beach Chamber of Commerce, 1920 Meridian Avenue, Miami Beach, FL 33139. ☎ 305/672-1270.

North Miami Chamber of Commerce, 13100 W. Dixie Hwy., North Miami, FL 33161. ☎ 305/891-7811.

North Miami Beach Chamber of Commerce, 41 NE 167th St., North Miami Beach, FL 33162. ☎ 305/653-1200.

Coconut Grove Chamber of Commerce, 2820 McFarlane Rd., Coconut Grove, FL 33133. ☎ 305/444-7270.

Coral Gables Chamber of Commerce, 50 Aragon Avenue, Coral Gables, FL 33134. ☎ 305/446-9900.

Bal Harbour Dept. of Tourism, 655 96th St., Bal Harbour, FL 33154. ☎ 800/847-9222.

Surfside Tourist Board, 9301 Collins Avenue, Surfside, FL 33154. ☎ 800/327-4557.

Key Biscayne Chamber of Commerce, 604 Crandon Blvd., Suite 203, Key Biscayne, FL 33149. ☎ 305/361-5207.

■ Greater Fort Lauderdale Area

Greater Fort Lauderdale Chamber of Commerce, 512 NE Third Avenue, Fort Lauderdale, FL 33301. ☎ 954/462-6000.

Greater Hollywood Chamber of Commerce, 2410 Hollywood Blvd., Hollywood, FL 33021. ☎ 954/923-4000.

Lauderdale-by-the-Sea Chamber of Commerce, 4201 Ocean Drive, Lauderdale-by-the-Sea, FL 33308. ☎ 954/776-1000.

Dania Chamber of Commerce, 102 W. Dania Beach Blvd., Dania, FL 33004. ☎ 954/927-3377.

Davie-Cooper City Chamber of Commerce, 4185 SW 64th Avenue, Davie, FL 33314. ☎ 954/581-0790.

Deerfield Beach Chamber of Commerce, 1601 Hillsboro Blvd., Deerfield Beach, FL 33441. ☎ 954/427-1050.

■ Palm Beach, Martin, St. Lucie & Indian River Counties

Greater Boca Raton Chamber of Commerce, 1800 N. Dixie Highway, Boca Raton, FL 33432-1892. ☎ 561/395-4433.

Boynton Beach Chamber of Commerce, 639 E. Ocean, Boynton Beach, FL 33435. ☎ 561/732-9501.

Greater Delray Beach Chamber of Commerce, 64 SE Fifth Avenue, Delray Beach, FL 33483. ☎ 561/278-0424.

Hobe Sound Chamber of Commerce, PO Box 1507, Hobe Sound, FL 33475. ☎ 561/546-4724.

Jensen Beach Chamber of Commerce, 1910 NE Jensen Beach Blvd., Jensen Beach, FL 34957. ☎ 561/334-3444.

Jupiter Tequesta Juno Beach (JTJB) Chamber of Commerce, 800 N. US Highway One, Jupiter, FL 33477. ☎ 561/746-7111, 800/616-7402, fax 561/746-7715. Web site www.jupiterfl.org.

Northern Palm Beach County Chamber of Commerce, 1983 PGA Blvd, #104, Palm Beach Gardens, FL 33408, ☎ 561/694-2300; fax 561/694-0126. Web site www.npbchamber.com.

Palm Beach Chamber of Commerce, 45 Cocoanut Row, Palm Beach, FL 33480. ☎ 561/655-3282.

Central Palm Beach County Chamber of Commerce, 6728 Forest Hills Blvd., West Palm Beach, FL 33413. ☎ 561/642-4260.

Stuart/Martin County Chamber of Commerce, 1650 S. Kanner Hwy, Stuart, FL 34994. ☎ 561/287-1088.

Vero Beach/Indian River County Chamber of Commerce, 1216 21st St., Vero Beach, FL 32961. ☎ 561/567-3491.

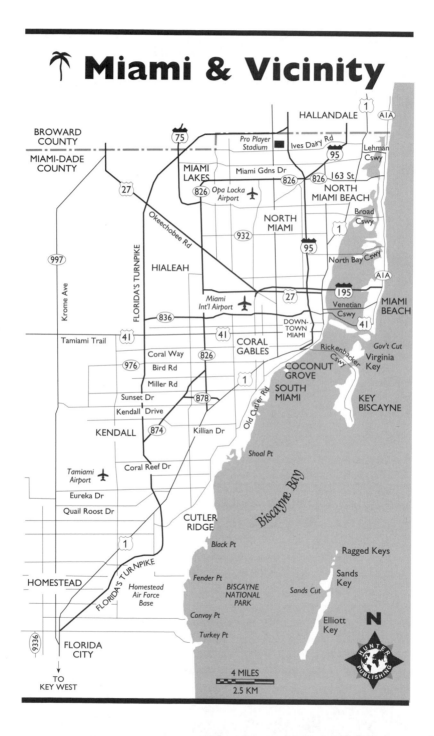

Miami & Vicinity

BROWARD COUNTY

MIAMI-DADE COUNTY

HALLANDALE

Pro Player Stadium

Ives Dairy Rd

Lehman Cswy

75

95

MIAMI LAKES

Miami Gdns Dr

826

826

163 St

Opa Locka Airport

826

NORTH MIAMI BEACH

27

Okeechobee Rd

NORTH MIAMI

932

Broad Cswy

1

997

FLORIDA'S TURNPIKE

HIALEAH

95

North Bay Cswy

Krome Ave

Miami Int'l Airport

27

A1A

195

Venetian Cswy

MIAMI BEACH

836

DOWN-TOWN MIAMI

41

Tamiami Trail

41

41

CORAL GABLES

Rickenbacker Cswy

Gov't Cut

Coral Way

826

COCONUT GROVE

Virginia Key

976

Bird Rd

Miller Rd

1

SOUTH MIAMI

Sunset Dr

878

Old Cutler Rd

KEY BISCAYNE

Kendall Drive

Killian Dr

874

KENDALL

Shoal Pt

Biscayne Bay

Coral Reef Dr

Tamiami Airport

Eureka Dr

Quail Roost Dr

CUTLER RIDGE

Black Pt

Ragged Keys

1

Sands Key

FLORIDA'S TURNPIKE

Fender Pt

Sands Cut

HOMESTEAD

Homestead Air Force Base

BISCAYNE NATIONAL PARK

Convoy Pt

Elliott Key

9336

FLORIDA CITY

Turkey Pt

N

TO KEY WEST

4 MILES

2.5 KM

HUNTER PUBLISHING

Miami & Surrounding Areas

"Miami is the most maddening, stimulating, life encouraging city in the world," wrote Florida's renowned environmentalist and author, Marjory Stoneman Douglas. There's nothing this prize-winning "centurion plus" doesn't know about her beloved city. In 1996, Miami celebrated Douglas' 100th birthday. It's hard to believe that in 1896 the population was 1,500; today it's over two million. Modern Miami has many nicknames: "Crossroads of the Americas"; "The Magic City"; and "Cruise Capital of the World." Away from the shops, restaurants, nightclubs, and dazzling skyline, it's definitely possible to find outdoor adventure. You just have to look.

■ Getting Here

Centrally located seven miles from downtown Miami, **Miami International Airport** ranks seventh in the US for passenger traffic. Some 32 million travelers pass through its portals each year. Tourist Information Counters are located outside the Customs exits, at the main Information Counter on the upper level at Concourse E, at the upper level of the Concourse E Satellite Terminal, and at Concourses D and G on the lower level of the Terminal. The airport telephone is ☎ 305/876-7000.

■ Getting Around

We recommend renting a car for your visit to Miami, especially if you'll be traveling outside the city for activities like boating, touring, golfing and sports events. Car rentals are available at Miami International Airport and other locations throughout the area.

If you picture yourself clad in black leather, try on a Harley Davidson. Available by the hour, day or week, the motorcycle fleet includes FLHR Road Kings, FLSTF Fat Boys, and XLH Sportster 1200s. Most bikes are equipped with saddlebags and detachable windshields. Available from **Harley Davidson**

Rentals at the Budget Rent A Car lot near the airport, 3901 NW 28th Street, ☎ 305/871-1040. Open 9 am-5 pm daily.

Rental Car Agencies

These agencies provide free shuttle buses from the airport to their rental locations:

Alamo Rent A Car . . . . ☎ 800/327-9633
3355 NW 22nd Street, Miami
Budget Car & Truck Rental . . . . ☎ 800/527-0700
2601 NW LeJeune Road, Miami
Enterprise Rent A Car . . . . ☎ 800/325-8007
3975 NW South River Drive, Miami
Hertz Rent A Car . . . . ☎ 800/654-3131
3795 NW 21st Street, Miami

Major Roadways

North-South: I-95 is the major north-south expressway, running through downtown Miami and into **US1** (also called Dixie Highway), and continuing south all the way to Key West. **A1A** (Collins Avenue) is the major thoroughfare in Miami Beach.

East-West: State Road 836 (Dolphin Expressway) is the major expressway connecting **Florida's Turnpike** (Homestead Extension) to **State Road 826,** I-95, and Miami Beach via **I-395.**

State Road 112 runs from Miami International Airport to I-95 and connects to Miami Beach via I-195. Seven **causeways** link Miami and Miami Beach: two of the major ones are **I-195** (Julia Tuttle) and **I-395** (MacArthur Causeway), both reached from I-95.

Look for **signs** showing an orange sun on a blue background: they identify primary routes from Miami International Airport to Coral Gables, Coconut Grove, downtown Miami, Key Biscayne, Miami Beach and the Seaport (Port of Miami). The orange sun also directs visitors returning rental cars to the "triangle area," home to more than 20 car rental agencies, east of Miami International Airport.

Public Transportation

Miami has safe and efficient public transportation, including buses, elevated rapid transit trains and a people mover system. Get maps and time schedules for the **Metromover, Metrorail,** and **Metrobus** by calling ☎ 305/638-6700. Full fares are $1.25 for Metrobus, $1.25 for Metrorail, and 25¢ for Metromover.

Personal Safety

Like any major metropolitan area, Miami has its share of crime. If you practice common sense, you will have a safe fun vacation. Here are a few tips:

- All rental car agencies have excellent city maps, which they provide free to customers. Discuss your driving route with the car rental agent, get a clear understanding of how to get to your destination, and outline it on your map.

- Before leaving the car rental agency, take time to familiarize yourself with car safety features, such as door locks, hazard/emergency lights, location of the spare tire, seat belts, etc.

- While on the road, if another car motions you to pull over for any reason, do not pull over. Do not respond to honking, flashing headlights or any strange behavior. Keep driving to your destination.

- If you become lost, do not pull over to the roadside to study maps or ask directions from strangers. Drive to the nearest well-lighted public restaurant, service station, or store, and ask for help.

- Drive with car doors locked and windows up, especially at night.

- Never pick up hitchhikers.

- Specially marked Metro-Dade Tourist-Oriented Police cars displaying the orange sun decal are there to assist tourists – don't hesitate to ask for their help.

In this chapter, we'll traverse the Miami area from south to north, beginning with the southernmost areas of Dade County.

South Dade 🌴

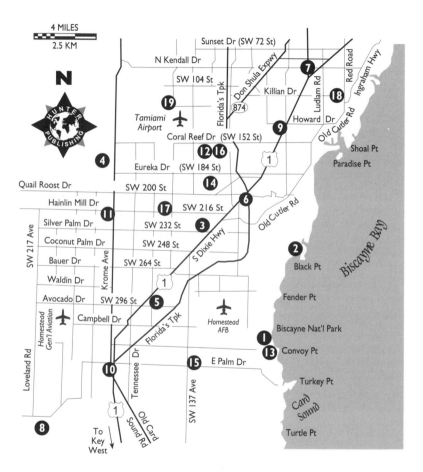

1. Biscayne National Park / Visitor Ctr
2. Black Point Marina
3. Cauley Square
4. Chekika State Park Recreation Area
5. Coral Castle
6. Cutler Ridge Mall
7. Dadeland Mall
8. Everglades Nat'l Park &
   Everglades Alligator Farm
9. The Falls Shopping Center
10. Florida Pioneer Museum
11. Fruit & Spice Park
12. Gold Coast Railroad Museum
13. Homestead Bayfront Park & Marina
14. Larry & Penny Thompson Park
15. Metro-Dade Motorsports Complex
16. Metrozoo
17. Monkey Jungle
18. Parrot Jungle & Gardens
19. Weeks Air Museum

South Dade

Historically the South Dade area was known as the Redland, named for the rich red soil that grows avocado, mango, lemon, lime, tomatoes, squash and pole beans. Today, the Redland is the United States' largest winter-season producer of vegetables. Many farms have stands selling fresh fruit and vegetables, or you can pick your own from their fields. Don't miss the creamy milkshakes made from farm fresh strawberries, sold at places like the "Robert is Here Fruit Stand."

Getting Here

We recommend renting a car for exploring South Dade County. To get here from Miami International Airport, take SR 836/Dolphin Expressway west to Florida's Turnpike, then south into Dade County. Or take SR 826/Palmetto Expressway south, intersect at US1, and head south.

■ Adventures

On Foot

Chekika State Recreation Area, Homestead

Whether you amble along a nature trail or boardwalk, be alert for snoozing alligators at Chekika State Recreation Area, off 177th/Krome Avenue, 15 miles north and west of Homestead, ☎ 305/251-0371; Web site www.nps. gov/ever. This 640-acre park is ideal for enjoying tropical foliage, mini-islands, and cascading waterfalls. Take a dip in the swim hole or enjoy a languid afternoon picnic.

South Dade Greenway Network, Everglades Trail

The 24-mile Everglades Trail passes through picturesque agricultural land. An unpaved off-road facility, the trail is ideal for hiking. Keep an eye out for birds, snakes, alligators and deer. Be sure to carry plenty of water and snacks. The trail parallels the eastern boundary of Everglades National Park along the C-111 canal. Parking is available the corner of the canal and SW 136th Street (don't leave valuables in your car). The trail is an unpaved, offroad facility designed for hiking, biking, and equestrian use. There are no facilities or services here. For trail maps and information, call the South Dade Greenway Network at The Redland Conservancy, ☎ 305/740-9007.

Golf

- **Palmetto Golf Course,** 9300 SW 152nd Street, ☎ 305/238-2922. Par 70, 18-hole championship course on 121 acres. Putting green, lighted driving range, snack bar and pro shop.

- **Briar Bay Golf Course,** 9375 SW 134th Street, ☎ 305/235-6667. Par 31, nine-hole executive course on 30 acres; restaurant.

- **Keys Gate Golf & Tennis Club,** 2300 Palm Drive, ☎ 305/230-0362. 18 holes, driving range, lessons, restaurant.

Tennis

There are numerous places for tennis buffs to work off some energy. Just a few are listed here.

- **Bent Tree Park,** SW 47th Street & 139th Avenue, ☎ 305/385-4750. Two courts.

- **Continental Tennis Center,** 10010 SW 82nd Avenue, ☎ 305/271-0732. Eight courts.

- **Coral Reef Tennis Center,** 7895 SW 152nd Street, ☎ 305/234-4907. Six courts.

- **Ron Ehmann Tennis Center,** 10995 SW 97th Avenue, ☎ 305/271-7731, has six courts.

On Wheels

Biking

 Metro-Dade Bicycle Program has created an excellent *Bike Miami Suitability Map* to help bikers select safe routes when biking within Dade County. The map rates specific roadways according to speed limits, road widths, amounts of traffic, and hazardous conditions. The map shows off-street paths, sidewalks, bike lanes, paved shoulders, and wide curb lanes. There's also information on bike rental shops, bike clubs, and parks with bike paths. To order the map ($3.50) or get information on cycling in Dade County, contact: Jeffrey Hunter, Coordinator, Metro-Dade Bicycle Program, 111 NW First Street, Suite 901, Miami, Florida 33128. ☎ 305/375-4507.

To get you started, here are some recommended safe bike routes in South Dade County.

- **In Homestead:** At the corner of US1 and SW 312th Street (Campbell Drive). Start at Thom J. Harris Field and ride east.

- **In Kendall:** At the corner of SW 136th Street/Howard Drive and Ludlam Road. Ride east and then north as the road turns into Old Cutler Road.

For additional information on biking in the South Dade area, contact the **Bicycle Club of Homestead,** PO Box 1155, Homestead, FL 33030.

On Water

Biscayne National Park

 You won't see them at first. Listen: just an exhale of breath. A small dog-like snout appears on the surface. Then a whoosh of air. Paddle quietly to the water bubbles. Peering into the clear water you see enormous ghostly bodies gliding like hot air dirigibles. Manatees are under your canoe. This unusual encounter occurred during my visit to **Biscayne National Park,** one of America's few aquatic national parks. Of its 180,000 acres, 95% is underwater, alive with **coral reefs, tropical fish, marine plants,** and endangered **manatees.** The other 5% of the park is made up of 44 keys forming a north-south chain 18 nautical miles long, bordered on the west by Biscayne Bay, on the east by the Atlantic Ocean.

Canoeing & Boating

Rent a **canoe** by the hour at the park's Visitor Center, and take a self-guided tour of Biscayne Bay. You may luck out as we did and meet wild manatees. At the very least you'll be eye to eye with pelicans, cormorants, egrets, and herons, as the Park is a habitat for over 179 bird species.

If you're not into canoeing, then take a three-hour **glass-bottom boat ride** over the coral reefs and see the park's underwater world. Check the Visitor Center for daily departures and fees.

Private boat launches are not permitted from the park, but if you've come by private boat from a nearby marina (see our list in this section), you can spend the day or **camp** at the park's Elliot Key. Or dock at Boca Chita Key Harbor on a first-come, first-served basis. Boaters are advised to use NOAA Nautical Chart #11451, and to pay close attention to channel markers. Use extreme caution when boating near divers or manatees.

An anhinga, seen here while kayaking through mangrove-lined waterways, holds out its wings to dry them in the sun.

Fishing, Lobstering & Crabbing

Fishing is excellent year-round at Biscayne National Park. Biscayne Bay is famous for eight- to 12-pound bonefish in the flats near the shore. North Biscayne Bay yields sea trout, jack, Spanish mackerel, and barracuda. Snapper, grouper and sea trout are also plentiful in the Bay, with hogfish and tuna found on the ocean side of the keys. A fishing license is required and you must follow Florida's regulations on size, number, season and method of take.

Lobsters may only be taken east of the Biscayne National Park islands (ocean side) during the legal seasons. During the two-day sport season, usually the last week of July, a maximum of 12 lobsters per person per day is allowed. During the regular season, usually August-March, commercial and sport fishermen may take a maximum of six lobsters per person per day or 24 per boat, whichever is greater. Lobsters may only be taken using hands, handheld nets or bully nets.

Stone crabs may be caught in season and blue crabs may be taken all year. For further information on lobstering and crabbing in Biscayne National Park, contact the park.

Diving & Snorkeling

"Anybody ever snorkeled or been diving here at Biscayne National Park?" inquired our dive master, Scott Windham. "You're in for a treat. We are probably the best-kept dive secret in the US."

I plunge overboard from the park's Boca Chita dive boat onto Ball Buoy Reef, a colorful world of elkhorn coral, purple sea fans, car-sized brain coral, and pointy-lipped angelfish. Parrotfish, squirrelfish and barracudas dart by. I understand why Miami's *New Times* newspaper voted Ball Buoy Reef one of the "Best Snorkel Spots in Miami." Although the water is 72° in January, I'm snug in my wetsuit, awed by 100-foot visibility.

Most divers and snorkelers visiting Southeast Florida head to John Pennekamp Park in Key Largo, but if you want to avoid the crowds, dive Biscayne National Park. The Visitors Center has a full-service PADI/NAUI dive shop that rents masks, fins, snorkels, buoyancy compensators, regulators, weight belts and air tanks. You must show your dive certification card.

Other popular reefs at the park are Triumph, Long and Ajax reefs, all less than five miles from Elliot Key. In depths averaging 15-20 feet, these reefs gently slope to 60 feet on the seaward side. Check with the Visitor Center for daily dive schedules and locations.

The beauty of diving at Biscayne National Park is you can be ogling an angelfish in the afternoon, and by sunset be back in South Miami for dinner.

Biscayne National Park, PO Box 1369, Homestead FL 33090, ☎ 305/230-PARK (7275). For boating and diving information, ☎ 305/230-1100. The park offers canoeing, glass-bottom boat tours, fishing, lobstering, crabbing, snorkeling and diving. Open-daily 8 am-5:30 pm. No park entrance fee.

Marinas

South Dade offers a number of marinas for boaters. These are some of the most popular:

> **Homestead Bayfront Marina.** Located next door to the Convoy Point Visitor Center headquarters for Biscayne National Park, with 173 wet slips, a bait and tackle shop, fuel, and 10 boat launch ramps. 9698 SW North Canal Drive, Homestead, 33090. ☎ 305/230-3033.

> **Black Point Marina.** North of Homestead Bayfront Park, with 178 wet slips, 10 boat launch ramps, bait and tackle shop, dry dock storage, boat rentals, fishing charters, dive shop, canoe ramps, fuel, restaurant. 24775 SW 87th Avenue, Homestead, 33032. ☎ 305/258-4092.

In the Air

When was the last time you were freefalling at 120 mph from a small aircraft? At **SkyDive Miami** in Homestead, adventurers do it every day. The company utilizes an advanced Tandem Parachute Training System, so you can jump after just a few hours of instruction. Your instructor will be attached behind as your guide while you sightsee downtown Miami and Biscayne Bay from the air. Once your parachute opens, you'll soar through the sky for about four minutes. If that sounds like a rush, call ☎ 800/SKYDIVE for further information. 28790 SW 217 Avenue, Homestead, at the Homestead General Aviation Airport.

✳ Snapshot

Meet Reed Robbings, Instructor, Skydive Miami.

SS: What's your background in skydiving, Reed?

RR: Well, I've made over 5,000 jumps. I've been a member of the Army Parachute Team & Flight School and the Golden Knights Jumping Team, so I guess you could say I love this sport!

SS: What's a typical reaction from a first-time jumper?

RR: They say things like "what a rush" and "fantastic." Some people want to jump again right away.

SS: Why do people jump?

RR: Why not? You're soaring among the clouds in a clear blue sky, the views are fantastic. And it's perfectly safe, because you have an instructor attached to your back. Plus you get a lot of training before the jump.

SS: What's been the most unusual jump situation for you?

RR: Well, a woman came in who was going to give birth in four weeks – she wanted to jump! I convinced her to wait until after the baby arrived. So I expect to see her out here any day now, accompanied by her newborn. We get folks from all over the country and all over the world. You never know who will try skydiving.

Miami

Skydiving in Homestead.

Other Adventures

The Homestead Motorsports Complex, SW 336th Street, ☎ 305/230-7223, is a 344-acre complex hosting NASCAR, Indy Car, Formula One, and American Motorcycle Association races. Seating 65,000 people, the complex features a 1½-mile quad-oval 8° track and a 2.21-mile road course. Call for their race schedule and tickets.

■ Sightseeing

The Florida Pioneer Museum, 826 N. Krome Avenue, Homestead, ☎ 305/246-9531, is housed in the old Homestead Florida East Coast Railway Depot and Station Agent's House. Built in 1904 from Dade County pine, there are interesting exhibits on pioneer life, agriculture and railroad memorabilia. At press time, the museum was temporarily closed for repairs. Call for reopening date.

Coral Castle, 28655 S. Dixie Hwy (US1 at 286th Street), Homestead, ☎ 305/248-6344, was created by Latvian immigrant Ed Leedskalnin. With homemade pulleys and levers salvaged from junk yards, he spent 28 years building this strange coral structure that some compare to Stonehenge. Why he built it is a mystery, but decide for yourself from the half-hour self-guided audio tour. Open daily, 9 am-6 pm. Admission.

Fruit and Spice Park, 24801 SW 187th Avenue, Homestead, ☎ 305/247-5727, is a tropical paradise in the heart of the Redland Historic district. Surrounded by thousands of acres of tropical agriculture, this is a showcase for the South Florida agricultural community. Over 500 varieties of exotic fruits, herbs, spices and nuts grow within the 20-acre park. The gift shop sells unusual jams, international spices, and cookbooks. Open daily 10 am-5 pm. Admission.

Tour the Everglades by airboat at **Everglades Alligator Farm,** 40351 SW 192nd Avenue, Homestead, ☎ 305/247-2628. This is South Florida's oldest working alligator farm, and they have alligator and snake shows, as well as a gift shop and snack bar. Open daily 9-6 pm. Admission.

Aircraft lovers will enjoy touring the **Weeks Air Museum,** 14710 SW 128th Street, Tamiami Airport, Miami, ☎ 305/233-

5197. The historic display of aircraft and aviation artifacts includes a B-29 cockpit, a P-51 Mustang, a Grumman J2F-6 Duck, and an A-26. Open daily 10 am-5 pm. Admission.

Miami Metrozoo, 12400 SW 152nd Street, Miami, ☎ 305/251-0400, is a 290-acre cageless zoo, home to white Bengal tigers, apes, elephants, giraffes and other endangered animals. Live shows run throughout the day, and kids will enjoy the petting zoo. Food courts. For a relaxing aerial view of the zoo's animals, take the monorail, which runs all day long. Open daily 9:30 am-5:30 pm. Admission.

Take a weekend train ride on a diesel or steam locomotive at the **Gold Coast Railroad Museum,** 12450 SW 152nd Street, Miami, ☎ 305/253-0063. Browse their collection of historic railroad cars, which includes the Presidential Pullman car, "Ferdinand Magellan," used by Roosevelt, Truman, Eisenhower, Reagan and Bush. Open daily 10 am-3 pm. Admission.

Monkeys roam freely at **Monkey Jungle,** 14805 SW 216th Street, Miami, ☎ 305/235-1611, and visitors are caged. Hundred of South American monkeys live in a lush tropical jungle setting. Enjoy continuous shows, a snack bar, and the gift shop. Open daily 9:30 am-5 pm. Admission.

Fruit & Vegetable Stands

Burr's Berry Farm sells strawberries, fresh produce and strawberry milkshakes at 12741 SW 216th Street, ☎ 305/235-0513. They open between Christmas and New Year's, and close mid-May. Open daily 9 am-5:30 pm.

Florida City State Farmer's Market sells fresh produce from September-May at 300 N. Krome Avenue, Florida City, ☎ 305/246-4727. Open Monday-Friday, 8 am-5 pm; Saturday and Sunday 8-noon.

Knaus Berry Farms, 15980 SW 248th Street, ☎ 305/247-0668, offers fresh baked goods, produce and fruit shakes. They open a week before Thanksgiving and close the last Saturday in April. Open Monday-Saturday 8 am-5:30 pm.

Robert is Here Fruit Stand, 19200 SW 344th Street, ☎ 305/246-1592, specializes in tropical fruits like lychee, carambola, papaya, mangos; vegetables, and fruit shakes. Open daily 8 am-7 pm.

■ Festivals & Events

January

Homestead Annual Chili Cookoff, Florida Keys Factory Shops, 250 East Palm Drive, Florida City, ☎ 305/247-2332.

Redland Natural Arts Festival, Fruit and Spice Park, 24801 SW 187 Avenue, ☎ 305/247-5727.

Homestead Rodeo, Harris Field, US 1 and SW 312 Street, Homestead. ☎ 305/248-5533.

February

Jazz Under the Stars, Miami Metrozoo, 12400 SW 152nd St, ☎ 305/238-1811.

March

Asian Arts Festival, call for location, ☎ 954/921-3315.

Marlboro Grand Prix of Miami, Homestead Motorsports Complex, ☎ 305/230-5214.

May

Great Sunrise Hot Air Balloon Race, Homestead Air Reserve Base, SW 127th Ave at SW 268th St, ☎ 305/273-3050.

July

Tropical Agricultural Fiesta, Fruit and Spice Park, 24801 SW 187 Avenue, ☎ 305/248-5533.

Annual Everglades Music and Crafts Festival, Miccosukee Indian Village, 30 miles west of Miami on Tamiami Trail (SW 8th St), ☎ 305/223-8380.

December

Annual Indian Arts Festival, Miccosukee Indian Village, 30 miles west of Miami on Tamiami Trail (SW 8th St), ☎ 305/223-8380.

■ Where to Stay

Florida City

 Best Western, One Strano Blvd., Florida City, ☎ 800/528-1234, is a 114-room hotel located within a few miles of Everglades and Biscayne National Parks. Near fishing, diving and the Homestead Motor Sports Complex. Ask for a room with a kitchen, since there is no restaurant in the hotel. $$

Hampton Inn, 124 E. Palm Drive, Florida City, ☎ 800/HAMPTON, is contemporary with pastel colors and 123 rooms. Also near Everglades and Biscayne National Parks, as well as shopping and sports attractions. No restaurant. $

Kendall

Miami Dadeland Marriott, 9090 S. Dadeland Blvd. Kendall, ☎ 800/228-9290 is an elegant hotel in the heart of Kendall across the street from Dadeland Mall. There are 302 rooms, a restaurant and lounge, pool, fitness center and valet parking. $$

Ramada Limited Dadeland, 7600 N. Kendall Drive, Kendall, ☎ 305/595-6000 offers a convenient location with easy access to US1, Dadeland Mall and area attractions. 110 rooms and a pool. No restaurant, but many are located nearby. $

Wellesley Inn Kendall, 11750 Mills Drive, Kendall, ☎ 800/444-8888 (reservations) or 305/270-0359 (hotel), has a suburban location just east of Florida's turnpike. Convenient location next to Town & Country Mall, with 106 rooms and a pool. No restaurant. $

Camping

City of Florida City Camp Site & RV Park, 601 NW 3rd Avenue, Florida City, ☎ 305/248-7889, features level grassy sites, seasonal recreational events, a dump station and security fencing. Shopping and the race track are only five minutes away. Open year-round. Amenities include picnic tables/shelters, pay phones, full hookups, 30 and 50 amp electricity, laundry, rec hall, playground and shuffleboard. Tenters welcome.

Southern Comfort RV Resort, 345 E. Palm Drive, Florida City, ☎ 305/248-6909, features 350 full hookup grassy sites, a tiki bar, bingo, crafts, dances, live music, 24-hour security. Other amenities include phone hookups, propane, food and snacks, grocery store, laundry, rec hall, swimming pool. Tenters welcome.

The Boardwalk, 100 NE 6th Avenue, Homestead, ☎ 305/248-2487, has a new recreation center, a heated swimming pool, and lighted shuffleboard. Open year-round, minutes away from Homestead's Motor Sports Complex, golf, baseball stadium and shopping. Other amenities: 30 and 50 amp electricity, full hookups, cable TV, pay phone, laundry, horseshoes and tennis.

Miami/Homestead KOA, 20675 SW 162nd Avenue, Homestead, ☎ 800/562-7732, is in a rural setting of avocado and mango groves. Open year round; just seven miles to Homestead Motor Sports Complex, with Monkey Jungle and MetroZoo nearby. Amenities: full hookups, 30 amp electricity, propane, food and snacks, grocery store, laundry, hot showers, hot tub, a pub, picnic shelters, rec hall, air-conditioned cabins, horseshoes, shuffleboard and a swimming pool. Tenters and pets welcome.

Biscayne National Park, SW 328th Street, Homestead, ☎ 305/230-7275, does not have camping on the park's mainland, but island camping is available, accessible only by boat. **Boca Chita Key** offers overnight tie-ups for boats, tent camping in designated areas, restrooms, picnic tables, grills and a short nature trail. Bring your own fresh water, food, supplies, and pack all trash out. On **Elliott Key,** accessible by private boat or tour boat, there are 40 primitive campsites. Showers, restrooms, and drinking water are available, but all trash must be packed out.

Gator Park, 24050 SW 8th Street, ☎ 800/559-2205, is north and west of Coral Gables, 12 miles west of Florida's Turnpike. Close to the Everglades, where you can airboat or fish in the campground's private lake. Other amenities include: full hookups, restaurant, gift shop, phone hookups, 30 amp electricity, boat ramp, ice, picnic shelters.

Camp Owaissa Bauer, 17001 SW 264th Street, Homestead, ☎ 305/247-6016, is on 119 acres of South Florida woodland and accommodates 146 overnight campers in its six cabins. This is a popular spot for family gatherings, group picnics, reunions etc. Amenities include a dining hall/social room for 200, swimming pool, baseball field, volleyball court, fire circle, nature trails, chickee hut and restrooms. A park manager is on the premises.

North of Homestead, adjacent to the Metrozoo is the **Larry and Penny Thompson Campground,** 12451 SW 184th Street, 505/232-1049. There are 270 acres of woodland, bridle trails, and hiking paths, with 240 campsites. Amenities include: space for recreational vehicles, full electrical and water hookups, restroom/laundry facilities with hot showers, a camp store, picnic shelters, a freshwater lake with a beach, boat rentals, tot lot, concession stand, fitness course, jogging and bike trail. Open year round, advance seasonal reservations recommended.

■ Where to Eat

Haitian

Café Creole, 12983 SW 112th Street, Kendall, ☎ 305/386-7070, prepares delicious crunchy malanga fritters dipped in a chili pepper sauce; or try the tender marinated conch served in a rich tomato Creole sauce. Whole snapper is wonderful, mild and sweet. $

Thai/Chinese

Chopsticks House, 20553 Old Cutler Rd., Kendall, ☎ 305/254-0080, serves expertly prepared spring rolls stuffed with shredded vegetables. The marinated bean curd is chopped and deep fried, and may be enjoyed with black bean or red curry sauce. Pad Thai is a delicious house specialty. $

K.C. Cagney & Co., 11230 SW 137th Avenue, West Kendall, ☎ 305/386-1555, has an eclectic menu, including Thai chicken salad and rice bowls topped with fresh fish in a pungent black bean sauce. They also serve more than 30 varieties of hamburgers, with sundaes and cream pies for dessert. $

Mexican

El Toro Taco, 1 Krome Avenue, Homestead, ☎ 305/245-8182 dishes up authentic chicken burritos with shredded white meat.

Miami

Fajitas filled with steak, onions, and peppers are also flavorful. $

Vietnamese

Mekong, 18073 S. Dixie Hwy, Cutler Ridge, ☎ 305/238-3500, has delectable salad rolls, noodles, meat and herbs wrapped in chewy rice paper, and unforgettable lemon grass chicken. Stir-fried garlic jumbo shrimp are a good bargain, as are the noodle soups. $

Indian

Punjab Palace, 11780 N Kendall Drive, Kendall, ☎ 305/274-1300, serves fresh-baked nan from their clay tandoor oven, dripping with butter. Try lamb curry or tandoori chicken, with a side of stewed lentils and chickpeas. $$

Italian

Romano's Macaroni Grill, 12100 N. Kendall Drive, Kendall, ☎ 305/270-0621, is a friendly family bistro with delightful focaccia bread and fresh caesar salad. Try their thin crust pizza with sun-dried tomatoes, mozzarella, basil and oregano. Pasta lovers will enjoy the penne with scallops and Italian peppers. $

American

White Lion Café, 146 NW 7th St, Homestead, ☎ 305/248-1076, is a café within an antique shop, with a Key West-style outdoor patio. Homemade soups and salad are tasty, as are cakes, pies and cobblers made daily by chef/owner Loryann Swank. $

Tourism Information

Greater Homestead / Florida City Chamber of Commerce, 43 N. Krome Avenue, Homestead 33030. ☎ 305/247-2332.

❦ ❦ ❦

Coral Gables & Coconut Grove

A bout 25 miles north of the South Dade area is Coral Gables, a city of serene parks, tropical gardens, and fountains reminiscent of Venice. Quiet tree-lined streets feature homes with architectural styles from Spain, Italy, New England, Dutch South Africa, France, and China. Designed by George Merrick and incorporated in 1925, Coral Gables is rightfully called the "City Beautiful."

North and east of Coral Gables is Coconut Grove, a town that hosts festivals and events like the **Coconut Grove Bed Race, Goombay Festival,** and **King Mango Strut.** This is a good place to take a break in between your adventures: shop, dine, see movies and plays, or hang out with locals.

Getting Here

A car is recommended for getting around in the Coral Gables and Coconut Grove area. From the airport, take 836/Dolphin Expressway east to I-95 south; intersect at US1, and take the appropriate street exits to Coral Gables or Coconut Grove destinations that interest you.

■ Adventures

On Foot

When not directing traffic at Miami International Airport, blonde, blue-eyed Dickie David is an enthusiastic volunteer at **Fairchild Tropical Garden,** located in the south part of Coral Gables at 10901 Old Cutler Road, ☎ 305/667-1651; Web site, www.ftg.org. On this rainy day she's driving us around the 83 stunning acres in a golf cart, so we can hop out and examine lush emerald palms as big as houses. "Did you know there are 2,700 kinds of palms?" she asks. "We have about 700 varieties here at Fairchild," she smiles proudly. This magnificent botanical garden features one of the world's largest collections of palms and cycads, as well as flowering vines, tropical fruits, century-old trees, lily ponds, 11 lakes, and a sunken garden. Colonel Robert Montgomery established the garden in 1938 to share his extensive collection of tropical and subtropical plants. The garden grew as Montgomery's friend, botanist David Fairchild, traveled the world and brought back thousands of plant species to Coral Gables. The garden was later named in honor of Fairchild's important contributions to botanical education and research, which the garden's world-renowned horticultural staff continue today.

The diversity of plants is astonishing, from fragrant **ylang-ylang** trees, whose blossoms create Chanel No. 5, to the giant African **baobab** trees. A 16,000-foot conservatory, "Windows to the Tropics," displays rare and exotic plants from around the world. Gardening books, prints, souvenirs, and tropical preserves are available at the gift shop. Free tram tours of the garden run hourly, but walking gets you really close. The **Rain Forest Café** is open on weekends. Located five miles south of Coconut Grove. Open 9:30 am-4:30 pm daily, except Christmas day. Admission.

Explore the winding trail meandering through thick mangrove hammocks at **Matheson Hammock County Park,** north of Fairchild Tropical Garden off of Old Cutler Road, ☎ 305/666-6979. A coconut plantation in the early 1900s, this 100-acre beach park offers several pleasant picnic spots. The manmade lagoon is ideal for shelling, or you can sunbathe on the tranquil beach. There's also a marina for boat launches into Biscayne Bay. Enjoy lunch or dinner at The Red Fish Grill. The park is open from 6 am to sunset. Parking fee.

Tennis

Tropical Park Tennis Center, 7900 SW 40th St., Miami, ☎ 305/223-8710. 12 courts.

Tamiami Park, 11201 SW 24th Street, Miami, ☎ 305/223-7076.

Coral Gables

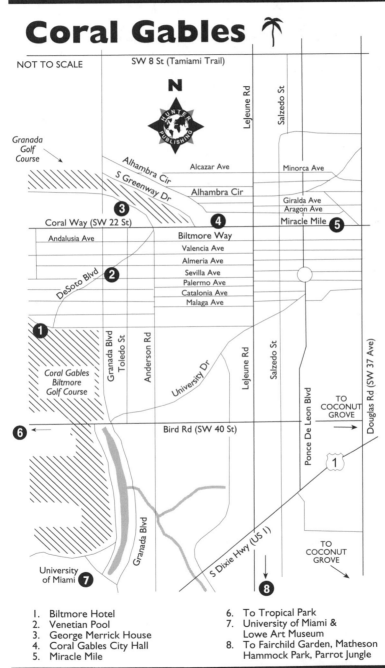

NOT TO SCALE

1. Biltmore Hotel
2. Venetian Pool
3. George Merrick House
4. Coral Gables City Hall
5. Miracle Mile
6. To Tropical Park
7. University of Miami & Lowe Art Museum
8. To Fairchild Garden, Matheson Hammock Park, Parrot Jungle

On Wheels

Metro-Dade Bicycle Program has created an excellent *Bike Miami Suitability Map* to help bikers select safe routes when biking within Dade County. The map rates specific roadways according to speed limits, road widths, amounts of traffic, and hazardous conditions. The map shows off-street paths, sidewalks, bike lanes, paved shoulders, and wide curb lanes. There's also information on bike rental shops, bike clubs, and parks with bike paths. To order the map ($3.50) or get information on cycling in Dade County, contact: Jeffrey Hunter, Coordinator, **Metro-Dade Bicycle Program,** 111 NW First Street, Suite 901, Miami, Florida 33128. ☎ 305/375-4507.

Some suggested bike routes are:

- In **Coral Gables:** At the corner of Coral Way/SW 24th Street and Galloway Road. Ride west along Coral Way to Tamiami Park.

- In **Coconut Grove:** At the corner of McFarlane Road and South Bayshore Drive, start at Coconut Grove Bayfront Park and cycle north along Bayshore Drive to the Museum of Science/Planetarium.

For additional information on bicycling in this area, contact:

Coral Way Bicycle Club, 2241 Coral Way, Coral Gables, FL 33145.

Coconut Grove Bicycle Club, Box 696, Coconut Grove, FL 33233.

On Water

Marinas

The recently renovated **Matheson Hammock Marina** has 242 modern aluminum wet slips, boat launching ramps, bait and tackle shop, fuel dock. 9610 Old Cutler Road, Coral Gables. 33156. ☎ 305/665-5475.

Pleasure Boating

If you'd prefer boating with a captain at the helm, book one of these cruises for dinner or sightseeing. All require reservations.

Miami Queen. Dining cruise. 700 Biltmore Way, Suite 204, Coral Gables. ☎ 305/445-7821. Call for boat location.

Biscayne America Co. Dining cruise. Boat location: Dinner Key Marina. For information, contact their office at 9401 SW 78th Street, Miami. ☎ 305/857-9000.

Castle Harbor Sailboat Rentals and Sailboat School. No food or beverages served. Boat location: Dinner Key Marina, 3400 Pan American Drive, Coconut Grove. ☎ 305/858-3212.

Celebration Excursions of Miami. Dining cruise. Call for boat location. Office: 3239 W. Trade Avenue, Suite 9, Coconut Grove. ☎ 305/445-8456.

Easy Sailing Yacht Charters. Dining cruise. Boat location: Dinner Key Marina. Office: PO Box 95, Coconut Grove. ☎ 305/858-4001.

Swimming

Do you dream of swimming like Esther Williams or Johnny "Tarzan" Weismuller? Then enjoy your laps in what's billed as "the largest hotel pool in the Continental United States." The famous 22,000-square-foot **Biltmore Hotel pool** in Coral Gables is where Esther performed and swimming instructor Johnny W. won his gold medal in the US Diving Championships. Newly renovated, the pool deck sports full-grown Canary Island palms, and lush gardens of bougainvillea and hibiscus. Don't be surprised if you see a film crew milling about, as the pool is popular for fashion shoots and music videos. Located at 1200 Anastasia Avenue, Coral Gables, 33134, ☎ 305/445-1926.

Another favorite pool of Esther and Johnny (were they ever dry?) was the **Venetian Pool,** also in Coral Gables. During its heyday, gondolas floated across the turquoise water, as orchestras serenaded dancers swaying beneath the stars. Bathing beauties promenaded across walkways in beauty contests, and William Jennings Bryan delivered political speeches. Once a quarry pit, the pool was created by George Merrick's uncle, Denman Fink, and architect Phineas Paist in 1924.

Today over 100,000 tourists visit the pool annually to enjoy cascading waterfalls, vine-covered loggias, and palm-fringed islands. Fed by underground artesian wells, the 800,000 gallons of water are replenished daily via natural ground filtration. Hidden behind pastel stucco walls and wrought iron gates, it's easy to drive past without ever knowing the pool exists. Most people stop, take a few snapshots, and move on. We recommend you spend a morning or afternoon actually swimming in this lovely pool, which is listed on the National Register of Historic Places. Enjoy the elegance of a bygone era. Admission. Hours: Open seven days, 11 am-7:30 pm mid-June through mid-August. Open 11 am-5:30 pm during September and October. Open 10 am-4:30 pm Nov-March. Closed Mondays in April and May. The pool is at 2701 DeSoto Boulevard, Coral Gables, ☎ 305/460-5356.

Other Adventures

Horse Shows

There are more than 30 horse shows a year at the **Equestrian Center** at Tropical Park, just west of Coral Gables at 7900 SW 40th Street, Miami, ☎ 305/554-7334. Registered Arabians, hunter/jumpers, Western-style, and Paso Fino horses all perform here. The 1,000-seat Center also hosts rodeos, so call for their schedule of shows and special events.

■ Sightseeing

Coral Gables

Many of the Coral Gables mansions were designed by George Merrick in the 1920s, and are still surrounded by grand entrances, elegant fountains, and tree-lined boulevards. Take a spin along **Riviera Drive**, where Chinese-style homes sport carved balconies, lattice, and curved tile roofs adorned with animal sculptures for good luck. Over on **Hardee Road,** Country French-style chateaus have square towers and wrought iron balconies. On **LeJeune Road,** homes are designed in the style of Dutch colonist farmhouses, with spiraling chimneys, scroll work, and high domed arches. Driving through these storybook neighborhoods is like being on a Hollywood movie backlot.

George Merrick House, 907 Coral Way, ☎ 305/460-5361, offers tours on Sundays and Wednesdays from 1-4 pm, but you can visit the charming gardens every day until sunset. The boyhood home of Coral Gables' founding father features coral rock construction and many of Merrick's original furnishings.

South of Merrick House is **Coral Gables City Hall,** 405 Biltmore Way, ☎ 305/446-6800. A 1920s limestone structure with both circular and square design, it's worth strolling through to see the antiques and rotunda mural.

On Saturday mornings from mid-January through the end of March, there's a European-style **Farmers' Market** in front of City Hall at Merrick Park. Call for details, ☎ 305/460-5310.

If you're not a guest at the Mediterranean revival-style **Biltmore Hotel,** 1200 Anastasia Avenue, ☎ 305/445-1926, take a free tour conducted by the Dade Heritage Trust on Sundays at 1:30, 2:30 and 3:30 pm. This landmark hotel features massive stone columns, intricately painted ceilings, Italian marble floors, and Spanish woodwork, as well as the largest and possibly most glamorous hotel swimming pool in the Continental US. The hotel's Web site is www.biltmorehotel.com.

South of The Biltmore, the **University of Miami** is the oldest university in Greater Miami, and largest private research university in the Southeastern United States. The **Lowe Art Museum** on campus, 1301 Stanford Drive, ☎ 305/284-3535, holds exhibits from a permanent collection of Italian Renaissance and Baroque Art, Greco-Roman antiquities, Spanish Old Masters, Native American, pre-Columbian, Asian and African art. There are also touring exhibits from international museums. If you'd like a guided tour, call for reservations. Open Tuesday-Saturday 10 am-5 pm, Sunday noon-5 pm. Admission.

Shoppers will enjoy browsing **Miracle Mile** (SW 22nd Street), among chic boutiques, book stores, and bridal shops selling wedding gowns for $500-$50,000. This neighborhood has over 120 restaurants, many the recipients of regional and national dining awards. You'll find everything from a French bistro to a rowdy Irish pub.

Miami

On the first Friday of each month, Coral Gables art galleries host free open house parties as part of **"Gables Gallery Night."** Call ☎ 305/461-2723 for the party calendar.

If you've got an extra $11,000, buy a teak replica of a 1904 Orient Express Dining Car. It's only 30 inches long, but who's counting? **The Gallery of Transportation,** 165 Aragon Avenue, ☎ 305/529-8599, features high end "Gauge One" model trains, cars, planes and ships. Most of the intricately detailed classic transportation models date from the 1960's to the present, and are made of brass, aluminum, teak and steel. Now you can have your dream 801 Formula One Ferrari, but in radio-controlled quarter-scale.

Just south of Coral Gables, enjoy a unique bird sanctuary and botanical garden at **Parrot Jungle & Gardens,** 11000 SW 57th Avenue, Miami, ☎ 305/666-7834; www.florida.com/parrotjungle/. Parrots fly free here and you can feed them and pose for pictures, as well as enjoy bird and wildlife shows. The park also is home to flamingos, apes, alligators, and giant tortoises. There's a children's playground, a gift shop, and The Parrot Café. Open daily 9:30 am-6 pm. Admission.

A bit farther west, **The Art Museum at Florida International University,** University Park, SW 8th Street and 107th Avenue, ☎ 305/348-2890, features national traveling and self-curated exhibitions, including the acclaimed American Art Today series. Browse ArtPark, the museum's outdoor sculpture garden. Open Monday 10-9 pm; Tuesday-Friday until 5 pm; Saturday noon-4 pm; closed Sunday. Free.

Coconut Grove

By the time Miami became a city in 1896, Coconut Grove was a thriving community with a school, several churches, a yacht club, a library, and the Biscayne Bay area's first Black settlement, Bahamian immigrants who helped build much of the town. Today "The Grove" has a style and flavor that's as unique and diverse as its residents.

The bayside home and grounds of Grove shipbuilder Ralph Munroe make for an interesting tour at the **Barnacle State Historic Site,** 3485 Main Highway, ☎ 305/448-9445. Built in 1891, tours of his five-acre estate are given Friday-Sunday at

10, 11:30, 1, 2:30. Stroll the old horse and buggy trail that wends through a hammock to the house or visit on a moonlit night when special events are planned. Call for the schedule.

Built in 1926, the **Coconut Grove Playhouse,** 3500 Main Highway, ☎ 305/442-4000, was destroyed by a hurricane, but rebuilt in 1927. The Rococo-style former movie theater, richly ornamented with columns and parapets, now presents contemporary theater and music productions.

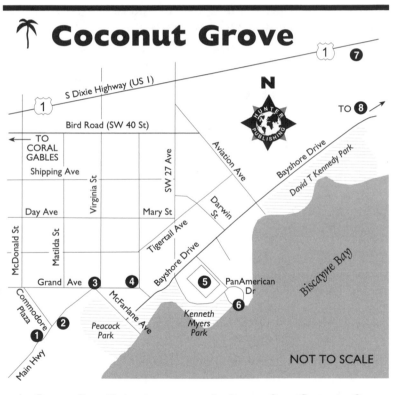

Coconut Grove

1. Coconut Grove Playhouse
2. The Barnacle State Historic Site
3. CocoWalk
4. Mayfair Shops and Hotel
5. Coconut Grove Convention Ctr
6. Dinner Key Marina
7. Museum of Science & Planetarium
8. Vizcaya

Miami

CocoWalk, 3015 Grand Avenue, ☎ 305/444-0777, draws thousands of shoppers with stores like The Gap, Banana Republic and Victoria's Secret. There's also a multi-screen cinema and a diversity of restaurants. For a sensational chocolate milkshake and some entertaining people watching, grab a curbside table at Johnny Rocket Restaurant, across the street.

Just east of CocoWalk is **Streets of Mayfair,** 2911 Grand Avenue, ☎ 305/448-1700, a newly renovated entertainment, dining and shopping emporium. Enjoy comedy at **The Improv Club,** try virtual reality on for size at **Virtua Café,** or shoot pool at **FatKat's Pool Bar.** Dozens of shops and restaurants make it easy to enjoy an afternoon or evening here.

When was the last time you were face to face with an Australian bearded dragon? How about a thick-necked giant tortoise? At the **Miami Museum of Science & Space Transit Planetarium,** 3280 S. Miami Avenue, ☎ 305/854-4247 (museum) and 305/854-2222 (planetarium information), the indoor exhibits are diverse: robotic dinosaurs, CD-ROM displays, and multimedia extravaganza star shows. I highly recommend a visit to the outdoor Wildlife Center. A rehab center for injured birds of prey (like an orange-beaked Florida crested caracara that was hit by a car, and an owl that had been shot), the center is an oasis for birds and an educational opportunity for wildlife lovers. There are also reptiles, like the spiny faced dragon, which volunteers will let you hold. The Space Transit Planetarium features hourly star shows, laser rock presentations, and live star lectures/telescope viewing on Saturday nights. Director Jack Horkheimer reaches 10 million people weekly on the PBS TV show Star Hustler. Open daily 10 am-6 pm, closed Thanksgiving and Christmas. The planetarium has evening shows as well; call for schedule. Admission.

If you only have time for one Coconut Grove stop, make it **Vizcaya,** 3251 South Miami Avenue, ☎ 305/250-9133. This 1916 Italianiate estate built by industrialist James Deering is a stunning example of what money and good taste can create. Inspired by Italian villas of the 16th and 17th centuries, the home is filled with antique furnishings and surrounded by 10 acres of formal gardens and fountains. The gift shop features replicas of antique pottery, metalwork, tapestry, Italian crafts and jewelry. Vizcaya Café is a relaxing spot for lunch, serving salads, sandwiches, desserts, and overlooking Deering's glamorous swimming pool. The house is open daily from 9 am-5 pm, the gardens from 9:30 am-5:30 pm. Closed Christmas day. Admission.

■ Festivals & Events

January

Vizcaya Moonlight Tours, 3251 S. Miami Avenue, Coconut Grove, ☎ 305/250-9133. Monthly, call for dates.

Taste of the Grove, Peacock Park, McFarlane Rd, and South Bayshore Drive, Downtown Coconut Grove, ☎ 305/447-1224.

Coconut Grove Cares Antique & Jewelry Show, Coconut Grove Convention Center, ☎ 305/444-8454. (Held monthly throughout the year.)

Annual Beaux Arts Festival, University of Miami Campus, 1301 Stanford Drive, Coral Gables, ☎ 305/284-3603.

February

Coconut Grove Arts Festival, downtown Coconut Grove, ☎ 305/447-0401.

Home Show, Coconut Grove Convention Center, Coconut Grove, ☎ 305/666-5944.

Annual South Miami Arts & Crafts Festival, Sunset Drive and US1, South Miami (a few miles southeast of Coral Gables), ☎ 305/558-1758.

March

Festival of Rides, Tropical Park, 7900 SW 40th Street, Miami, ☎ 305/226-8315.

Italian Renaissance Festival, Vizcaya Museum and Gardens, 3251 S. Miami Avenue, Coconut Grove, ☎ 305/758-4595.

The Dade County Fair & Exposition, Tamiami Park, 11201 SW 24th Street, west of Coral Gables, ☎ 305/223-7060.

In the Company of Women celebrates Women's History Month, recognizing the achievements of women based on their professional accomplishments and community service. Vizcaya, 3251 S. Miami, Coconut Grove, ☎ 305/857-6878.

Annual Miami International Orchid Show, Coconut Grove Convention Center, ☎ 305/285-0107.

April

The Biltmore International Wine Festival, Biltmore Hotel, Coral Gables, ☎ 305/445-8066, ext. 2340.

Taste of the Gables, Ponce Circle Park, Coral Gables, ☎ 305/447-9299.

Merrick Festival, Ponce Circle Park, Coral Gables, ☎ 305/447-9299.

Springtime Harvest Festival, Dade County Fair & Exposition Center, Coral Way and SW 112th Ave (west of Coral Gables), Tamiami Park, ☎ 305/373-1492.

May

Coconut Grove Bed Race, downtown Coconut Grove, ☎ 305/624-3714.

The International Hispanic Theater Festival, El Carrusel Theater, 235 Alcazar Ave, Coral Gables, ☎ 445-8877.

June

Miami/Bahamas Goombay Festival, Coconut Grove, ☎ 305/372-9966.

July

Moon Over Miami Dance, Coconut Grove Convention Center, 2700 S. Bayshore Drive, Coconut Grove, ☎ 305/579-3400.

August

Boat Show, same address as above, ☎ 305/442-4012.

September

Festival Miami, Maurice Gusman Concert Hall, on the University of Miami campus, 1314 Miller Drive, Coral Gables, ☎ 305/284-4940.

October

The Florida Shakespeare Theatre, The Biltmore Hotel, 1200 Anastasia Avenue, Coral Gables, ☎ 305/446-1116.

Caribbean Carnival, Coconut Grove Convention Center, 2700 S. Bayshore Drive, Coconut Grove, ☎ 305/579-3310.

Sunday in the Park with Art, Fairchild Tropical Garden, 10901 Old Cutler Road, Coral Gables, ☎ 305/667-1651.

Antique & Jewelry Show, Coconut Grove Convention Center, 2700 S. Bayshore Drive, Coconut Grove, ☎ 305/444-8454.

Annual Historical Museum Golf Classic, Biltmore Hotel & Golf Course, 1200 Anastasia Ave, Coral Gables, ☎ 305/375-1492.

November

Santa's Enchanted Forest, Tropical Park, 7900 SW 40th Street, a few miles west of Coral Gables, ☎ 305/893-0090.

Coral Gables International Festival of Craft Arts, Alhambra Plaza and Ponce de Leon Blvd, Coral Gables, ☎ 305/445-9973.

The White Party Against HIV/AIDS, Vizcaya, ☎ 305/759-6181.

Banyan Arts and Crafts Festival, Fuller Street and Commodore Plaza, Coconut Grove, ☎ 305/444-7270.

Annual South Miami Art Festival, Sunset Drive between Red Road and US1, South Miami, just southeast of Coral Gables, ☎ 305/661-1621.

December

Annual Holiday Stroll, Merrick Park and Miracle Mile, Coral Gables, ☎ 305/446-1657.

King Mango Strut, annual spoof of the Orange Bowl Parade, Coconut Gove, ☎ 305/445-1865.

Fairchild Tropical Garden Ramble, gardening festival and plant sale, Fairchild Tropical Garden, 10901 Old Cutler Rd, Coral Gables, ☎ 305/667-1651.

Junior Orange Bowl International Tennis Championship, Biltmore Tennis Center, 1150 Anastasia Drive, and University of Miami, Coral Gables, ☎ 305/662-1210.

Orange Bowl International Junior Golf Championship, The Biltmore Golf Course, 1210 Anastasia Drive, Coral Gables, ☎ 305/662-1210.

Miami

Junior Orange Bowl Parade, along Miracle Mile, Coral Gables, ☎ 305/662-1210.

■ Where to Stay

Coral Gables

Biltmore Hotel, 1200 Anastasia Avenue, Coral Gables, ☎ 800/727-1926 or 305/445-1926, www.biltmorehotel.com, is a National Historic Landmark Hotel with Mediterranean architecture. Roman columns, hand-painted ceilings and marble floors create an elegant setting. Three restaurants, three lounges, 10 tennis courts, a superb golf course, fitness center, and the "largest hotel swimming pool in the continental US." $$$

David William Hotel, 700 Biltmore Way, Coral Gables, ☎ 800/327-8770, offers one- and two-bedroom suites for families requiring extended stays. 124 rooms, some with kitchens, a restaurant and lounge, pool and golf course. $$

Holiday Inn Downtown Coral Gables, 2051 LeJeune Rd, Coral Gables, ☎ 305/443-2301 is right in the heart of Coral Gables, within walking distance of Miracle Mile shops and the city's many restaurants. 167 rooms, restaurant, lounge, pool and fitness center. $$

Hotel Place St. Michel, 162 Alcazar Avenue, Coral Gables, ☎ 800/848-HOTEL, is a charming European-style hotel built in 1926, recently renovated. The hotel offers a complimentary Continental breakfast, fruit basket and newspaper. 27 rooms, restaurant and lounge. Within walking distance of Miracle Mile. $$

Hyatt Regency, 50 Alhambra Plaza, Coral Gables, ☎ 800/233-1234, is an elegant Mediterranean-style hotel inspired by the Alhambra Palace in Spain. The 242 spacious guest rooms are luxuriously appointed, and there is a restaurant, two lounges, a pool, and fitness center. Walking distance to Miracle Mile. $$$

Riviera Court Motel, 5100 Riviera Drive, Coral Gables, ☎ 800/368-8602, is geared for families on a budget. Located on the Coral Gables Waterway, it's near the University of Miami,

Miracle Mile shopping and Dadeland Mall. 30 rooms, some with kitchens, pool. No restaurant. $

Coconut Grove

Cherokee Rose Lodge, 3734 Main Highway, Coconut Grove, ☎ 305/858-4884, is a private walled-in estate in the historic section of town. Walk to shops, restaurants, and the Coconut Grove Playhouse. Suites overlook the garden, or choose a cottage by the pool. $$

DoubleTree Hotel, 2649 S. Bayshore Drive, Coconut Grove, ☎ 305/858-2500 (central reservations, ☎ 800/222-8733), is within walking distance of Coconut Grove shops, restaurants, movies, nightclubs, galleries and theaters. 192 rooms, a restaurant, lounge, pool, and two tennis courts. $$

Grand Bay Hotel, 2669 S. Bayshore Drive, Coconut Grove, ☎ 800/327-2788, offers luxurious accommodations, a pool and fitness center, restaurant and lounge. 180 rooms. $$$

Grove Isle Club & Resort, 4 Grove Isle Drive, Coconut Grove, ☎ 800/88-GROVE, has panoramic views of Biscayne Bay and Miami's skyline. The newly renovated resort is on a private island, and all guest rooms have large private balconies and floor-to-ceiling windows. The Dining Room features gourmet cuisine such as golden crab and yuca soufflé, all prepared by executive chef Doug Reiss. The resort has a full-service tennis center, fitness facility, waterfront walking/jogging path, outdoor pool, and hydro-massage whirlpool. $$$

Hampton Inn Hotel, 2800 SW 28th Terrace, Coconut Grove, ☎ 305/442-8655, is one of the town's newest hotels, with 137 rooms, a pool and fitness center. No restaurant. $

The 185-room **Mayfair House Hotel,** 3000 Florida Avenue, Coconut Grove, ☎ 800/433-4555, has luxurious all-suite accommodations. Each has a private terrace and a Japanese spa; some have kitchens. Amenities include a restaurant, two lounges, pool, and fitness center. It's right downtown, within walking distance of shops and entertainment. $$$

■ Where to Eat

American

☆ If you only eat one meal in southeast Florida, dine at **Norman's,** 21 Almeria Avenue, Coral Gables, ☎ 305/446-6767. Chef Norman Van Aken's beautiful and delectable "New World Cuisine" has garnered numerous awards, such as *Gourmet Magazine's* "Best Restaurant in South Florida," and was the James Beard Nominee for "Best Restaurant in America." Try an appetizer of "peeky toe" crabcakes with West Indian guacamole, then the yuca-stuffed crispy shrimp salad. One of Chef Van Aken's many signature entrées is his Key West yellowtail with grilled asparagus spears, garlicky mashed potatoes, and citrus butter. For dessert, the papaya sorbet is sublime. A truly memorable dining adventure. Reservations suggested. $$$

Rodeo Grill, 2121 Ponce de Leon Blvd., Coral Gables, ☎ 305/447-6336, is a carnivore's delight. Sausages, chicken, turkey, lamb, short ribs, top sirloin, ham, and pork loin are grilled over hot coals and served on skewers. Seafood kebabs are a good choice for non-meat eaters. $$

Greenstreet Café, 3110 Commodore Plaza, Coconut Grove, ☎ 305/567-0662, is a pleasant sidewalk café serving soups, sandwiches and salads with a Mediterranean and Caribbean flair. Jamaican chicken wings are popular, as are eggs Benedict al fresco. $

Continental

Two Sisters, Hyatt Regency, 50 Alhambra Plaza, Coral Gables, 305/441-1234, serves an unusual blend of Spanish and Pacific Rim cuisine. Crispy whole yellowtail snapper is delicious, as are the tasty tapas. Don't miss the banana flan. $$

Grand Café, Grand Bay Hotel, 2669 S. Bayshore Drive, Coconut Grove, ☎ 305/858-9600, has soft shell crabs over springy buckwheat linguine, thick New York strip steak with wild mushrooms, and Chilean salmon in a sherry vinaigrette. $$$

French

Le Bouchon du Grove, 3430 Main Highway, Coconut Grove, ☎ 305/448-6060, is a charming open-air French restaurant, known for friendly service and bubbly kir royales. Try the homemade duck paté, steak with green peppercorn sauce, or chicken en papillote. $$

Le Provencal, 382 Miracle Mile, Coral Gables, ☎ 305/448-8984, is all about leeks, tomatoes, garlic, onions, and olive oil in the best French tradition. Bouillabaisse gets raves, as does the piquant red pepper rouille. $$

Italian

Bocca di Rosa, 2833 Bird Avenue, Coconut Grove, ☎ 305/444-4222, serves delicious gnocchi, tender filet of beef in white peppercorn and red wine sauce, and potato-mushroom soup garnished with edible rose petals. $$$

Spanish

Las Rias Gallegas, 804 Ponce de Leon Blvd., Coral Gables, ☎ 305/442-9058, serves excellent paella and grilled sandwich treats like swordfish or tuna steaks on hoagie rolls. They also have another location in Coconut Grove at 2890 SW 27th Avenue, ☎ 305/443-0037. $

Tourism Information

Miami Visitor Center at CocoWalk, 3015 Grand Avenue, Coconut Grove, Florida 33133. ☎ 305/569-9142. Open Monday-Thursday noon-10 pm, Friday-Sunday until 11 pm.

Coconut Grove Chamber of Commerce, 2820 McFarlane Rd. Coconut Grove 33133. ☎ 305/444-7270. Visit their Web site at www.coconutgrove.com.

Coral Gables Chamber of Commerce, 50 Aragon Avenue, Coral Gables 33134. ☎ 305/446-1657; fax 305/446-9900.

🌴 🌴 🌴

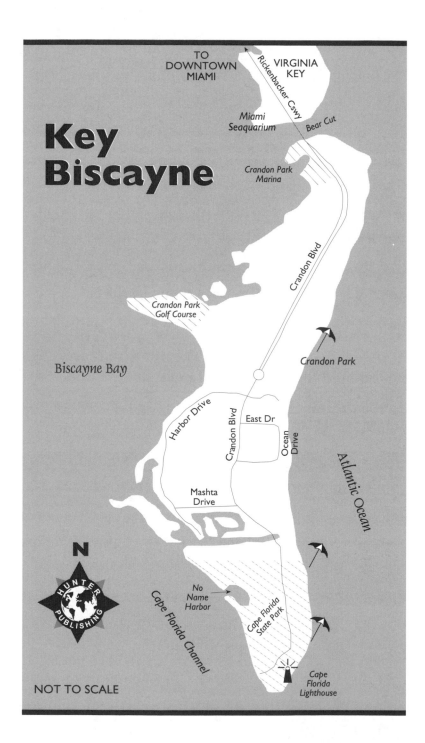

Key Biscayne

At first it seems Key Biscayne is only for the mega-rich: a sign in the Häagen Dazs ice cream store implores, "No $100 bills please!" Women shopping at the grocery sport chic couture sun dresses, bronzed aerobicized bodies, and blonde tresses. Glamourous condos along Biscayne Bay, second homes for many residents, casually advertise half-million-dollar sales tags. Mercedes, Jaguars, and BMWs are the local cars of choice. But adventure lovers will find plenty of affordable fun on Key Biscayne, from fishing to swimming, surfboarding, boating, biking, beaching and sightseeing. John Festa, Key Biscayne's mayor and a NOAA oceanographer, lauds the island as "a tropical paradise, with the safety and serenity of seclusion, a diverse population, and proximity to a big city." I agree.

Getting Here

We recommend you rent a car to get around Key Biscayne. From Miami International Airport, take 836/Dolphin Expressway east to I-95 and head south. Watch for signs to Rickenbacker Causeway. Take the Causeway (there is a toll) across Biscayne Bay and you'll be on Crandon Boulevard, the main street throughout Key Biscayne.

■ Adventures

On Foot

The **Cape Florida Lighthouse** at Bill Baggs Cape Florida State Recreation Area, 1200 S. Crandon Boulevard, Key Biscayne, ☎ 305/361-5811, has faithfully stood guard over the coast of South Florida for more than 170 years Built in 1825, its beacon has guided sailors past Key Biscayne's treacherous sandbars and coral reefs, standing stalwart against hurricanes, Seminole Indian attacks, fire, and environmental degradation. It was rebuilt to its current 95-foot height after hurricane damage in 1855, and in 1971 was placed on the National Register of Historic Places. Through the support of volunteers, funding from government and private grants, and private donations, the lighthouse was recently restored to its authentic 1855 condition. Climbing the 109 interior spiral steps to the top reveals splendid views of the park's award-winning beach and sparkling Biscayne Bay. The former light-keeper's cottage next door, now **Key Biscayne History House,** features cultural displays and videos depicting early island life. Ranger-guided walks are at 10:30 am and 1, 2:30, and 3:30 pm daily, except Tuesday and Wednesday. Free with park admission.

Golf

In the heart of Crandon Park are the Links of Key Biscayne, recently renamed **Crandon Park Golf Course,** 6700 Crandon Blvd., ☎ 305/361-9129. Winding through natural mangroves and around saltwater lagoons, the course is consistently rated as one of the best public golf courses in the US. Every hole is a challenge: steep, gaping bunkers; long, undulating greens; and mangrove-lined fairways. If you play from the blue tees, there's a track stretching over 7,000 yards. The course hosts the Senior PGA Tour for the Royal Caribbean Classic every winter, where golfers enjoy great weather and Miami's skyline. Call for reservations and greens fees.

Tennis

The **Tennis Center** at Crandon Park, 7300 Crandon Blvd., ☎ 305/365-2300, hosts the Lipton Championships each March, where players like Agassiz, Sampras, Graf and Seles meet their match. The rest of the year it's open to the public, featuring 17 hard courts (six of which are lighted), eight clay courts and two grass courts. Fees are per hour; call for reservations.

Next door to the Tennis Center is another first-class facility, **Key Biscayne Tennis Association,** 6702 Crandon Blvd., ☎ 305/361-5263. There are seven clay courts and three hard courts, all lighted for night play. Adult and junior clinics and private lessons are available. Call for reservations and fees.

If you really want to improve your game, then study with Mike Belkin, head tennis pro at the **Sonesta Beach Resort Key Biscayne,** 350 Ocean Drive, ☎ 305/361-2021. Mr. Belkin won tournaments over Jimmy Connors and Arthur Ashe, and was ranked the #1 Canadian tennis pro for eight years. His extensive experience as a pro tennis player and coach can only mean more wins for you.

On Wheels

 Biking Key Biscayne is the most pleasurable way to experience the island. There's less traffic than other areas of south Florida, with many easy bike paths. Along Crandon Boulevard are several shops that rent bikes by the hour, day or week.

One highly recommended path is along **Rickenbacker Causeway,** from the toll booth to Crandon Park. This route has beautiful views of Biscayne Bay, ocean and beach, winding past golf courses and the Tennis Center and ending near Crandon Park Beach. Just north of the beach is a wooded area with a bike path. Keep an eye out for possums, rabbits, reptiles and raccoons living among the dense vegetation.

Another enjoyable ride is along **Crandon Boulevard,** first heading west on Harbor Drive, which makes a half circle, then east on W. Mashta Drive and ending back at Crandon. This tour winds through Key Biscayne's pristine neighborhoods of lovely homes, posh condos, and beachside mansions. A third option is the 1½-mile bike path within **Bill Baggs Cape Florida State Recreation Area.** Start at the entrance (you must pay the park fee), then follow the marked bike path running west along Biscayne Bay. You'll see pelicans, fishermen casting from the seawall, and Biscayne Bay while biking alongside mangrove jungles. Bikes are available for rent at the park's concession stand.

Key Biscayne Bike Rental Shops

Intra Mark, Rickenbacker Causeway, ☎ 305/365-9762.

Key Cycling, 61 Harbor Drive, ☎ 305/361-0061.

Mangrove Cycles, 260 Crandon Blvd, ☎ 305/361-5555.

To get in touch with area bikers, write: **Biscayne Bay Bicycle Club,** 9617 Park Drive, Key Biscayne, 33149.

Miami

Many of the bike shops in town also rent **in-line skates,** as does the Bill Baggs Cape Florida State Recreation area concession stand. You can skate on the same bike paths suggested above. Try **Sergio's Skate Zone,** 180 Crandon Blvd. ☎ 305/361-6610.

On Water

Are you ready to get wet? Key Biscayne is renowned for some of most exhilarating boating, fishing, diving, windsurfing, and swimming in southeast Florida.

Boating

For one-stop "shopping," **Crandon Marina** in Crandon Park, 4000 Crandon Boulevard, ☎ 305/361-1281, has the most diverse selection of boats. **Sailboats of Key Biscayne,** at the marina, ☎ 305/361-0328, has eight 22- to 25-foot-long Catalina sailboats. You can also enroll in sailing school with instructor Gary Sprague. Special packages are available for lessons, full day, and overnight sailboat rentals.

Club Nautico, also at Crandon Park Marina, ☎ 305/361-9217, rents powerboats like 200 Horizons, 207 Quests, and 205 Sundowners.

Key Biscayne Boat Rentals, 3301 Rickenbacker Causeway, ☎ 305/361-7368, rents Monza boats with bimini tops and Yamaha 150-HP outboard engines. They also rent jet boats, waverunners, and waterskis.

One of the most delightful features of Key Biscayne is that you can be lazing the beach one minute and boating the Atlantic Ocean the next. At **Bill Baggs Cape Florida State Recreation Area,** 1200 S. Crandon Blvd., ☎ 305/361-5811, the park's east side concession rents Sunfish, kayaks, pedal boats, and hydrobikes right at the water's edge. As a guest at **Sonesta Beach Resort Key Biscayne,** 350 Ocean Drive, ☎ 305/361-2021 ext. 7938, you have easy ocean access via Hobie Cats, Sunfish, waverunners, or sea kayaks. Kids love careening around on the resort's six-seater banana boats. Sports directors at the Sonesta are helpful with instruction and boat launches.

Fishing

Deep-sea fishing is easy from **Crandon Marina,** Crandon Park, 4000 Crandon Blvd., ☎ 305/361-1281. There's a variety of sports fishing charter boats to choose from for half- or full-day trips. Bait and equipment are included, as you try to land dolphin, kingfish or snapper. One boat captain boasted that Key Biscayne bonefish average seven to nine lbs., as opposed to the "three-pounders you get everywhere else."

If you like shore fishing, spend the day at **Bill Baggs Cape Florida State Recreation Area,** 1200 S. Crandon Blvd., ☎ 305/361-5811. There are eight wooden fishing platforms along Biscayne Bay seawall and holes to hold your pole, making it easy to catch redfish, snook, snapper, and pompano. Another popular shore fishing spot is the old **Rickenbacker Causeway Bridge,** an inactive bridge next to the active Rickenbacker Causeway. There's parking on either side of the bridge.

To hire a fishing guide, call **Capt. Frank Garisto,** ☎ 305/361-9258, or **Bad to the Bone,** ☎ 305/361-5155.

Diving & Snorkeling

Southeast of Key Biscayne is good for wreck diving. Check out the freighter *Proteus,* the *Arida,* the Woolworth yacht *South Seas,* the *Orion,* and the *Ultra-Freeze.* Most of these wrecks are in depths of 55 to 120 feet, and teem with marine life. At depths below 100 feet you'll spot sharks and 300-pound groupers.

Crandon Marina, 4000 Crandon Blvd., has a PADI diveschool, **Divers Paradise,** ☎ 305/361-3483. Dive equipment is for rent or purchase, and they have a swimming pool for dive certification courses. Their three boats are ready to take you out to any of the wrecks off Key Biscayne.

Park rangers at **Bill Baggs Cape Florida State Recreation Area,** 1200 S. Crandon Blvd., provide guided snorkeling tours with advance reservations. ☎ 305/361-5811.

Windsurfing

Imagine learning to windsurf in two hours, or your money back? That's the promise made by instructors at **Sailboards Miami,** Rickenbacker Causeway, Hobie Beach, ☎ 305/361-SAIL. Innovations in equipment, teaching tools and instruction methods make it possible to "run off the wind on a screaming plane at 25 knots," brags their sales brochure. The school also offers "Jimmy's 10-Hour Guide to Windsurfing Greatness," if greatness is your goal.

Swimming

With so many gorgeous beaches on Key Biscayne, you can spend a different day on each one. Our favorites are: **Crandon Park Beach, Bill Baggs Cape Florida State Recreation Area Beach** (rated in the top 10 US beaches by *Condé Nast Traveler* magazine) and **Virginia Key Beach.** All are clean, with soft beige sand, and uncrowded, especially during the week.

If you're tired of salt in your eyes, take a dip in one of the prettiest and largest pools in South Florida. "Swimming is good for your heart, your muscles, and your circulation," says Alex Ballora, Pool and Beach Manager at **Sonesta Beach Resort Key Biscayne,** 350 Ocean Drive, ☎ 305/361-2021. The resort's inviting pool is 45 feet wide and 85 feet long, varying in depth from three to 10 feet. The temperature is a soothing 80° year round, and in only 62 laps you've completed a mile. So close that trashy novel and dive in.

Other Adventures

Sea Turtle Nesting

In the past few years, increasing numbers of sea turtles are nesting on Key Biscayne beaches; over 230,000 baby turtles hatch each year. Of the eight species of sea turtles worldwide, three nest on Virginia Key and Key Biscayne: the endangered **loggerhead** (400-500 lbs.), the endangered **green sea turtle** (500 lbs.), and the endangered **leatherback** (weighing up to 2,000 lbs.). Crandon Park presents a 50-minute slide presentation during turtle nesting season and offers a hatchery tour; for reservations, ☎ 305/365-3018. There's also one turtle watch a year at Bill Baggs Cape Florida State Recreation Area, with a park ranger lecture on turtle nesting habits. ☎ 305/361-5811 for reservations.

■ Sightseeing

 At **Miami Seaquarium's** Discovery Bay exhibit, the world is wild. Stingrays chase sea turtles as a turquoise parrotfish looks on. Twelve brown pelicans roost in a green mangrove while gulls fight over fish. Cormorants and egrets wade the shallows looking for snacks. Nurse sharks, tarpon, snook, and pink flamingoes round out the neighborhood.

❋ Snapshot

Meet Robert Rose, Director of Training, Miami Seaquarium.

SS: Robert, what exciting encounters with animals have you experienced?

RR: Watching killer whales, sea lions, and dolphins give birth is very rewarding. The time I've spent interacting with the animals in the water is exciting.

SS: What does Seaquarium offer wildlife lovers?

RR: Even in the wild you won't see as many animals as we have here. You can observe manatees, feed a sea lion, and get close to a killer whale. You get eye-to-eye with all our animals, even smelling them.

SS: Is there an educational aspect to Seaquarium?

RR: We think of our animals as ambassadors to animals in the wild. As trainers, our goal is to entertain and educate people about endangered species. For example, there are only about 2,000 manatees left in the wild; some 200 a year are killed. Most likely, by the time my child is grown, he'll only be able to see a manatee at a facility like Seaquarium. So we're valuable in that we're offering a haven for endangered or injured animals, as well as providing a close-up encounter for wildlife lovers.

Miami

The Seaquarium is famous for their killer whale, Lolita, and for bottlenose dolphin BeBe, who played in the *Flipper* TV show. "Salty the Sea Lion" still poses for pictures, and manatee families live in a larger-than-life outdoor tank. Continuous animal shows feature rock music and water splashes, which kids love.

Few people know the Seaquarium has a marine research and conservation program in conjunction with the University of Miami and the National Marine Fisheries Service. If a marine animal needs assistance, Seaquarium divers and vets are on call 24 hours to offer medical care and a home at the Seaquarium. 4400 Rickenbacker Causeway, Key Biscayne, ☎ 305/361-5705; Web site www.miamiseaquarium.com. Open seven days, 9:30 am-6 pm. Admission.

Key Biscayne Branch Library, 299 Crandon Blvd., ☎ 305/361-6134, invites you into their garden. Volunteer gardeners have transformed the grounds into an oasis of flowering plants and trees. Madagascar royal poincianas, palm trees, magnolias, ground orchids, and wild roses create a habitat for frogs, turtles, and ducks. The garden is an idyllic place to while away a long hot afternoon.

■ Festivals & Events

January/February

Key Biscayne Art Festival, Crandon Blvd., ☎ 305/361-9100, Chamber of Commerce.

Annual Ball, Rusty Pelican Restaurant, 3201 Rickenbacker Causeway, ☎ 305/361-5207.

Royal Caribbean PGA Golf Classic, Crandon Park Golf Course, 6700 Crandon Blvd., ☎ 305/365-0365.

March

The **Lipton Tennis Championship,** Tennis Center at Crandon Park, 7300 Crandon Blvd., ☎ 305/442-3367.

April

Spring Egg Hunt, The Village Green, 400 Crandon Blvd., ☎ 305/365-8900.

June

Pig Roast, Key Biscayne Beach Club, 685 Ocean Drive, ☎ 305/361-8144.

July

4th of July Parade, Picnic, Concert and Fireworks, Crandon Blvd., ☎ 305/365-8900.

October

Columbus Day Regatta, between Key Biscayne Island and Dinner Key Channel on Biscayne Bay, ☎ 305/666-8353.

November

Annual Key Biscayne Lighthouse Run, 5K and 10K runs, 5K walk, wheelchair event. Open to all ages. 400 Crandon Blvd., ☎ 305/365-8901.

December

Winterfest, 400 Crandon Blvd., ☎ 305/365-8900.

■ Where to Stay

Key Colony for Guests, 121 Crandon Blvd., ☎ 305/361-2170, features 24 rooms, all with kitchens, a restaurant, lounge, three pools, a fitness center, 12 tennis courts and a golf course. $$

Key Islander Executive Suites, 290 Sunrise Drive, ☎ 305/361-6273, are fully furnished apartments with a private beach. All have kitchens, and the suites share a pool. $$

☆ **Sonesta Beach Resort Key Biscayne,** 350 Ocean Drive, ☎ 800/ SONESTA, is a 300-room, five-star resort with every imaginable luxury. Each beautifully appointed room has a private balcony with breathtaking island or ocean views. The beach is inviting for strolls or sunning, with a variety of watersports including kayaks, catamarans, Sunfish, windsurfing and banana boats. Tennis courts are open day and night, with tennis pro Mike Belkin available for private/group lessons. A state-of-the-art fitness center offers weight training and aerobics classes. The Purple Dolphin Restaurant and Terrace serves delicious breakfasts, lunches, dinners, and Wednesday Italian Night features operatic arias. The staff is extremely hospitable. $$-$$$

■ Where to Eat

Cuban/Latin

☆ **La Carreta,** 12 Crandon Blvd., ☎ 305/365-1177, serves beef, pork, seafood and chicken dishes. The black bean soup is delicious, as is the paella Valenciana with seafood, chicken and rice. At lunch try the Calle Ocho special: ham, turkey, cheese and bacon on toasted Cuban bread. $

Italian

Stefano's, 24 Crandon Blvd., ☎ 305/361-7007, features calamari fritti, and delicious antipasto. Try the paillards of veal or homemade pasta. Very popular spot on weekends. $$$

Health Food

Soundness of Body, 260 Crandon Blvd., ☎ 305/365-0696, is a quaint little health food restaurant serving thick fruit smoothies and pita sandwiches. Try the mock egg salad made from tofu or the creamy hummus. The arame (seaweed) salad with tofu and soy ginger sauce is a real energy booster. $

Casual Seafood

Bayside Hut, 3501 Rickenbacker Causeway, ☎ 305/361-0808, is a tiki bar seafood shack serving "catch of the day," like grouper or snapper. Fish is flaky and served with delicious seasoned fries. $

☆ **The Lighthouse Café,** Bill Baggs Cape Florida State Recreation Area, 1200 S. Crandon Blvd., ☎ 305/361-5811, is beachside with spectacular ocean views. The menu includes fresh grilled shrimp, grouper, dolphin, tuna, red snapper and lobster. Conch salad is zesty. For dessert, try the flan or cheesecake. You must pay park admission to dine here. $

Continental

☆ **The Purple Dolphin** restaurant, Sonesta Beach Resort Key Biscayne, 350 Ocean Drive, ☎ 305/361-2021, serves excellent soups, salads, sandwiches, fresh fish, steaks, and chicken dishes for breakfast, lunch, dinner. Wednesday "Italian Night," is a sumptuous buffet of antipasto, breads, desserts and a "create your own pasta" station. A festive evening with operatic arias. $$

Key Biscayne Chamber of Commerce, 328 Crandon Blvd., Suite 217, 33149, ☎ 305/361-5207.

🌴 🌴 🌴

Downtown & Greater Miami

Ultra-modern skyscrapers designed by I.M. Pei and Philip Johnson vault proudly into a cobalt sky. The world's largest cruise port is surrounded by a fascinating tapestry of Latin-American, Haitian, Jewish and African-American neighborhoods. Downtown in Miami's frenetic business districts, you're apt to hear more Spanish, Portuguese, and Japanese than English. Shops overflow with fashions, electronics, and crafts from all over the world. And there's always a festival of art, music or culture going on: from Goombay, the largest African-American heritage festival in the US, to world film premieres at Miami's Film Festival.

Urban pleasures are easy to find here. Shopping at Bayside Marketplace is convenient with over 100 stores and a covered parking lot, hip nightclubs swing until dawn, and restaurants serve everything from salsa to sushi to salmon. Hotels vary from ultra-luxe high-rises with views of Biscayne Bay to warm and friendly B&Bs.

Even with all these creature comforts at hand, adventure is easy to find: bike paths wend through serene parks, cruising yachts set sail under the moonlight, lakes are alive with bass and mullet. Relax with a game of golf or tennis, or amble around the city on a historic walking tour. If you're a sports fan, get a ticket and cheer the Miami Dolphins, Florida Marlins, Miami Heat, or

Florida Panthers on to victory. You won't be bored in Greater Miami.

■ Adventures

On Foot

For an unusual walking tour, visit the **Miami Cemetery** with Dr. Paul George, historian for the Historical Museum of Southern Florida, 101 W. Flagler Street, Miami, ☎ 305/375-1625. Dr. George was named "Best Local Historian," for his dramatic ability to make South Florida history come alive. "So many spicy stories to tell he can't possibly cram them into a 2½-hour tour," applauds the *Sun Sentinel*.

Dr. George's other walking tours include Miami's Historic Churches, Little Havana, and Coconut Grove. Call for schedule and reservations.

Golf

Call to reserve tee times.

- **Costa Del Sol,** 100 Costa del Sol Blvd., ☎ 305/592-3300. An 18-hole, par 72 course.

- **Don Shula's Hotel & Golf Club,** 15255 Bull Run, Miami Lakes, ☎ 305/821-1150. Par 72; 18 holes.

- **Doral Golf Resort,** 4400 NW 87th Avenue, ☎ 305/591-6453. Four 18-hole courses, ranging from par 70 to 72.

- **Doral Park Silver Course,** 5001 NW 104th Street, ☎ 305/594-0954. 18 holes; par 72.

- **Fontainebleau Golf Club,** 9603 Fontainebleau Blvd., ☎ 305/221-5181. Two 18-hole, par 72 courses.

- **Golf Club of Miami,** 6801 NW 186th Street, ☎ 305/829-8456. Two 18-hole courses; par 70,72.

- **Golf Club of Miami,** 6881 NW 179th Street, ☎ 305/556-8485. One 18-hole course; par 62.

Downtown Miami 🌴

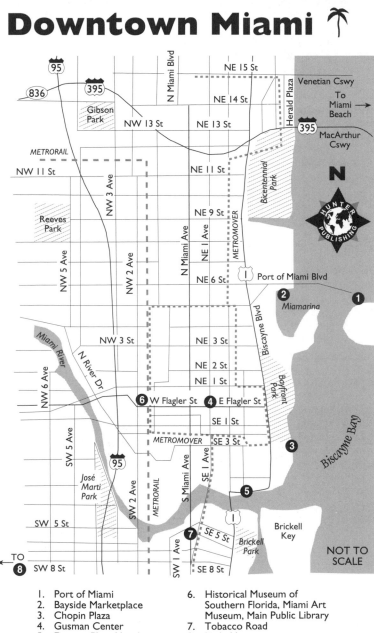

1. Port of Miami
2. Bayside Marketplace
3. Chopin Plaza
4. Gusman Center
5. Dupont Plaza Hotel
6. Historical Museum of Southern Florida, Miami Art Museum, Main Public Library
7. Tobacco Road
8. Little Havana

Miami

- **Melreese Golf Course,** 1802 NW 37th Avenue, ☎ 305/635-6770. An 18-hole course; par 72.

- **Miami Shores Country Club,** 10000 Biscayne Blvd, Miami Shores, ☎ 305/795-2366. An 18-hole course; par 71-72.

- **Miami Springs,** 650 Curtiss Parkway, Miami Springs, ☎ 305/888-2377. 18 holes; par 72.

Tennis

- **Sans Souci Tennis Courts,** 1795 Sans Souci Blvd., North Miami, ☎ 305/893-7130.

On Wheels

 Although Miami has the heavy traffic associated with any frenetic urban center, there are a number of paths and streets suitable for bike riding.

Here are some suggested bike tours to get you started:

- Look for a bike path that starts at The Dupont Plaza Hotel, corner of US1 and 4th Street in downtown Miami. This path heads north into Bayfront Park and ends at the Amphitheater next to Bayside Marketplace. Lots of greenery and nice views of Biscayne Bay.

- Farther northwest, there's a bike path at 21st Avenue where it intersects with 54th Street. It heads north along 21st and goes up to NW 79th Street through a residential area.

- A third bike path winds inside Amelia Earhart Park in Hialeah, an area of the city that's north of Miami International Airport. Start at the corner of Gratigny Drive and 4th Avenue. Take 4th Avenue north into the park and enjoy the lakes and greenery.

The Bike Miami Suitability Map *rates off-street paths, roads with low traffic volume, parks with paths, and lists contacts for area bike clubs. To order the map, contact Jeffrey Hunter, Coordinator, Metro-Dade Bicycle Program, 111 NW First Street, Suite 910, Miami 33128.* ☎ *305/375-4507.*

On Water

Whether you're speeding to the rooftop of a mirrored high-rise in an elevator, or speeding across MacArthur Causeway in a convertible, water is a consistent sight. Cruising, sailing, fishing, swimming or diving, the best way to enjoy Miami is in or on the water.

Cruises

Some three million travelers a year make their way to The Port of Miami, 1015 North America Way, Miami 33132, ☎ 305/347-4860, sailing for distant horizons. You might want to spend a week exploring Miami, then book yourself on a cruise to faraway ports.

Port of Miami Cruise Lines:

Carnival Cruise Lines, 3655 N W 87th Avenue, Miami 33178, ☎ 800/327-9501.

Discovery Cruise Line, 1850 Eller Drive, Ft. Lauderdale 33316, ☎ 800/937-4477.

Dolphin Cruise Line, 901 South America Way, Miami 33132, ☎ 800/222-1003.

Majesty Cruise Line, 901 South America Way, Miami 33132, ☎ 800/645-8111.

Norwegian Cruise Line, 95 Merrick Way, Coral Gables, 33134, ☎ 800/327-7030.

Royal Caribbean Cruise Line, 1050 Caribbean Way, Miami 33132, ☎ 800/327-6700.

Tropicana Cruises, Port of Miami, Pier 6, Miami 33132, ☎ 800/965-3999.

Pleasure Boating & Sailing Charters

Bayside Marketplace, 401 Biscayne Blvd., Miami, is a retail, dining and entertainment complex located on beautiful Biscayne Bay in downtown Miami. On the east side of the Marketplace is a marina, where dozens of sailboats, yachts, and power cruisers run sightseeing tours. Some of our favorites:

Pau Hana, ☎ 305/822-2428, a catamaran sightseeing cruise with a narrated tour past homes of the "rich and famous," Port of-Miami, South Beach, and Miami's skyline.

Island Queen Cruises, ☎ 305/822-2428, two-deck power cruising yachts offering tours of "Millionaire's Row" and moonlight cruises.

Heritage of Miami II, ☎ 305/442-9697, an 85-foot two-masted schooner with lounge areas, restrooms, and a ship's store, offers one- and two-hour daily trips around Biscayne Bay.

Celebration's Bay Brunch, ☎ 305/445-8456, a luxury dinner yacht with a brunch buffet and narrated 1½-hour cruise to "Millionaire's Row," Miami's Outer Islands, and Fisher Island. Saturday/Sunday.

In addition to these, the **Historical Museum of Southern Florida,** 101 West Flagler Street, Miami, ☎ 305/375-1625, runs boat tours on the Miami River, into Biscayne Bay, and out to the water community of Stiltsville throughout the year. Tours are conducted by historian Dr. Paul George, lauded by the *Miami Herald* as "a bubbling spring of fascinating information." Call for tour schedules and reservations.

Jet Ski Rental

Minutes from downtown Miami, at the marina of the Miami Airport Hilton, is **Fun Watersports,** 5101 Blue Lagoon Drive, ☎ 305/261-7687. You can rent a jet ski and head off on your own, or take a waterskiing or jet ski lesson with staff instructors. The Blue Lagoon is a contained area of water, which makes it safe for beginners. Showers, food, and soft drinks are available.

Snorkeling Trips

Enjoy a snorkeling trip south of Miami to Key Largo with **Aqua-World,** ☎ 800/595-2746. Their bus will pick you up from Bay-side Marketplace or one of 10 Miami area hotels, and transport you down to Key Largo. Light snacks and soft drinks are served on the bus. If you prefer not to take the bus, a water taxi from Miami's Holiday Inn will whisk you to Key Largo.

Once there, you'll board AquaWorld's "Party Boat" for an after-noon of snorkeling, swimming and sunbathing. They also have a "Sub See Explorer," a semi-submersible air-conditioned craft that tours Key Largo's coral reef. Snorkeling gear is provided, and you'll be back at your hotel by dinner.

Lake Fishing

The five lakes at **Amelia Earhart Park,** 401 E. 65th Street, Hialeah, ☎ 305/769-2693 make this 515-acre park one of Flori-da's largest fresh water spots for bass, brim and mullet. The park also has a boat rental and food concession.

Fishing for bass, oscar, bluegill and mudfish is good at any of the three lakes at **Milton E. Thompson Park and Campground,** 16665 NW 177 Avenue, Miami, ☎ 305/821-5122.

Other Adventures

Miami Area Sports Arenas

Miami is a sports capital, with top teams and world-class sports facilities. Here are just a few that are within an easy drive from the downtown area:

■ Catch exciting championship games at **Pro Player Stadium** (formerly Joe Robbie Stadium), 2269 NW 199th Street, ☎ 305/452-7000, home to both the Mi-ami Dolphins football team and baseball's new Major League team, the Florida Marlins. The Dolphins have been to the Super Bowl five times, and the Florida Marlins won the World Series in 1997 during their fifth season.

- The NBA and NHL also have teams in Miami. Both the Miami Heat basketball team and the newest entry in the National Hockey League, the Florida Panthers, play home games at downtown's 15,000 seat Miami Arena, 721 NW 1st Avenue, ☎ 305/530-4402.

- Collegiate sports fans can enjoy the **University of Miami Hurricanes,** ☎ 305/284-2263, and the **Florida International University Golden Panthers,** at SW 8th Street, ☎ 305/348-4263.

- The competition is high-speed at **Miami Jai-Alai,** 3500 NW 37th Avenue, ☎ 305/633-6400. There's a court-view restaurant, parimutuel wagering, and it's open year-round. Admission. Other parimutuel venues include **Calder Race track,** 21001 NW 27th Avenue, ☎ 305/625-1311; **Flagler Dog Track,** 401 NW 38th Court, Miami (corner of NW 37th Street and NW 37th Avenue), ☎ 305/649-3000, is open from June 1 through November 30; **Gulfstream Park,** 901 S. Federal Hwy, Hallandale, ☎ 954/931-7223; and **Hialeah Park,** 2200 E. 4th Avenue, Hialeah, ☎ 305/885-8000.

■ Sightseeing

The heart of downtown Miami is Flagler Street, jammed with noisy electronics shops, discount jewelry stores, South American clothing, and knick-knacks from all over the world. One of the most elegant downtown buildings is **Gusman Center for the Performing Arts,** 174 East Flagler, ☎ 305/374-2444. Built in the mid-1920s as the Olympia Theatre, today the ornate theater showcases comedians, Broadway musicals, and world symphonies.

Two blocks east is the three-building **Metro-Dade Cultural Center,** 101 West Flagler, a Mediterranean plaza with cascading fountains. The complex includes the **Historical Museum of Southern Florida,** ☎ 305/375-1492; the **Miami Art Museum of Dade County,** ☎ 305/375-1700; and the four-story **Miami-Dade Public Library,** ☎ 305/375-2665. The Historical Museum also has a Web site, www.historical-museum.org.

The Historical Museum has hands-on displays and exhibits on the people and events that shaped South Florida: pioneer sailboats, European explorers, a 1925 Miami streetcar, the Art Deco era, cigar factories, and Audubon's *The Birds of America*. The Museum gift store has an excellent book department, specializing in publications by Florida authors. Each month, the museum hosts historic walking and boat tours by Dr. Paul George. Call ☎ 305/375-1625 for tour schedules and reservations.

Designed by architect Phillip Johnson, the Art Museum presents international art since WWII, with a focus on the Western Hemisphere. Open Tuesday, Wednesday, Friday 10 am-5 pm; Thursdays until 9 pm; Sat-Sun noon-5 pm.

Another popular Miami art museum is the **Museum of Contemporary Art,** 770 NE 125th Street in North Miami, ☎ 305/893-6211. The state-of-the-art facility was designed by Charles Gwathmey, and features works by Jean-Michel Basquiat and Robert Chambers and examples of Mexican Modernism. The gift shop sells handcrafted jewelry. Tours are given Tuesday, Saturday and Sunday at 2pm. Open-Tuesday, Wednesday, Friday, and Saturday, 10 am-5 pm; Thursday until 9 pm; Sunday noon-5 pm. Admission. To get here from I-95, take the 125th Street Exit and go east to Bal Harbour, until you reach 7th Avenue.

■ Entertainment

The beat goes on in Miami, from dawn to dusk. Whether you're a jazz lover, rocker, blues hound or Broadway buff, Miami has just the right tune.

- **Victor's Café,** 2340 SW 32nd Avenue, ☎ 305/445-1313, presents live music and one of the city's best cabaret shows at the Cabaret Babalu.

- **Tobacco Road,** 626 S. Miami Avenue, ☎ 305/374-1198, is a longtime favorite for rock, blues and homegrown talent.

- **Jensen's Lounge,** 1516 NW 27th Avenue, ☎ 305/635-0569, swings with country music. They offer The Bob Music Show on Friday and Saturday.

- **La Paloma,** 10999 Biscayne Blvd., North Miami, ☎ 305/891-0505, is an intimate piano bar, presenting Broadway musical favorites.

For a complete listing of clubs and musicians, pick up an issue of *Miami New Times,* a free weekly tabloid of what's happening around Miami in film, theater, dining and music. Available at all city newsstands and many hotels.

■ Festivals & Events

January

Three Kings Day Parade, SW 8th Street, ☎ 305/445-4020.

Miami Modernism Art Deco Antique Show, 400 SE Second Avenue, ☎ 305/372-0277.

Chopin Music at Chopin Plaza, 301 N. Biscayne Blvd., ☎ 305/868-0624

Martin Luther King Jr. Birthday Celebration, 6101 NW 32nd Ct., ☎ 305/633-4150.

Miami Film Festival, Gusman Center for the Performing Arts, 174 E Flagler St, ☎ 305/377-FILM.

February

Annual Miami International Map Fair, Historical Museum of Southern Florida, 101 W Flagler St, ☎ 305/375-1492.

Carnaval Miami Latin festival, various locations, including the Orange Bowl, Calle Ocho, and South Beach. ☎ 305/644-8888.

Doral-Ryder Open, PGA tour, Doral Golf Resort & Spa, 4400 NW 87th Ave, airport area. ☎ 305/365-0290.

March

Scottish Festival and Games, Hialeah Park, ☎ 305/757-6730.

Dade Heritage Days, throughout the city, ☎ 305/358-9572.

Calle Ocho Festival, SW 8th St, ☎ 305/644-8888.

Subtropics New Music Festival, various locations throughout the city, ☎ 305/758-6676.

April

Dade Heritage Days, throughout the city, ☎ 305/358-9572.

Baynanza, annual celebration that includes recreational and educational events relating to Biscayne Bay and its history. Various locations throughout the city, ☎ 305/372-6770.

June

Black Music Month, 5400 NW 22nd Avenue, ☎ 305/636-2350.

Miami/Bahamas Goombay Festival, throughout the city, ☎ 305/ 445-8292.

July

America's Birthday Bash (July 4), Bayfront Park, 301 N. Biscayne Blvd. ☎ 305/358-7550.

Bayside's Independence Day Celebration (July 4), Bayside Marketplace, Biscayne Blvd, ☎ 305/577-3344, ext 7020.

Summer Olympic Soccer Games, Orange Bowl, 1501 NW 3rd Street, ☎ 305/643-7100.

Congo de Oro, Bayfront Park, 301 N. Biscayne Blvd., ☎ 305/591-2229.

August

Miami Reggae Festival, Bayfront Park, 301 Biscayne Blvd. ☎ 305/891-2944.

Latin Rock, same location as above, ☎ 305/264-2641.

NFL Town Center Concert, same location as above, ☎ 305/279-0118.

September

Brazilian Festival, Bayfront Park, ☎ 305/794-2925.

Central American Independence Festival, Bayfront Park, ☎ 305/448-9532.

October

Caribbean American Carnival, Miami Bicentennial Park, ☎ 305/381-9200.

Hispanic Heritage Festival, various locations, ☎ 305/541-5023.

Miami

Discovery of America Day Festival, Bayfront Park, 301 Biscayne Blvd. ☎ 305/541-5023.

November

Tropic Hunt, Bayfront Park, ☎ 305/376-2773.

Wind in the Willows, 400 SE 2nd Avenue, ☎ 305/372-0277.

Family Day, Bayfront Park, ☎ 305/576-1071.

Pan American Festival, Bayfront Park, ☎ 305/944-7272.

Miami Book Fair International, Miami-Dade Community College, 300 NE 2nd Avenue, ☎ 305/237-3258.

Power and Motoryacht Rendezvous at Fisher Island, ☎ 954/537-1010.

December

Junior Orange Bowl Parade, Biscayne Blvd., ☎ 305/371-4600.

Kwanzaa Fest, 6161 NW 22nd Avenue, ☎ 305/638-6771.

Bayside Holiday Celebration, Bayside Marketplace, ☎ 305/577-3344.

Metropolitan South Florida Fishing Tournament, various locations, ☎ 305/376-3698.

Handel's Messiah, performed by the Florida Philharmonic, Gusman Center, 174 E. Flagler Street, ☎ 305/374-2444.

Orange Bowl Classic, Miami Arena, 701 Arena Blvd., ☎ 305/530-4400.

Orange Bowl Parade, along Biscayne Blvd., ☎ 305/371-4600.

Big Orange New Year's Eve Celebration, Bayfront Park, 301 N. Biscayne Blvd., ☎ 305/358-7750.

Federal Express Orange Bowl Classic, Pro Player Stadium, 2269 NW 199th Street, ☎ 305/371-4600.

■ Where to Stay

Downtown

 Biscayne Bay Marriot Hotel & Marina, 1633 N. Bayshore Drive, 33132, ☎ 305/374-3900, has a 220-slip marina and a multi-level deck overlooking Biscayne Bay. 603 rooms, a restaurant, lounge, pool, fitness center. $$

Crowne Plaza Miami, 1601 Biscayne Blvd., 33132, ☎ 800/2CROWNE, is newly renovated. The 528 rooms have Bay and downtown Miami views. Located above the Omni International Mall, the hotel's Metrorail stop provides convenient access around the city. Complimentary airport shuttle, two restaurants, two lounges, pool, fitness center. $$

DoubleTree Grand Biscayne Bay, 1717 N. Bayshore Drive, 33132, ☎ 800/872-7749 has 152 luxurious rooms, some with kitchens. Breathtaking views of Biscayne Bay, three restaurants and lounges, pool, fitness center. $$

Howard Johnson Port of Miami, 1100 Biscayne Blvd., 33132, ☎ 305/358-3080, is newly renovated in the heart of downtown. Complimentary transportation to the Port of Miami makes it convenient if you're booked on a cruise. $

Miami River Inn, 226 NE 1st Avenue, 33130, ☎ 800/HOTEL-89, is a historic bed and breakfast with 40 nicely appointed rooms in a lush garden setting. Pool. $

Sheraton Biscayne Bay, 495 Brickell Avenue, 33166, ☎ 800/325-3535, offers 598 rooms on historic Brickell Point. Walking distance to a tropical park, financial district, downtown shopping and Metro-Dade Cultural Center. $$$

North Miami Area

Holiday Inn Hialeah/Miami Lakes, 6650 W. 20th Avenue, Hialeah 33016, is a beautifully furnished five-story hotel with 144 comfortable rooms, all with separate living rooms. Close to Florida's Turnpike and Miami Airport. Restaurant, lounge, pool, fitness center. $

Don Shula's Hotel & Golf Club, 15255 Bull Run Rd., Miami Lakes 33014, ☎ 305/821-1150, is home base for many professional sports teams throughout the year. 301 rooms, some with kitchens. Amenities include restaurants, two lounges, two pools, fitness center, nine tennis courts, two golf courses. $$

Holiday Inn Calder/Pro Player Stadium, 21485 NW 27th Avenue, 33056, ☎ 305/945-2621, is conveniently located next to thoroughbred racing at Calder Race Course and sports action at Pro Player Stadium. Scenic views from the rooftop lounge. 214 rooms, some with kitchens; restaurant, lounge, pool, fitness center. $$

Miami

Camping

The **Milton E. Thompson Campground,** 16665 NW 177th Avenue, Miami 33192, ☎ 305/821-5122, can accommodate 10-12 tents and 40 recreational vehicles with full electrical hook-ups. The campground has a laundry room, bathrooms with hot showers, and on-duty security. Campfires are permitted. Open year-round, with RV storage available. Two miles south of US27, or 12 miles north of US41 on SR 997 (Krome Avenue).

■ Where to Eat

Spanish

 Casa Juancho, 2436 SW 8th Street, ☎ 305/642-2452, specializes in fresh snapper browned with butter, topped with mushrooms, ham and shrimp. For dessert try the crema Catalana. $$$

El Bodegon de Castilla, 2499 SW 8th Street, ☎ 305/649-0863, presents authentic Spanish seafood, like snapper in green sauce with garlic and parsley. *Cazuela de Mariscos* (seafood casserole) is a signature dish. Finish with the fried custard. $$

Victor's Café, 2340 SW 32nd Street, ☎ 305/445-1313, features meaty plantain baskets overflowing with fricasseed shrimp, as well as shredded/fried steak with garlicky onions. $$

Mexican

Cisco's Café, 5911 NW 36th Street, ☎ 305/871-2764, offers standard Mexican favorites: burritos, tacos, fajitas, tamales. Corn and flour tortilla chips are homemade, as is the spicy salsa. Try the guacamole, too. $

Cuban

Covadonga, 6480 SW 8th Street, ☎ 305/261-2406, serves clams in green sauce and whole baby squid stuffed with ham in brown sauce. It's considered one of Miami's best Cuban restaurants. $$

Islas Canarias, 285 NW 27th Avenue, ☎ 305/649-0440, is tiny, but portions are ample. Order *bistec Uruguayo* (breaded *palomilla* steak filled with Swiss cheese and ham), and share it with at least four other friends. Best dessert: flan, rich with egg yolks and cinnamon syrup. $

La Casona, 6355 SW 8th Street, ☎ 305/262-2828, showcases singers who belt out Spanish/English favorites, while guests enjoy fried green plantains with sour cream and caviar, and grilled fish. $$

Nicaraguan

El Novillo, 6830 Bird Road, ☎ 305/284-8417, serves tender and hearty *churrasco* (their house steak special) and pepper steak in cream sauce. $$

American

S&S Diner, 1757 NW 2nd Avenue, ☎ 305/373-4291, always has a long line, but the roast turkey, fried sole, and mashed potatoes are worth the wait. Homemade rice pudding is a perfect finish. $

New Hickory Bar-B-Que, 3170 Coral Way, ☎ 305/569-0098, will satisfy any craving for beef ribs, chicken livers, or BBQ pork. Sides of rice and black beans round out the hearty fare. $

Tourism Information

Greater Miami Convention & Visitors Bureau, 701 Brickell Avenue, Suite 2700, Miami, Florida 33131, ☎ 305/539-3063 or 800/283-2707.

Miami Visitor Center at Bayside, Bayside Marketplace, 401 Biscayne Blvd., Miami, Florida 33132, ☎ 305/539-8070. Open Monday-Thursday 10 am-10 pm; Friday-Saturday until 11 pm; Sunday 11 am-9 pm.

❦ ❦ ❦

Miami Beach

Miami Beach wakes up to another perfect day. Lycra-clad joggers lope along the Atlantic Ocean. Musclemen and women stride off to the gym. Clusters of chatty seniors and

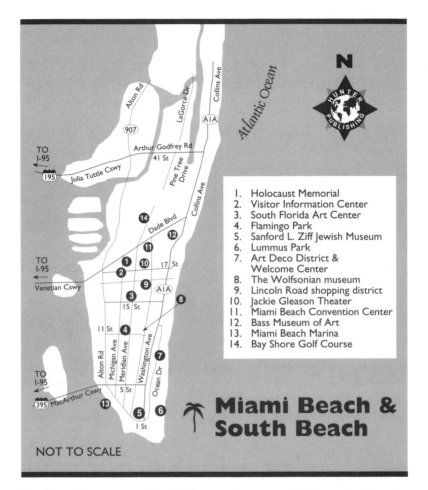

Miami Beach & South Beach

1. Holocaust Memorial
2. Visitor Information Center
3. South Florida Art Center
4. Flamingo Park
5. Sanford L. Ziff Jewish Museum
6. Lummus Park
7. Art Deco District & Welcome Center
8. The Wolfsonian museum
9. Lincoln Road shopping district
10. Jackie Gleason Theater
11. Miami Beach Convention Center
12. Bass Museum of Art
13. Miami Beach Marina
14. Bay Shore Golf Course

NOT TO SCALE

hordes of moms pushing baby carriages walk along the beachside boardwalk. Even at 8 am a rock n' roll salsa pulses the air. Miami Beach is in great shape. Besides, how can you be crabby when so many Art Deco buildings are pink? Lighten up, hang loose. You're in Miami Beach.

Getting Here

From the Miami airport, take SR 836 East to I-95, then watch for the turnoff to I-395 (MacArthur Causeway). From other areas of Miami, take I-95 toward the downtown area, then turn east on either I-195 (Julia Tuttle Causeway) or I-395 (MacArthur Causeway).

■ Adventures

On Foot

Why is walking South Beach an adventure? Take a look. Hundreds of long-legged beauties, mostly wannabe models and actresses, decorate the beach. Strutting along the water's edge, they show off sculpted buttocks and voluptuous 36Cs, reminding me of a favorite song, *The Girl from Ipanema* – "Tall and tanned, and young and lovely, the girl from Ipanema goes walking, and when she passes each one she passes goes ahhhhhh."

Add to this mix some high-spirited seniors: 60+ women sport pearls with their leopard bikinis, while their boyfriends wear headsets on bald pates. They too are beautiful, healthy, and glad to be on the beach.

Then there are the kids: toddlers waddling to the water's edge with buckets, beaming with the excitement of building a castle with daddy, or flirting with the crashing waves. Little girls wear curls and itsy-bitsy polka-dot bikinis; baby boys wear little more than big blue eyes.

The whole human race is nearly naked, having a ball on Miami Beach.

Golf

- **Bayshore Golf Course,** 2301 Alton Road, Miami Beach, ☎ 305/532-3350, is an 18-hole golf course with par 72, 73.

- **Bayshore Par 3 Golf Course,** 2795 Prairie Avenue, Miami Beach, ☎ 305/674-0305. Nine holes; par 27.

- **Normandy Shores,** 2401 Biarritz Drive, Miami Beach, ☎ 305/868-6502, has 18 holes and a par of 71, 72.

Tennis

- **Flamingo Park,** 1000 12th Street, Miami Beach, ☎ 305/673-7761.

- **North Shore Park,** 501 72nd Street, Miami Beach, ☎ 305/993-2032.

On Wheels

Bicycling

It's Sunday morning in Miami Beach and we're touring the famous Art Deco District by bike. Our guide Sharon Hartley, a volunteer historian with the Miami Design Preservation League, is dressed in Art Deco peach shorts. She's all fired up with historic and architectural tales to share with us. We meet at **Miami Beach Bicycle Center,** 601 5th Street, ☎ 305/674-0150, to pick up our bikes, and off we go.

An ocean breeze keeps us cool as we wend our way among private neighborhoods, savoring these architectural treasures. We learn to identify arches, columns, asymmetrical roofs, and cantilevered projections called "eyebrows." Sharon explains that Miami Beach homes were once mostly white with turquoise and sapphire trim. But when *Miami Vice* featured a few pastel buildings in the 1970s TV series, pastel got "hot." Miami Beach residents decided to paint their homes shades of peach, pink, baby blue, purple and lemon yellow. Today these rainbow beauties are owned by devoted Art Deco lovers committed to their preservation.

We ride along, stopping under shady trees to learn of Miami Beach's history, then continue along Collins Road admiring stunning Art Deco hotels. Our tour ends on South Beach along Ocean Drive, across the street from the mansion of the late Gianni Versace, a private palace with a garden and a pool.

If you'd like to bike on your own, Miami Beach has plenty of pleasant places to ride, both on oceanside paths and on the streets. In Lummus Park along Ocean Drive, there's a bike path that parallels the ocean, from 9th Street to 15th Street. Farther north is another oceanfront bike path, running from 24th Street to 28th Street.

For a pleasant street ride on Miami Beach's west side, start on Alton Road at 8th Street, and head north on Alton Road to La Gorce Island. Circle around the island on La Gorce Circle, then return south on Bay Road.

Another bike shop is **Cycles on the Beach,** 713 Fifth Street, ☎ 305/673-2055, which also has rentals by the hour, day, and week.

On Small Wheels

How about skating past art galleries and outdoor restaurants into a chic café for a latte and biscotti? In-line skating is a way of life in Miami Beach. Locals "blade" to work, go grocery shopping, and run errands. Wearing as little as possible, they show off tight bods earned at the gym. Why walk or drive when you can blade? It's great exercise and fun, once you're feeling confidently balanced.

☀ Snapshot

Meet Vesna Galesic, Miami Beach "Rollerblade Queen" and front-desk clerk at the Indian Creek Hotel.

SS: What's adventurous about in-line skating in Miami Beach?

VG: Well, even though I'm 40-something, skating makes me look young. When I'm dressed in short-shorts, tank top, Walkman, and sunglasses, the young kids still flirt with me. Then they realize I'm their mom's age, which is good for my ego.

SS: Where's your favorite place to skate?

VG: On Ocean Drive, from 5th to 16th street, there's a smooth track right by South Beach. Gentle curves, no cars, and skaters all ages from tiny kids to seniors. There are always skaters there even when I skate, which is often at midnight!

SS: How did you get started skating?

VG: I saw all these people skating and decided I wanted to do it. I spent hours practicing in a garage in the building where I live, trained myself for three weeks, and I learned. It looked like too much fun not to do it.

SS: Any advice for first-time skaters?

VG: Wear knee and wrist pads. A helmet if you want. And rent skates first before buying; see if you really like it. Maybe even take a lesson. Just relax. Skating is so much fun, especially here in Miami Beach.

If you've never tried it, or even if you have, make **Fritz's Skate Shop,** 726 Lincoln Road Mall, Miami Beach, ☎ 305/532-1954, your first stop. Manager Mitch Wentworth and his staff will share skating basics and get you fully outfitted in rental gear. If you decide to buy, they'll make sure everything fits correctly. This skate shop is jammed with hundreds of K2 Rollerblade styles, hats, backpacks, wrist/knee guards, helmets, T-shirts etc. You can rent skates by the hour, day, or overnight.

For beginners, here are tips on in-line skating from Mitch:

- Keep your knees bent.

- Wear protective gear.

- Fall forward on your hands and knees, not backward on your rear.

- Skate on a flat surface, avoiding oil, cars and people.

- Practice on grass to get your balance and confidence.

If you'd like to take lessons with a Certified Rollerblading Instructor, the shop recommends Donna, ☎ 305/674-1559 or 305/880-3074.

On Water

Boating, Fishing, Diving

 Palm Trees and elegant stone picnic tables decorate the very beautiful **Miami Beach Marina,** 300 Alton Road, Miami Beach 33139, ☎ 305/673-6000. Adjacent to Government Cut, this Marina affords easy accessibility to great fishing, sailing, cruising and scuba diving. Over 400 boat slips provide dock space for vessels up to 250 feet, and slips are complete with fresh water, electricity, telephone and cable hookups. The Marina features a control tower with state of the art weather service, 24-hour dock attendants and security patrol, a heated swimming pool, laundry facilities, air-conditioned restrooms, a lighted parking lot and US customs clearing. On the premises are restaurants, a gourmet grocery/provisioning market, a marine hardware/ bait/tackle shop, a full-line scuba dive shop, Club Nautico boat rentals, yacht and sailboat charters, sport and drift fishing charters, dine/dance cruises and Miami Beach's Water Taxi service.

Talk with the dockmaster about your interests in fishing, sailing, cruising, or diving, and he'll put you in touch with the appropriate boat captain. Here are just a few recommendations for vessels docked at Miami Beach Marina:

- ■ *Sissy Baby,* Deep Sea Sportfishing Charters, ☎ 305/531-4223, offers half-day, ¾-day, and full-day charters for sailfish, marlin, dolphin, wahoo, kingfish, tuna, amberjack, grouper. They have a 45-foot Hatteras with full tuna tower and three fishing chairs. Takes 106 people per trip by reservation.

- ■ **Deep Sea Fishing,** Reward Fleet, ☎ 305/372-9470. They offer two 70-foot charter boats for one to six passengers. Three trips daily by reservation.

- ■ *Luv Cats,* ☎ 305/673-6000. A 53-ft. Marquis catamaran with four spacious cabins and a dining area with wet bar that seats 12. Available for evening cruises as well as week-long adventures, with captain or as a bareboat.

- ■ *Europa Sun,* ☎ 305/538-8300. Cruise line with a casino, blackjack and slot machines. Food and beverage served, reservation required.

Water Taxi

Miami Beach's water taxis are a fun way to get around and sightsee. They hold 19-49 passengers and depart from Miami Beach Marina and area hotels. Call ☎ 305/728-8417 for their schedule and locations.

Swimming

When it comes to swimming, a 1927 editorial said it all: "Miami Beach should set a precedent in dress and become known throughout the world as 'the bathing suit city.' Businessmen should go to their offices in bathing suits and robes. The natural therapy that makes Miami Beach the most healthful playground city in the world is a combination of sunshine and ocean waters."

Need we say more? Beaches are blankets of soft clean sand, stretching north and south for miles. Waves curl and crash like blue-green molten glass. The sky is cobalt, the sun is blazing. Swim, snooze, tan, enjoy. It doesn't get any better than this.

In the Air

Wearing purple suede Boreal climbing shoes, I feel like a ballet dancer. I am, in fact, preparing to vertically scale a wall. Like a velcro-clad Spiderwoman, my feet adhere to the rocks, my fingers grab the hand holds, and into the air I go. I'm not scaling Mt. Everest. I'm wall-climbing at the **Eden Roc Resort & Spa,** 4525 Collins Avenue, Miami Beach, ☎ 305/674-5585. Their state-of-the-art indoor wall is 24 feet high, constructed of fiberglass with a stone coating. Black and blue toe and finger holds jut out at various heights and widths, some an easy grab, others... well, perhaps if were six feet tall I could reach *that* one.

There are no mountains in Florida, but you can sharpen your climbing skills on the Wall at the Eden Roc Hotel, Miami Beach.

Todd Carter, a movie-star-handsome rock climbing instructor, coaches me up the wall. "Go for that hold," "remember to keep your arms straight," he encourages. Todd's got me harnessed and roped so I'll just dangle in the air if I slip. "You won't fall," Todd promises. And I don't. I make it almost to the top and, a few minutes later, Todd has assisted me safely to the ground. "When can I go up again?" I ask, exhilarated.

Call for the schedule of climbing workshops and one-on-one training sessions. For experienced climbers, the wall is available for open climbing Monday-Friday 6-9 pm; Saturday and Sunday 10 am-1 pm.

✳ Snapshot

Meet Todd Carter, wall climbing Instructor, Eden Roc Resort & Spa, Miami Beach.

SS: Why is climbing a wall an adventure?

TC: It's 90% mental. If you can overcome your fear of heights and trust other people, you're in your own little world down to your feet and out to your hands. Anything that's been bothering you is gone. It's just you, the rock, where you're at, and where you're going. Just like life. Once your mind allows you to let go of what's keeping you in that one place you can move forward.

SS: Sounds like the Zen of rock climbing, Todd.

TC: It can be a very spiritual experience. In fact I've heard rock climbers say they handle tough situations by "Zen-ing through it."

SS: What are the physical requirements for climbing?

TC: Some people think you have to be built like Arnold or Sylvester, but it's not that way. Thin and wiry people actually do much better; they don't have the bulk to carry up. You need strong legs and you use your hands for balance.

SS: What's special about this climbing wall?

TC: There aren't many like it in South Florida. It's a state-of-the-art wall system with a fiberglass wall panel on top, a steel structure underneath. Interchangeable holes make the climb easy or tough.

SS: Is climbing becoming a popular sport?

TC: Many people are tired of spectator sports like football and basketball. Climbing enables people from different backgrounds to be together: husband and wife teams, fathers and sons, mothers and daughters. Climbing is good for relationships. You start developing a trust right away because the person on the ground is in charge of the other person's life. You won't get that kind of trust out on the dance floor! Your mind is busy figuring out the puzzle of the climb, overcoming fear, how to get up, how to use the different holds. That's the challenge, that's the fun.

Miami

■ Sightseeing

Lincoln Road: 11 Blocks of Style

 Few cities in the US have a neighborhood this stylish and imaginative. In the stretch from Collins Avenue to West Avenue, a day or evening stroll along **Lincoln Road** will tempt you with antiques, fashion, art, home furnishings and leather goods. In between shopping and browsing, dine al fresco to live music among palm trees and fountains. There's even a psychic shop, at 817 Lincoln Road, where they'll be happy to predict your next adventure.

The Holocaust Memorial

The Holocaust Memorial, 1933-45 Meridian Avenue, ☎ 305/538-1663, is a dramatic tribute to the six million Jewish victims of Nazi terrorism during WWII. Sculptures, photos, and personal stories presented in a peaceful garden create a deeply moving experience. Designed by acclaimed sculptor Kenneth Treister, the Memorial is created from Jerusalem stone and marble. Free admission; group tours available.

Memorial to victims of the Holocaust.

Museums

Miami Beach is home to world-class museums and galleries, as well as the New World Symphony, the Miami City Ballet, and Ballet Flamenco La Rosa. On any given day or night, choose among historic and contemporary art exhibits, music, ballet, flamenco, musicals or dramatic theater productions.

Bass Museum of Art, 2121 Park Avenue, Miami Beach, ☎ 305/673-7530, has South Florida's most comprehensive permanent collection of Old Master paintings, sculptures, textiles, period furniture, objets d'art and ecclesiastical artifacts. Special exhibits throughout the year focus on contemporary European, American and Hispanic arts, as well as historic art from around the world. Open Tues.-Sat. 10 am-5 pm; Sunday 1-5 pm. Every second and fourth Wed., open 1-9 pm. Closed Mondays and holidays. Admission.

The Wolfsonian, 1001 Washington Avenue, Miami Beach, ☎ 305/531-1001, is a state-of-the-art international museum and study center containing over 70,000 American and European objects produced between 1885 and 1945. The collection includes furniture, industrial design, glass, ceramics, metalwork, books, works on paper, paintings and sculptures. Open Tues-Sat. 11 am-6 pm and Thursday evenings until 9 pm; Sunday noon-5 pm. Admission charge; free on Thursdays from 6-9pm.

Sanford L. Ziff Jewish Museum of Florida, 301 Washington Avenue, Miami Beach, ☎ 305/672-5044, is in a former synagogue for Miami Beach's first Jewish congregation. Built in 1936, now on the National Register of Historic Places, it features Art Deco architectural design, a marble bimah (reading table), and 80 stained-glass windows. The museum presents a variety of exhibits, cultural and educational programs, and houses a Collections & Research Center. Tours available. Open Tues-Sunday 10 am-5 pm, Friday until 3 pm. Closed Monday. Admission.

South Florida Art Center, 924 Lincoln Road, Miami Beach, ☎ 305/674-8278, is comprised of four buildings, housing over 85 artists. The exhibition spaces are Art 800, Common Space, Ground Level and Clay Space. Art classes in all media are offered, and the center sponsors lectures, workshops and forums.

Tours available. Free. Call for gallery hours and individual studio hours.

Ticket Information

The New World Symphony, performing at the Lincoln Theatre, 555 Lincoln Road, Miami Beach, ☎ 305/673-3331.

Schedule of shows at **Lincoln Theatre,** ☎ 800/939-8587.

Colony Theater, 1040 Lincoln Road, ☎ 305/674-1040.

Jackie Gleason Theater, 1700 Washington Avenue, ☎ 305/673-7300.

Miami City Ballet, 905 Lincoln Road, ☎ 305/532-7713.

Ballet Flamenco La Rosa, ☎ 305/672-0552.

■ Festivals & Events

January

Art Deco Weekend, Ocean Drive, ☎ 305/672-2014.

Art Miami Expo, Miami Beach Convention Center, ☎ 305/220-2690.

South Florida International Wine and Food Festival, Doral Ocean Beach Resort, ☎ 305/531-4851.

Miami Beach Antique Show, Miami Beach Convention Center, ☎ 305/754-4931.

February

Festival of the Arts, Collins Avenue, ☎ 305/673-7733.

Miami International Boat Show, Miami Beach Convention Center, ☎ 305/531-8410.

AIDS Walk Miami, Art Deco District. One of the largest AIDS walks in the nation. ☎ 305/759-6181.

April

South Beach Film Festival, ☎ 305/448-9133.

Yamaha Outboards Miami Billfish Tournament, Miami Beach Marina, 300 Alton Road, ☎ 954/561-2868.

South Beach Film Festival, The Colony Theater, 1040 Lincoln Rd, ☎ 305/532-1233.

Taste of the Beach, South Pointe Park, 300 Biscayne St, ☎ 305/672-1270.

May

Miami International Home & Garden Show, Miami Beach Convention Center, ☎ 305/66-5944.

June

South Florida Boat Show, Miami Beach Convention Center, ☎ 305/946-6164.

July

Fourth of July Fireworks, 73rd & Collins, ☎ 305/865-4147.

October

International Women's Show, Miami Beach Convention Center, ☎ 305/673-7311.

November

South Florida International Auto Show, Miami Beach Convention Center, ☎ 305/758-2643.

Baron's Antique Show, Miami Beach Convention Center, ☎ 305/754-4931.

December

World's Largest Indoor Flea Market, Miami Beach Convention Center, ☎ 305/651-9530.

■ Where to Stay

☆ **The Indian Creek Hotel,** 2727 Indian Creek Drive, 33140, ☎ 305/531-2727. Enter this hotel and you're swept back to a 1930s style of graciousness. Antique suitcases with international hotel decals echo a bygone era, sleek upholstered club chairs beckon, and a Western Electric Teletalk radio suggests that announcer Walter Winchell may speak any second.

Proprietor Marc Levin has created an authentically restored Art Deco hotel with 61 inviting rooms and suites, a romantic garden and pool, and the intimate Pan Coast Restaurant. The Indian Creek is a favorite of international models, photographers, and film crews who showcase Miami Beach in feature films, fashion spreads, and TV commercials around the world. Some of the models staying at The Indian Creek are too beautiful to be let out of their rooms, but they find their way to the lobby anyway, much to the embarrassment of lesser mortals.

We love this hotel not just for its élan, but for the sincere warmth and hospitality extended by Marc Levin, Vesna Galesic, and the staff. The Indian Creek is just like home, only better. $$

The Albion Hotel, 1650 James Avenue, ☎ 888/665-0008, has 110 newly renovated rooms, several indoor-outdoor penthouse suites, lush landscaping, a lobby bar, and private solariums for sunbathing. $$

Banana Bungalow, 2360 Collins Avenue, ☎ 305/538-1951, is a lively, 60-room youth hostel close to the beach. The hostel has a café, bar, movie theater, kitchen, pool, billiards room, and free gym access. A good choice if you're on a tight budget. $

Colours, The Mantell Guest Inn, 255 W. 24th Street, ☎ 800/ARRIVAL. The 35-room hotel has furnished studio apartments, some with kitchens. It's located one block from the beach and boardwalk, and serves a complimentary continental breakfast. Lounge and pool. $

Doral Ocean Beach Resort, 4833 Collins Avenue, ☎ 800/22-DORAL, is a contemporary high-rise resort with 417 rooms, some with kitchens and oceanfront views. It's close to shopping, nightlife and area attractions. There are three restaurants, four lounges, a pool, fitness center, and two tennis courts. $$-$$$

Eden Roc Resort & Spa, 4525 Collins Avenue, ☎ 800/327-8337, is a beautiful tropical Art Deco hotel with 349 rooms, some with kitchens. The two outdoor pools are spectacular, and the full-service spa has everything from massage to aerobics. The hotel has a state-of-the-art climbing wall, two restaurants, three lounges. $$-$$$

Fontainebleau Hilton Resort and Towers, 4441 Collins Avenue, Miami Beach 33140, ☎ 800/548-8886, is an elegant seaside resort hotel with 1,206 rooms. Amenities include free supervised children's activities, complimentary evening shows, and a shopping arcade, as well as seven restaurants, five lounges, two pools, a fitness center, and seven tennis courts. $$$

Hotel Brazil, 6525 Collins Avenue, Miami Beach, 33141, ☎ 305/861-0911, is a good choice if you're on a tight budget. There are 62 rooms, many with kitchens, a pool, and a private beach. Complimentary continental breakfast is served. The hotel is close to restaurants, nightlife and shopping. $

Lorraine Hotel Beach Resort, 2601 Collins Avenue, Miami Beach, 33140, ☎ 800/545-3905, is an oceanfront hotel with 40 rooms, all with kitchens. It's within walking distance of the Miami Beach Convention Center, Lincoln Road Mall, and the Art Deco District. Restaurant. $

The National Hotel, 1677 Collins Avenue, Miami Beach, ☎ 800/327-8370, recently underwent a $5 million renovation, which included the addition of a spectacular 203-ft. lap pool. The hotel has 154 rooms, the Oval Restaurant, 24-hour room service, the Deco Lounge, and beach access. $$

Sol Miami Beach Hotel, 8925 Collins Avenue, Miami Beach 33140, ☎ 800/336-3542, is an Art Deco hotel with 271 rooms. It has a restaurant, lounge, pool, and fitness center. $$

South Beach Royal Hotel, 2469 Collins Avenue, Miami Beach, 33140, ☎ 800/327-3110, is a 120-room Art Deco hotel with bay and ocean views. Walking distance to Ocean Drive. $$

Tides, 1220 Ocean Drive, Miami Beach, ☎ 800/OUTPOST (for reservations) or 305/604-5000 (hotel), is an Art Deco high-rise with 45 ocean-view rooms, a high-tech gym, and a private restaurant. Owned by Island Records' CEO, Chris Blackwell. $$-$$$

Miami

■ Where to Eat

☆ **The Original Wolfies,** 21st & Collins Avenue, Miami Beach, ☎ 305/538-6626, opened here in 1947. Waitresses greet their favorite customers with "where ya been honey," and everyone stands in line for the best hot pastrami in town. *Zadies* and *bubbehs* pass around pix of the grandkids, babies in designer sweats howl, cute young things in flowered minidresses devour truck-sized portions of cheesecake. The decor is corny, but fun: cardboard cutouts of dancing pickles, 3D art of hotdogs. But it's the food you've come for: bowls of borscht with hot potato, sliced tender Nova salmon on toasted bagels, grilled reubens, chicken in a pot and homemade desserts so caloric you'll gain weight just looking. If you haven't eaten at Wolfies, you don't know great deli. $

☆ **Café Papillon,** 530 Lincoln Road, Miami Beach, ☎ 305/673-1139, serves a delicious Greek salad and fresh filet of grouper complemented with tomatoes and new potatoes. Service is attentive, and it's fun to read the free *International Herald Tribune* while your meal is being prepared. For dessert, try a gourmet coffee with homemade chocolate cake. $

☆ **Sushi Hana,** 1131 Washington Avenue, Miami Beach, ☎ 305/532-1100, is extremely chic, with fountains, intimate tatami enclosures and outdoor café dining. People watching is fun: lithe models in clogs and skintight pants; clusters of Men in Black sporting tattoos, silver earrings and cell phones. The sushi is very fresh; they also serve tempura, teriyaki and stir fry. $$

☆ **Pan Coast Restaurant,** Indian Creek Hotel, 2727 Indian Creek Drive, Miami Beach, ☎ 305/531-2727 is an intimate restaurant featuring Pan Asian/Caribbean cuisine. Cordon bleu chef Mary K. Rohan serves imaginative dishes like steamed papaya ponzu scallops, salmon, tempura shrimp, cellophane noodles and wasabi ginger; or honey Dijon veal chop with warm orange tomato salsa and scotch bonnet sour cream. Dine indoors or in the garden by the pool. $$

American

Lulu's, 1053 Washington Avenue, ☎ 305/532-6147, offers fried farm-raised catfish, fried boneless chicken breast with pecan cream gravy, and corn fritters, all served in a decor of Elvis memorabilia. $

Models America Café, 1440 Ocean Drive, ☎ 305/531-7011, is a fun hangout serving salads, fresh fruits, sandwiches and burgers. They also have 12-oz. ribeye steaks and seafood gumbo. $

Italian

Mezzaluna, 834 Ocean Drive, ☎ 305/674-1330, offers brick-oven pizza and fresh pasta specials. Chef Aldo Marcon makes his own flavored olive oil. Dine on the terrace for a romantic evening. $$

Mexican

Moe's Cantina, 616 Collins Avenue, ☎ 305/532-MOES, features eight different margaritas, but don't try them all at once. They serve authentic Cal-Mex cuisine, such as *gambas negras* and beefsteak *tampiquena* with chili pepper mashed potatoes. $

Seafood

Monty's Stone Crab, 300 Alton Road, ☎ 305/673-3444, has delicious stone crabs year-round. Order by size and portion or the "all you can eat" special. Lunch and dinner are served daily, and the raw bar is open almost all night on weekends. A great hangout for late-night seafood lovers. $$

Tourism Information

Miami Beach Chamber of Commerce, 1920 Meridian Avenue, Miami Beach, 33139, ☎ 305/672-1270. Open Mon-Fri, 9 am-5 pm, Sat., 10 am-4 pm. Tourist complaint hotline: ☎ 305/673-7400.

🌴 🌴 🌴

North Miami Beach

I f Miami Beach's "super hip scene" has worn you out, head north. The towns of Surfside and Sunny Isles Beach have gorgeous beaches too, but a more peaceful ambiance. Bad weather? There's always America's favorite indoor sport: shopping. At the Bal Harbour Mall, try on a $3,000 designer gown or a pair of $200 gold-studded sneakers. You never know when either might come in handy.

■ Adventures

On Foot

Golf

- **Greynolds Park,** 17530 W. Dixie Hwy., ☎ 305/949-1741. Nine holes; par 36.

- **Haulover Park,** 10800 Collins Avenue, Miami Beach, ☎ 305/940-6719. Nine holes; par 27.

- **Turnberry Isle Resort & Club,** 19999 W. Country Club Drive, Aventura, ☎ 305/932-6200. 36 holes; par 72.

Tennis

- **Haulover Beach Tennis Center,** 10800 Collins Avenue, ☎ 305/940-6719.

- **Desert Inn Beach & Tennis Club,** 17201 Collins Avenue, ☎ 305/947-0621.

- **RUI Pan American Ocean Resort,** 17875 Collins Avenue, ☎ 305/932-1100.

- **Suez Oceanfront Resort,** 18215 Collins Avenue, ☎ 305/932-0661.

- **Turnberry Isle Resort & Club,** 19999 W. Country Club Drive, Aventura, ☎ 305/932-6200.

On Wheels

 Surfside has a paved **bike path** with spectacular ocean views. Start at Altos Del Mar Park, 81st Street and Atlantic Way. Continue north on Atlantic Way to 87th Street. Another paved bike path is south of Sunny Isles in Haulover Park, also along the ocean. Start at the Haulover Park Fishing Pier and continue north parallel to Collins Avenue.

Across the Intracoastal Waterway, just west of Haulover Beach Park is **Oleta River State Recreation Area.** On the east side of this park is a scenic 1½-mile bike trail.

For picturesque Oleta River and Intracoastal Waterway views, try the paved bike path along Sunny Isles Boulevard. You'll cross both bodies of water on this path. Start east at Sunny Isle Causeway and A1A, then head west on Sunny Isles Boulevard, also known as 163rd Street and Route 826.

North of Sunny Isles, ride around **Turnberry Isle Country Club.** Start at the 192nd Street Causeway and E. Country Club Drive. Ride north on E. Country Club Drive and follow the horseshoe-shaped road that ends back at the causeway.

Hun-Fun Bicycle Rentals, 220 Sunny Isles Boulevard, North Miami, ☎ 305/940-3889, rents bikes by the day or week. Bikes are also for rent at **Urban Trails Kayak** at Haulover Beach Park, ☎ 305/947-1302.

To learn more about these and other bike routes, order the *Bike Miami Suitability Map* from the Metro Dade Bicycle Program, 111 NW First Street, Suite 910, Miami 33138, ☎ 305/375-4507.

On Water

Fishing

The best boating and fishing in this area is at **Haulover Park Marina & Deep Sea Fishing Center,** 10800 Collins Avenue, ☎ 305/947-3525. Choose from a number of charter boats that fish for snapper, yellowtail, mackerel, grouper or kingfish. Most supply fishing rods, bait & tackle and instruction. Two charters at this Marina:

- **The Kelley Fleet,** in operation since 1957, provides half-day, full-day and night excursions for drift and bottom fishing. They also offer two- and three-day Bahama fishing trips. Call for reservations, ☎ 305/945-3801.

- *Therapy IV,* a 58-ft. air-conditioned twin diesel fishing yacht, goes out for big game fish: shark, sailfish and marlin. Maximum six people. Reservations, ☎ 305/945-1578.

Along Collins Avenue in south Sunny Isles, the **Haulover Beach Park Fishing Pier** is a scenic spot to fish for snapper, grunt, mackerel and yellowtail. Farther north, there's **Newport Pier** at Collins Avenue and 170th Street. You can rent fishing equipment and buy bait here as well.

Saltwater fishing is permitted at **Oleta River State Recreation Area,** 3400 NE 163rd Street, ☎ 305/947-6357. Located on the banks of the scenic Oleta River and the Intracoastal Waterway, this park has abundant birdlife, as well as porpoises and manatees.

Mini-Cruising

If you'd rather cruise than fish, contact the captain of *Kon Tiki Dee* at the Haulover Marine Center, ☎ 305/947-0750, who will arrange a pleasant outing on his boat.

Kayaking

At the north end of Haulover Beach Park is **Urban Trails Kayak,** 10800 Collins Avenue, ☎ 305/947-1302, located on the shore of Biscayne Bay just a short paddle away from uninhabited islands and the Oleta Recreation Area. The Oleta is Dade County's last free-flowing river, and is teeming with herons, ibises, spoonbills, kingfishers, and ospreys. Look for raccoons and manatees. Steve Schuemann has owned Urban Trails Kayak since the late 1980s and he's an enthusiastic and knowledgeable guide. Kayak with Steve on Saturday mornings, or get a map and explore on your own anytime during the week.

Scuba Diving & Snorkeling

Off the Sunny Isles Beach coastline, four wrecks were sunk in 1985-1991 to encourage **coral reef** formation. The ships are *Conception, Cone, Andro* and *Narwal.* For information on dive sites, contact the Metro-Dade County Department of Environmental Resources Management (DERM) at ☎ 305/375-DERM.

Two area dive shops providing snorkel and dive instruction, gear rental and sales, and supervised day and night dives are:

- **H2O Scuba,** 160 Sunny Isles Blvd., ☎ 305/956-DIVE. The PADI Course Director is Larry Friedman.

- **The Diving Locker,** 223 Sunny Isles Blvd., ☎ 305/947-6025.

Jet Ski Tour

If you're a jet ski maniac, join a six-hour "Out Back Jet Ski Tour." The tour starts 10:30 am at **D&D's Watersports,** Hawaiian Isle Beach Resort, 17601 Collins Avenue, ☎ 305/932-8445. You'll visit six islands, Port of Miami cruise ships, Bayside Marketplace, the Miami River, Star Island, Flagler Island, and enjoy an island barbecue, returning to D&D's by 4 pm. Don't forget your sunblock.

■ Sightseeing

The Ancient Spanish Monastery, 16711 W. Dixie Highway, North Miami Beach, ☎ 305/945-1462, was built in Segovia, Spain in 1141. It was brought to America by newspaper magnate William Randolph Hearst in 1954. Open Mon-Sat. 10 am-4 pm, Sunday noon-4 pm. Admission.

■ Shopping

If you've just gotta shop, browse **Bal Harbour Shops,** 9700 Collins Avenue, Bal Harbour, ☎ 305/866-0311. You'll be in company with Chanel, Armani, Brooks Brothers, Gianni Versace and Ralph Lauren. Shoppers at this mall look chic, so don't come in cut-offs. Take plenty of credit cards.

■ Where to Stay

☆ **Bay Harbor Inn,** 9601 East Bay Harbor Drive, Bay Harbor Islands, 33154, ☎ 305/868-4141, fax 305/867-9094, is a comfortable inn along the Intracoastal Waterway, near Bal Harbour Shops close to the beach. The 24 rooms are furnished with elegant antiques, some with king-sized four-poster beds. A complimentary continental breakfast is served aboard a docked yacht, the *Celeste,* which is also available for catered dinners. If you arrive by boat there is space available for you to tie up. Amenities include a pool, conference center, free valet parking and complimentary newspapers. Many of the European and US guests are professors and chefs, as the Inn is managed by Johnson & Wales University, the largest culinary arts college in the world. The University also has schools of business, technology and hospitality; many of their students intern at Bay Harbor Inn as chefs and hotel staff. It's a quiet, friendly hotel. Islands Café serves lunch and dinner inside and outdoors on the terrace. The London Tavern offers cocktails, wine, and beer. $$

Best Western Surf Vista, 18001 Collins Avenue, Sunny Isles Beach, ☎ 800/992-4786, has 119 rooms, some non-smoking, some with kitchenettes. There's a coffee shop/restaurant, lounge, in-room movies and a pool. $

Golden Strand Resort, 17901 Collins Avenue, Sunny Isles Beach, ☎ 305/931-7000, has 152 one- and two-bedroom apartments with kitchenettes. There's a coffee shop/restaurant, health spa with sauna, steam room, whirlpool, beauty shop, masseuse, manicurist, heated pool. $$

Marco Polo Resort Hotel, 19201 Collins Avenue, Sunny Isles Beach, ☎ 800/432-3664, has 550 rooms, some with kitchenettes. Persian and International night clubs, disco, lounge, restaurant, heated pool, shopping arcade. $$

Newport Pier Beachside, Crowne Plaza Resort, adjacent to the Newport Pier at 16701 Collins Avenue, Sunny Isles Beach, ☎ 800/327-5476, has 355 rooms, some non-smoking. There is a coffee shop/restaurant, live dinner theater and shows, lounge, heated pool, children's pool, Jacuzzi, watersports program. Pets welcome. $$$

The Baymar Ocean Resort, 9401 Collins Avenue, Surfside, ☎ 800/8BAYMAR, offers 100 rooms and suites with full kitchens and terraces. Right on Surfside Beach. Heated oceanfront pool, tiki bar/grill, sundeck with panoramic views, restaurant/lounge, live entertainment, gameroom. $$

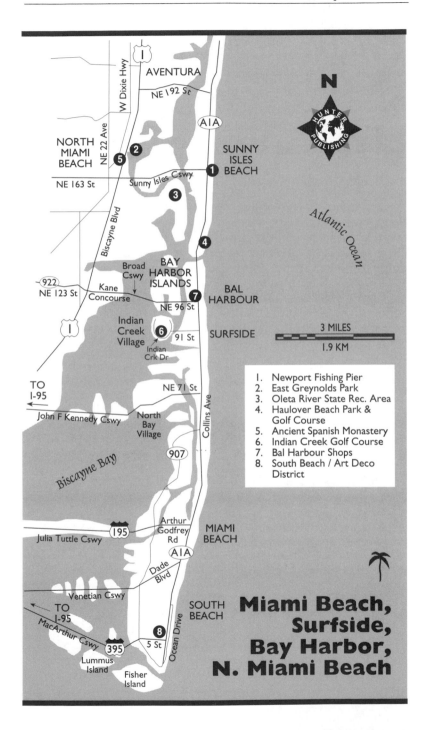

Miami

1. Newport Fishing Pier
2. East Greynolds Park
3. Oleta River State Rec. Area
4. Haulover Beach Park & Golf Course
5. Ancient Spanish Monastery
6. Indian Creek Golf Course
7. Bal Harbour Shops
8. South Beach / Art Deco District

Miami Beach, Surfside, Bay Harbor, N. Miami Beach

■ Where to Eat

☆ **Wolfie Cohen's Rascal House Restaurant,** 172nd and Collins Avenue, ☎ 305/947-4581. You'll wait in line behind chains to be seated. Waitresses in tight white uniforms and well-worn sneakers rush madly from table to table carrying overstuffed sandwiches. It's so noisy you have to shout, and tables are so close you'll touch elbows. But Wolfie's is always mobbed, and open 24 hours a day, because of their food. Melt-in-your-mouth hot pastrami on fragrant homemade rye; succulent Nova salmon on a bagel with cream cheese. Trout, fish cakes, omelettes, pancakes, homemade soup, and chopped steak are all served in portions only a halfback could eat. The cheesecake is so rich your arteries harden before the plate is empty, and it's worth every bite. $

☆ **Prezzo,** at Loehmann's Fashion Island Mall, 18831 Biscayne Blvd., Aventura, ☎ 305/933-9004, has delicious salads: a bed of organic greens, mushrooms and tomatoes is topped with grilled fresh yellowfin tuna in a sun-dried tomato vinaigrette. Entrées include artichoke pizza, veal chops, strip steak, and even that favorite comfort food, meatloaf. A popular spot with locals. $

☆ **Tuna's Waterfront Grille,** 17201 Biscayne Blvd, North Miami Beach, ☎ 305/945-2567, has some of the freshest seafood in the area. Florida stone crab, soft shell crabs, blue crab crakes, Maine and Florida lobster, shrimp creole, broiled scallops, grilled tuna, salmon, swordfish. The homemade chocolate decadence and custard pudding desserts are superb. A late-night menu is served from 10 pm-2 am. $$$

Tourism Information

Surfside Tourist Board, 9301 Collins Avenue, Surfside, 33154, ☎ 305/864-0722.

Sunny Isles Beach Resort Association, 17100 Collins Avenue, Suite 208, Sunny Isles Beach, 33160, ☎ 305/947-5826. Call or write for their *Information Guide* and *Discount Certificate Booklet.*

❦ ❦ ❦

Greater Fort Lauderdale

In this chapter we share our favorite adventures in Hollywood, Davie, Dania, Fort Lauderdale, Pompano Beach, Hillsboro Beach, Deerfield Beach, and Coconut Creek.

■ Getting Here

Fort Lauderdale/Hollywood International Airport is at 3629 N. 19th Street, ☎ 954/359-1200. This airport is served by Air Canada, Air Jamaica, American, American Trans Air, Canadian Airlines International, Carnival, Continental, Delta, Halisa Air, Icelandair, Laker Airways, Liberty, Midwest Express, Northwest, Southwest, Spirit, TWA, United and US Air.

Rental Car Agencies

Alamo	☎ 800/327-9633
Avis	☎ 800/331-1212
Budget	☎ 800/527-0700
Dollar	☎ 800/800-4000
Hertz	☎ 800/654-3131
National	☎ 800/227-7368

Other Transportation:

Greyhound/Trailways	☎ 800/231-2222
Broward Mass Transit	☎ 954/357-8400
Amtrak Trains	☎ 800/872-7245
Water Taxi of Fort Lauderdale	☎ 954/467-6677

■ Getting Around

From the Airport, take US Highway 1 north to S.E. 17th Street. Turn east and you'll be on A1A which parallels Fort Lauderdale's famous beach. Along A1A you can access downtown Fort Lauderdale via Las Olas Boulevard or Sunrise Boulevard.

Hollywood

■ Adventures

On Foot

If you enjoy beachwalking, we recommend you visit two beaches in this area. **Hollywood Beach** is a beautiful five-mile stretch of pearl-colored sand and elegant palm trees. The Broadwalk, a strip of pavement closed to cars but open for walkers and bikers, borders most of the beach. Swimming is wonderful here, and there are picnic spots, bathrooms, showers, lifeguards, snack shops and restaurants in the area. Off route A1A, the beach is accessible from Greenbriar to Sherman Street.

Our second recommendation is the 56-acre **Hollywood North Beach Park,** located between Hollywood Beach and Dania Beach. This lush park has dense vegetation, oak trees, sea grapes, and boardwalks built over dunes. North Beach has a sea turtle protection program, and you may see them in holding tanks, prior to their ocean release. Facilities include picnic spots, bathrooms, lifeguards, snack shops, walking paths, and a 60-foot-high observation tower. Access to this park is at Route A1A and Sheridan Street.

John U. Lloyd Beach State Recreation Area, 6503 North Ocean Drive, Dania, ☎ 954/923-2833, has a self-guided nature trail that meanders through a semi-tropical coastal hammock. Birders and photographers will love hiking here. An ocean walk along the white sandy beach is dramatic.

Dania Beach, off Route A1A at Oak Street, is a lovely half-mile beach with soft khaki-colored sand. Palm trees and a newly re-built pier create a nice setting for a short seaside stroll.

⌇ Greater Ft. Lauderdale

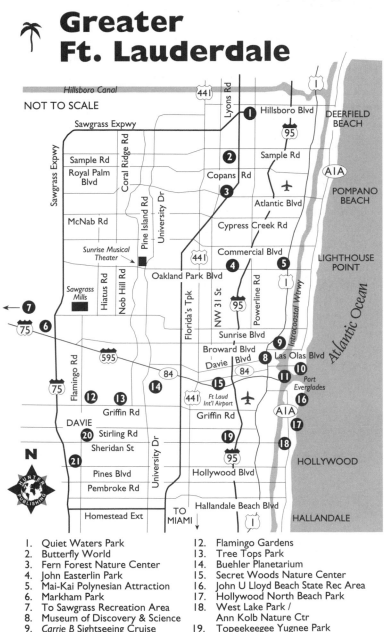

Ft. Lauderdale

1. Quiet Waters Park
2. Butterfly World
3. Fern Forest Nature Center
4. John Easterlin Park
5. Mai-Kai Polynesian Attraction
6. Markham Park
7. To Sawgrass Recreation Area
8. Museum of Discovery & Science
9. *Carrie B* Sightseeing Cruise
10. *Jungle Queen* Sightseeing Cruise
11. Swimming Hall of Fame
12. Flamingo Gardens
13. Tree Tops Park
14. Buehler Planetarium
15. Secret Woods Nature Center
16. John U Lloyd Beach State Rec Area
17. Hollywood North Beach Park
18. West Lake Park / Ann Kolb Nature Ctr
19. Topeekeegee Yugnee Park
20. Brian Piccolo Park
21. C.B. Smith Park

On Wheels

Biking & Skating

Take a spin along the **Broadwalk**, an asphalt promenade that hugs Hollywood beach for two miles between Simms and Georgia Streets. You'll pass family motels, snack shacks, and souvenir shops, as well as joggers, sun bathers, and senior citizens. This is a pleasant way to enjoy the sun and surf and get some exercise, too.

If you're feeling athletic, try the challenging velodrome at **Brian Piccolo Park,** 9501 Sheridan Street, Cooper City, ☎ 954/437-2600. The velodrome has a 333-meter cycle track and a 200-meter banked in-line skate track. Bikes and skates are available for rent, and lessons are available. The park also has a regular bike path.

Topeekeegee Yugnee Park (also known as T.Y. Park), 3300 N. Park Road, Hollywood, ☎ 954/985-1980, rents bicycles for use on the park's bike path, which circles around a fishing and boating lake.

Bike rentals are available at the **Anne Kolb Nature Center** in West Lake Park, 1200 Sheridan Street, Hollywood, ☎ 954/926-2410. This is one of the largest parks in Florida, preserving over 1,400 acres of coastal mangrove wetlands in an urban landscape. The center has observation platforms, boardwalks, and numerous bike trails.

On Water

Boating & Fishing

There's a small **fishing lake** in Brian Piccolo Park (address and phone given in the *On Foot* section, above). Catch-and-release fishing is encouraged, and the park closes at dusk. A license is required if you are 16 or over.

C.B. Smith Park has an 80-acre lake with three fishing piers. They also encourage catch-and-release fishing. Fish from the piers, from shore, or rent a boat. 900 N. Flamingo Road, Pembroke Pines, ☎ 954/437-2650.

Topeekeegee Yugnee Park has a 40-acre lake with shore or boat fishing permitted. Again, a license is required for those 16 or over. The park rents canoes, paddleboats, and john boats. (Address and phone in *On Foot,* above.)

West Lake Park, 1200 Sheridan Street, Hollywood, ☎ 954/926-2410, is the marine gateway to West Lake's 1,500 acres, running east from Johnson Street north to Port Everglades. You can rent canoes or launch your own boat from the park's marina. Within the park is a smaller lake that offers good shore fishing.

Canoeing

West Lake Park/Anne Kolb Nature Center (address above) has three different self-guided interpretive **canoe trails** meandering through one of southeast Florida's largest mangrove estuarine habitats. Keep your eyes open for fiddler crabs, mangrove crabs, coffee bean snails and snapping shrimp. Birds living here include the yellow crowned night heron, white ibis, osprey, roseate spoonbill, and peregrine falcon. On Saturdays in January, February and March, guided canoe tours leave from West Lake Marina at 10 am and 1 pm. Call ☎ 954/926-2480 for current schedules.

John U. Lloyd Beach State Recreation Area, 6503 North Ocean Drive, Dania, 33004, ☎ 954/923-2833, rents canoes. Keep a look out for manatees. Fishing is excellent off the jetty at the park's north end.

Kayaking

Past the chic high rises of Miami Beach is a quiet neighborhood of low-rise motels in Hollywood. Tucked among them is one of Florida's only kayak schools. **Water Ways Kayak,** 1406 N. Ocean Drive, ☎ 954/921-8944, offers excellent half-day clinics for beginning or advanced kayakers. A brief part of the class is on land, but the best part is in West Lake, where you'll practice paddle strokes and boat maneuvering as white egrets watch from dense mangroves. After four hours you'll feel completely in control of your kayak, ready for the advanced class or a day at sea. Instructors are experienced and enthusiastic, bestowing personal attention on each student. After class, browse the pris-

Ft. Lauderdale

tine shop overflowing with state-of-the-art kayaks and top quality sports clothing.

✳ Snapshot

Meet Jeffrey Bingham, Instructor, Water Ways Kayak, Hollywood.

SS: What attracted you to kayaking?

JB: The tremendous availability of water in South Florida. There are so many places to go. I started in canoeing, but as soon as I saw a sea kayak I fell in love with its sleek lines and beauty. The fact they are completely sealed against the weather is a plus.

SS: How did you get so comfortable in kayaking?

JB: Well, at first I felt pretty tippy, but I learned a lot about kayaking from reading books. Once I got formal training I really fell in love with the sport. What is fantastic is the ability to go anywhere in Florida by water: the Intracoastal Waterway goes all the way to Maine! I can paddle out into the ocean down to the Keys; Florida's west coast is beautiful too. You see birds and manatees much more often than when you are in a powerboat!

SS: What advice do you have for someone who has never kayaked?

JB: You need good navigation and paddling skills, especially if you're out among islands and mangroves. So I recommend you get instruction. It's the one thing that will provide you with the skills, comfort, and ability to handle any situation that comes up – storms, ocean swells, bay chop. Lessons will really open up the sport for you.

In the Air

Helicopter Flying

Blonde, blue-eyed Alice Butler may look like a magazine cover girl, but she has nerves of steel. She's been an air traffic controller, a skywriter, an airline transport pilot, commercial pilot, and flight instructor. Now she's found her place in the sky as President/Flight Instructor of **Rotors in Motion,** North Perry Airport, 7499 Pembroke Road, Hollywood, ☎ 954/981-4000. If you've always yearned to pilot a helicopter,

Opposite: The historic Cape Florida Lighthouse on Key Biscayne.

Above: *Windsurfing is very popular in breezy Biscayne Bay.*
Opposite: *The Biltmore Hotel in Coral Gables* (courtesy of the Biltmore Hotel)
Below: *Sea kayak instruction.*

Above: *An endangered hawksbill turtle watches visitors.* (© Miami Seaquarium)
Opposite: *Atlantic bottlenose dolphins show off their natural grace.* (© Miami Seaquarium)
Below: *One of Miami Beach's Art Deco hotels.*

Above: *The Florida Everglades has a rich biodiversity.*

Below: *A purple gallinule adds color to the Everglades.*

Above: *Kayaker navigating small falls on Jupiter's Loxahatchee River.*

Below: *Sunrise over the Atlantic.*

Alice will have you flying in one hour. Her Demo Flight includes a half-hour of ground instruction and half-hour flight for just $85. Of course Alice will be alongside as coach, so why not take the challenge?

✳ Snapshot

Meet Alice Ursula Butler, President/Pilot Instructor, Rotors in Motion, Hollywood.

SS: Why try helicopter piloting?

AB: It's really the ultimate when it comes to flying. The maneuverability allows you to do things you can't do in an airplane: fly backwards, in any direction, land on a spot without needing a runway. We fly with our doors off, so you're part of the environment. I sometimes feel like I'm in a *Jetsons* TV show, flying around in my little pod! With the helicopter's huge bubble out front and doors open on the sides, it's the most wonderful feeling.

SS: If I don't want to pilot the helicopter, can I just take a sightseeing ride?

AB: Yes, we tour the Everglades to see birds and alligators out in the sawgrass. We speed along five feet above the water, and the intense feeling is exhilarating. We also hover above The Port of Miami or Coconut Grove, looking at cruise ships, shops, restaurants, and marinas. We visit luxurious Fisher Island and Miami Beach's Art Deco district at sunset. When the city lights come on it's gorgeous. A whole new viewpoint.

SS: Tell me about your demo flights for would-be pilots.

AB: They are ideal for adults interested in aviation. We spend the first 30 minutes in ground school in an accelerated course learning basic helicopter aerodynamics. Students learn how the controls work, and are taken through the flight step by step: taxi, takeoff, flying, and the relationship of the helicopter to the horizon. We discuss and practice emergency situations. Then, up we go for 30 minutes, and the student does most of the flying, with me next to him or her at the controls. The demo class is 60 minutes and you get a souvenir Rotors in Motion T-shirt at completion. I've got over 1,200 hours of instruction, so you can feel completely confident. My relationships with my students are personal; they know I care about them. Everyone always leaves with a smile on their face.

Ft. Lauderdale

Opposite: Key Biscayne, off the south tip of Miami Beach. Beaches like this stretch for hundreds of miles up the Florida coast.

Other Adventures

Spectator Sports

Home to the Florida Derby and the world-renowned Breeders Cup, **Gulfstream Park** races thoroughbreds from January-March and offers parimutuel betting. 901 S. Federal Highway, Hallandale, ☎ 954/454-7000. Open Wednesday-Monday, post time 1:15 pm. Admission. At **Hollywood Greyhound Track,** fleet-footed greyhounds chase a mechanical rabbit nightly from December 26 to April 26 for parimutuel wagering. Watch the action while dining at the track restaurant or relaxing over cocktails in the lounge. 831 Federal Highway, Hallandale, ☎ 954/454-8666. Nightly from 7:30 pm; matinees Tuesday, Thursday and Saturday at 12:30 pm. Admission.

Handball players armed with a curved basket throw a ball at speeds up to 100 mph at the glass-fronted **Dania Jai-Alai** fronton, which features parimutuel betting, dining and a cocktail lounge. 301 E. Dania Beach Boulevard, Dania, ☎ 954/920-1511. Open Tuesday-Saturday from 7:15 pm; Tuesday, Thursday and Friday at noon; Sunday at 1 pm. Admission.

Davie

■ Adventures

On Foot

 Set among 60 lush acres of palms, flowers, and hundred-year-old trees, **Flamingo Gardens** is a haven for bird and tropical plant lovers.

Pink flamingos strut their sandy beach on impossibly thin legs that bend backwards at the joints. Some sleep balanced on one leg, heads facing backward. Inside the Aviary, double-crested cormorants, woodstorks and 200 other bird species fly freely or bathe in bubbling ponds. Feeding time at 2:30 pm is fun, as the birds go into a frenzy of squawking and flapping.

Trails lead among magnificent gardens of African tulip, pink trumpet vine, bread nut and floss silk trees. At the Learning Center, a great horned owl stars in a lecture on birds of prey. If you only have time for one walk in this area, don't miss Flamingo Gardens, 3750 Flamingo Road, Davie, ☎ 954/473-2955.

Tree Tops Park, 3900 SW 100th Avenue, Davie, ☎ 954/370-3750, has 358 acres of nature trails through dense woods and a live oak hammock. The historic Pine Island Ridge area has archaeological sites dating

Flamingo Gardens.

back to the Tequesta Indians, circa 1565. A 1,000-foot boardwalk along a 23-acre freshwater marsh is a good spot for wildlife and nature photography.

On Wheels

There are bike rentals and pleasant biking paths at **Plantation Park** and **Markham Park.** Tree Tops Park has a bike path, but no rentals. See the *On Water* section for park addresses and phone numbers.

On Water

Boating & Fishing

Tree Tops Park, 3900 SW 100th Avenue, Davie, ☎ 954/370-3750, has a marina renting canoes and paddleboats for exploring 15 acres of waterways. Rentals are on weekends and holidays only. Fishing is permitted from a boat, on shore, or from the pier. License required if you are 16 or older.

Ft. Lauderdale

Plantation Heritage Park, 1100 S. Fig Tree Lane, Plantation, 33317, ☎ 954/791-1025, offers paddleboat and canoe rentals, and permits fishing from shore. License required if you are 16 or older.

Markham Park, 16001 W. State Road 84, Sunrise, 33326, ☎ 954/389-2000, has a 26-acre lake with ramps for launching private boats into the New River Canals. Canoes, paddleboats, and johnboats are available for rent. Shore fishing is permitted in the lake and canal. License required if you are 16 and older.

Everglades Holiday Park, 21940 Griffin Road, Fort Lauderdale 33332, ☎ 954/434-8111, offers fishing guides, boat rentals, fishing gear, bait, and licenses for Everglades fishing. The park is located west of Davie.

Airboating

Everglades Holiday Park, 21940 Griffin Road, Fort Lauderdale (west of Davie), 33332, ☎ 954/434-8111. Admission. See the **snapshot** of Captain Dan Coltrane on the next page.

Airboat rides through the Everglades are a sensory thrill and give access to a variety of wildlife, from alligators to anhingas.

✳ Snapshot

Meet Captain Dan Coltrane, Everglades Holiday Park airboat captain

"Which ride do ya want: meek and mild or wild and crazy?" airboat captain Dan Coltrane asks in a deep throaty voice. Piled into an 800-horsepower Excaliber airboat, we're out for an Everglades adventure. "Wild and crazy," we shout. Why not, life is short.

"Keep your hands inside the boat. There's 27 kinds of snakes out here, all finger eaters," he snorts. Captain Dan fires up the boat, setting off a brain-rattling din, as we career into Florida's river of grass. Yellow-bellied turtles sun on Japanese water lilies, spiky sawgrass stretches to the blue horizon, and clouds reflect in a kaleidoscope of blue/green water/sky.

We stop on a small island to sample fresh fried alligator tails, while local Seminoles hawk 'gator heads, Indian drums, and toy tomahawks. Jacob Pitawanakwat from the Ojibwa Tribe enters a fenced yard where alligators snooze in the sun. He grabs a four-footer, clamps his hand around the jaw, and holds him out for petting. One by one we cautiously reach out, caressing the smooth hide, awed by this monstrosity. What if Jacob releases the gator's jaw?

Seconds later he's straddling an eight-footer, opening the jaw to show the gator's very large, very pink tongue. "He's got 600 lbs. of biting pressure with these teeth," grins Jacob. Somehow he looks comfortable sitting there. (Maybe I could try 'gator sitting.)

Two 12-foot alligators in the murky pool behind Jacob emit hissing sounds. One lunges at Jacob when he taunts the critter with a stick. "Don't try this at home, kids," he laughs. "Never feed a wild animal," he cautions more seriously, "or they'll come looking for more. And it might be you they eat."

Back in the boat, Captain Dan searches for wild 'gators. He points out white-faced coots and purple gallinules wading through the grass, as great blue herons flap by. In minutes, we're eye-to-eye with a four-foot 'gator hidden among sawgrass and cattails. He glides swiftly to our boat like a hungry pet. Looking for fingers, I think. I contemplate wrestling the cold-eyed beast into submission, riding him bareback like a proud rodeo queen.

Instead, I stay in the boat. Adventure has its limits.

On Horseback

To amuse your cowboy or cowgirl soul, pull on your boots and hat for an evening at **Davie Arena's 5 Star Rodeo,** 6591 Orange Drive, behind Town Hall, ☎ 954/797-1166. Competitions in bareback riding, steer wrestling, calf roping, saddle bronc riding, team roping, barrel racing and bull riding make for a Wild West event.

If you're in the Davie area the end of February or beginning of March, get tickets to the "Biggest Country Western Festival East of the Mississippi," the **Florida WestFair.** Ten fun-filled days of country music stars, monster truck shows, a parade, and carnival rides. For the monthly calendar of rodeos, or WestFair schedule, call ☎ 954/797-1166 or 954/791-WEST.

Fort Lauderdale

■ Adventures

On Foot

Hiking

Secret Woods Nature Center, 2701 W. State Road 84, Ft. Lauderdale, ☎ 954/791-1030, features guided nature walks through a 55-acre park. The New River Trail is a 3,200-foot wheelchair accessible boardwalk through oak hammock, freshwater and saltwater wetlands. The Laurel Oak Trail is a 1,200-foot woodchip trail wending through an oak hammock. A self-guided trail booklet from the park office makes it easy to enjoy park trails on your own. A Designated Urban Wilderness Area.

Another Designated Urban Wilderness Area is **Easterlin Park,** 1000 NW 38th Street, Oakland Park, ☎ 954/938-0610. The park's ¾-mile Woodland Nature Trail winds through oak hammock, cypress and maple forest. A self-guided trail map is available at the park office. The 250-year-old cypress trees create a peaceful setting for walking and relaxing.

Golf

- **Arrowhead Golf & Sports Club,** 8201 SW 24th Street, Fort Lauderdale, ☎ 954/475-8200. Par 71.

- **Bonaventure Country Club,** 200 Bonaventure Blvd., Fort Lauderdale, ☎ 954/389-2100. Par 70.

- **Colony West Country Club,** 6800 NW 88th Avenue, Fort Lauderdale, ☎ 954/726-8430. Par 71.

- **Rolling Hills Resort,** 3501 Rolling Hills Circle, Fort Lauderdale, ☎ 954/475-3010. Par 72.

- **Sabal Palms Golf Courses,** 5101 West Commercial Blvd., Fort Lauderdale, ☎ 954/731-2600. Par 72, 74.

Tennis

- **Bass Park,** 2750 NW 19th Street, Fort Lauderdale, ☎ 954/396-3621. Five lighted hard courts.

- **Bayview Park,** 4400 Bayview Drive, Fort Lauderdale, ☎ 954/396-3621. Five lighted hard courts.

- **Joseph C. Carter Park,** 1450 W. Sunrise Blvd., Fort Lauderdale, ☎ 954/761-5410. Six lighted courts.

- **Coral Ridge Tennis Club,** 3801 Bayview Drive, Fort Lauderdale, ☎ 954/564-7386. Two lighted hard courts, nine non-lighted clay courts.

- **Fort Lauderdale Tennis Club,** 600 Tennis Club Drive, Fort Lauderdale, ☎ 954/763-8657. Twenty non-lighted clay courts; four lighted hard courts.

- **Lafayette Hart,** 2851 NW Eighth Road, Fort Lauderdale, ☎ 954/791-1041. Six lighted courts.

On Water

Boating

Bahia Mar Yachting Center, 801 Seabreeze Boulevard, Fort Lauderdale, ☎ 954/764-2233, is the area's largest marina with 350 slips and a 44-acre beach. While strolling the docks, you'll see some of the world's largest yachts, international flags flapping in the breeze. There's a new Marina Service Center that provides assistance with reservations, fueling, yacht maintenance, cable TV, business and telephone services. The Marina Store has nautical resort wear, gifts, charts, books, sunglasses, sundries and ice. Stock up on groceries from the Bahia Mar Beach Market Deli, or dine on fresh seafood at Bahia Mar Bar & Grille. If you need some R&R, check into the Bahia Mar Beach Resort for a few days of tennis, swimming and beachwalking. The marina also hosts the annual Fort Lauderdale International Boat Show.

Southeast Yachting School & Charters, Inc., 2170 SE 17th Street Causeway, Suite 304, Fort Lauderdale, ☎ 800/966-BOAT, is an American Sailing Association training facility. Classes are taught by ASA certified instructors who are also licensed Coast Guard Captains. All courses are taught aboard an outstanding fleet of ocean going Sail and Power yachts. Weekly bareboat charters for powerboats and sailboats are also available year-round. See the **snapshot** of Captain Carolyn Williams and Captain Nadine Nack on the next page.

Scuba Diving & Snorkeling

Pro Dive International, 801 Seabreeze Boulevard, Bahia Mar Yachting Center, Fort Lauderdale, ☎ 954/761-3413, offers PADI specialty courses in night diving, navigation, search and recovery, wreck diving, deep diving, and underwater photography. There are also PADI Open Water Certification courses and advanced Certification courses.

If you're already certified, sign up to dive off the company's *Pro Diver II,* a 61-foot glass-bottom vessel that can accommodate up to 30 divers. There are plenty of wrecks in the area, such as the cargo freighter *Rodeo* at 130 feet, the barge *Hog Heaven* at 80 feet, and the Tenneco Platforms at 118 feet.

On Tuesdays through Saturdays, glass-bottom snorkel trips leave the dock at 9:30 am. Two-tank dive charters depart at 12:30 pm. On Sundays, the schedule is reversed. On Tuesdays, Thursdays and Saturdays there are twilight/night dives.

✳ Snapshot

Meet Captain Carolyn Williams and Captain Nadine Nack, Owners/Instructors, Southeast Yachting School & Charters, Inc., Ft. Lauderdale.

SS: When did you start teaching sailing and powerboating?

CW: Back in 1983 we were asked to bring our sailing and powerboat programs to Bahia Mar Yachting Center in Ft. Lauderdale. We were the first to have a powerboat school in this area. In 1994 we launched our own corporation, branching more into sailing, chartering boats, and offering the captain's license program.

SS: What sailing programs are offered?

NN: We have basic sailing courses through the American Sailing Association, intermediate coastal cruising courses, and bareboat chartering, a live-aboard situation. Also navigation courses. The first two levels are weekend courses, both on the water and in the classroom. Students then take a test, get a logbook and a written certification, so they can go to any ASA facility in the country, show that and pick up on the next level of training. We can customize a course for families with different schedule needs. We're flexible for our students, and they come from all over the world to study with us.

SS: What specifics do students learn in the sailing classes?

NN: Line handling, knots, raising and lowering the sails, pointing into the wind, coming about and jibing, terminology of the rigging, parts of the boat, rules of the road, man overboard drills, giving commands, docking, and teamwork.

SS: What about powerboating classes?

CW: We offer the same kind of in-depth instruction appropriate to powerboats, both on the water and in classroom training. By the end of the second day, I have my female students backing up the powerboat into the slip by themselves. They're quite proud and their husbands are happy that the family can learn to enjoy boating together.

SS: What attracted you to sailing?

CC: When you're out sailing, it's quiet – just you and the ocean. You feel the strength of the water; it's terrific therapy. It's a great way to find yourself.

SS: And powerboating?

NN: Working together and learning about the boat itself. There are always new places to explore. With a powerboat you can travel quickly to a destination. It's a comfortable and fun way to explore the world with your family.

Ft. Lauderdale

Fort Lauderdale's waterways attract many large yachts.

Deep-Sea Fishing

If 20 minutes to the fishing grounds sounds perfect to you, climb aboard the *Flamingo* at Bahia Mar Yachting Center, 801 Seabreeze Boulevard, Fort Lauderdale, ☎ 954/462-9194. They run three trips daily at 8 am, 1 pm, and 7 pm, and supply bait, rods and fishing instruction. The drift fishing boat has restrooms and a glass-enclosed lounge. Expect to reel in wahoo, cobia, grouper, bonita, kingfish, barracuda, dolphin and sailfish.

Speedboats & Parasailing

Fort Lauderdale has dozens of watersports centers renting waverunners, jet skis, mini-cigarettes, and speedboats. Some offer parasailing. We can recommend these companies:

- ■ **Bill's Sunrise Watersports,** 2025 E. Sunrise Boulevard, Fort Lauderdale, ☎ 954/462-8962.

- ■ **Sea Screamer,** 85 Las Olas Circle, Fort Lauderdale, ☎ 954/463-4110.

- ■ **Watersports Unlimited, Inc.,** 301 Seabreeze Boulevard, Fort Lauderdale, ☎ 954/467-1316.

Sightseeing Boats

The *Carrie B,* a charming replica of a 19th-century riverboat, cruises the New River and the Intracoastal Waterway in a 1½-hour narrated tour. The upper deck is open air, the lower deck is air-conditioned, and beverages/snacks are available. Restrooms and comfortable seating on board. Cruises depart at 11 am, 1 pm and 3 pm from Riverwalk at SE 5th Avenue & Las Olas Boulevard, Fort Lauderdale, ☎ 954/768-9920. No reservations are necessary.

The *Jungle Queen* cruises the New River past waterfront homes and downtown Fort Lauderdale, and also stops at the Jungle Queen Indian Village, a tropical island where macaws live. The three-hour sightseeing cruises depart daily at 10 am and 2 pm; four-hour dinner cruises depart at 7 pm. Dinners feature barbecue ribs, chicken and shrimp. Alcoholic beverages are available, and there's an after-dinner Variety Revue. Departures are from Bahia Mar Yachting Center, 801 Seabreeze Boulevard, Fort Lauderdale, ☎ 954/462-5596. Reservations suggested.

Fort Lauderdale **Water Taxis** travel the area's 300 miles of rivers and canals, functioning both as sightseeing rides and convenient transportation around the city. They operate daily from 10 am to 2 am. Taxis will pick you up from one of 56 locations; call ☎ 954/467-6677. Fees vary.

Swimming

The **International Swimming Hall of Fame Aquatic Complex** is an extensive outdoor swimming and diving facility open daily for lap swimming and water aerobics. The complex hosts national and international aquatic competitions. At the museum, browse the exhibits on Johnny "Tarzan" Weissmuller, Esther Williams, Greg Louganis and other swim stars. 501 Seabreeze Boulevard, Fort Lauderdale, ☎ 954/468-1580. Open daily 8 am-4 pm; Monday-Fridays, 6 pm-8 pm. Admission for swimming and museum.

Ft. Lauderdale

An excellent book and gift shop is **Bluewater Books & Charts,** Southport Center, 1481 SE 17th Street, Fort Lauderdale, ☎ 954/763-6533 or 800/942-2583. They stock some 35,000 nautical books, flags, cruising guides, travel guides, marine software, NOAA charts, marine videos, calendars, postcards and magazines.

■ Sightseeing

Museums & Culture

 Fort Lauderdale Historical Museum features exhibits that depict growth and development of the city from the 1870 to 1930. 219 SW 2nd Avenue, Fort Lauderdale, ☎ 954/463-4431. Open Tuesday-Friday, 10 am-4 pm. Admission.

Museum of Art has a permanent art collection, and touring exhibits such as Salvador Dali and Grandma Moses. 1 E. Las Olas Boulevard, Fort Lauderdale, ☎ 954/763-6464. Open Tuesday 10 am-9 pm; Wednesday-Saturday 10 am-5 pm; Sunday noon-5 pm. Admission.

Museum of Discovery and Science/Blockbuster Imax Theater, 401 SW 2nd Street, Fort Lauderdale, ☎ 954/467-6637, features dynamic hands-on exhibits and a five-story Imax theater. The museum conducts turtle walks on selected summer evenings; call for dates and reservations. Open Monday-Saturday 10 am-5 pm; Sunday, noon-5 pm. Admission.

Old Dillard Art and Cultural Museum, 1009 N.W 4th Street, Fort Lauderdale, ☎ 954/765-6952, is a National Historic Landmark school, now home to African art, jewelry and tribal masks. A storyteller performs in a thatched hut. Open Tuesday-Saturday noon-4 pm; Wednesday, noon-8 pm. Free.

Bonnet House, a historic seaside estate built in 1926, features antique family paintings by the home's original artist-owners and 35 acres of swans, orchids and monkeys. 900 N. Birch Road, Fort Lauderdale, ☎ 954/563-5393; www.bonnethouse.com. Open Wednesday-Friday 10 am to 2 pm, Saturday and Sunday noon-3 pm. Tours Wednesday-Friday at 10 am and 1 pm; Saturday and Sunday at 1 pm and 2 pm. Admission.

Stranahan House, 335 E. Las Olas Boulevard (at S.E. 6th Avenue), Fort Lauderdale, ☎ 954/524-4736, is the tiny, beautifully restored turn-of-the-century riverside home of Fort Lauderdale's founder. Furnished in period antiques, it's the city's oldest residence. Open Wednesday-Saturday, 10 am-4 pm; Sunday 1-4 pm. Admission.

Ah-Tha-Thi-Ki Museum, one hour from Fort Lauderdale, 17 miles north of Interstate 75, Exit 14, on the Seminole Big Cypress Reservation, ☎ 941/902-1113. To arrange group tours, contact the Seminole Reservation main office at ☎ 954/792-0745. Ah-Tha-Thi-Ki is the world's first comprehensive museum dedicated to the history and culture of Florida's Seminole Indians. The museum features a five-screen orientation theater, Seminole culture dioramas, artifacts, interactive computers, and a gift shop with a variety of Native American arts, crafts and music. The living Seminole village shows how the tribe lived over 100 years ago in the Everglades. Traditional Seminole dances are performed at the ceremonial grounds. A one-mile boardwalk nature trail winds through ferns, vines and trees, providing information on the Big Cypress Swamp. Open Tuesday-Sunday, 9 am-5 pm. Admission.

Buehler Planetarium, Broward Community College, 3501 SW Davie Road, Davie, ☎ 954/475-668, presents state-of-the-art laser light shows at their astronomy center. Admission.

Las Olas Horse and Carriage Tours, SE 8th Avenue and E. Las Olas Blvd., Carriage Stand, Fort Lauderdale, ☎ 954/763-7393, is a delightful way to tour the city's historic district. Fee.

Mai Kai Polynesian Revue, 3599 N. Federal Highway, Fort Lauderdale, ☎ 954/563-3272, recreates a Polynesian village with dance and cuisine. On Sunday evenings from June through September the show features Polynesian children. Admission.

Riverwalk, SW 7th Avenue to SW 2nd Avenue, Fort Lauderdale, ☎ 954/468-1541, is a new park along the banks of the historic New River. Landscaped paths, engraved brick walkways, and yachts in the harbor create a picturesque setting. Arts festivals and free outdoor jazz concerts are held here.

Ft. Lauderdale

Performing Arts

Bailey Hall, Broward Community College, 3501 SW Davie Road, Fort Lauderdale, ☎ 954/475-6880, presents a wide variety of dance, music, and professional touring theater groups.

Brian C. Smith's Off-Broadway at 26th Street Theater offers contemporary plays in a theater seating 300. 1444 NE 26th Street, Fort Lauderdale, ☎ 954/566-0554.

Broward Center for the Performing Arts, presents Broadway, dance and operatic stars in concerts and performances, along the banks of the New River. 201 SW 5th Avenue, Fort Lauderdale, ☎ 954/462-0222.

Parker Playhouse, 707 NE 8th Street, Fort Lauderdale, ☎ 954/764-0700, hosts Broadway shows from October-April.

Pompano Amphitheater, 1801 NE 6th Street, Pompano Beach, ☎ 954/946-2402, holds pop and rock concerts, like Hootie and the Blowfish and REO Speedwagon.

Sunrise Musical Theater, 5555 NW 95th Avenue, Sunrise, ☎ 954/741-8600, is a 4,000-seat auditorium presenting top stars and music groups.

■ Festivals & Events

February

Taste of Fort Lauderdale, ☎ 954/485-3481.

Wild West Fair, ☎ 954/537-1010.

Sistrunk Historical Festival, ☎ 954/357-7514.

Florida Renaissance Festival, ☎ 954/771-7117.

Annual Seminole Tribal Fair, ☎ 954/966-6300.

Davie Orange Blossom Festival and Rodeo, ☎ 954/581-0790.

March

Honda Golf Classic, ☎ 954/346-4000.

St. Patrick's Day Parade and Festival, ☎ 954/943-1012.

Museum of Art Las Olas Art Festival, ☎ 954/525-5500.

Fort Lauderdale Festival of the Arts, ☎ 954/761-5363.

April
Fort Lauderdale Seafood Festival, ☎ 954/463-4431.
Fort Lauderdale Spring Boat Show, ☎ 954/764-7642.

May
Gold Coast Wine Celebration, ☎ 954/467-6637.
Cajun Zydeco Crawfish Festival, ☎ 954/489-3255.

July
Fourth of July Family Celebration, ☎ 954/761-5363.

August
Big League World Series of Little League Baseball, ☎ 954/462-9644.

September
Art à la Carte, ☎ 954/525-5500.

October
Broward Navy Days Fleet Week, ☎ 954/767-NAVY.
Fort Lauderdale International Boat Show, ☎ 954/764-7642.
Oktoberfest, ☎ 954/761-5365.
Via Broward, ☎ 954/527-0627.

November
Promenade in the Park, ☎ 954/764-5973.
Broward County Fair, ☎ 954/FAIR.
Riverwalk Blues Fest, ☎ 954/489-3255.
Fort Lauderdale International Film Festival, ☎ 954/563-0500.

December
Christmas on Las Olas, ☎ 954/523-1200.

Ft. Lauderdale

Candy Cane Parade, ☎ 954/931-3407.

New River Boat Parade, ☎ 954/791-0202.

Winterfest Continental Airlines Boat Parade, ☎ 954/767-0686.

Winterfest Light Up Lauderdale, ☎ 954/767-0686.

■ Where to Stay

Note: Establishments designated as "Superior Small Lodging" are members of a county program designed to promote clean, safe, well-run lodgings. Member lodgings are reviewed and inspected annually, have fewer than 50 rooms and are distinguished by their friendly ambiance and personal service.

☆ **The Winterset Apartment/Motel,** 2801 Terramar Street, Fort Lauderdale, ☎ 800/888-2639, is a charming and relaxing property owned and managed by Mr. and Mrs. Robert Poirier. We enjoyed our second floor corner unit with a large living room, dining area, and fully equipped kitchen. Our bathroom window let in lovely morning sunshine. We could relax on our balcony or by one of two pools surrounded by exotic plants and palm trees. On-site laundry facilities and soft drink machines were an added convenience. The Winterset is a short walk to shops, restaurants, and the beach. They offer hotel rooms, efficiencies, and one- and two-bedroom units. The gracious Poiriers make sure you're having a wonderful vacation. English and French spoken. A *Superior Small Lodging* member. $-$$

Embassy Suites, 1100 S.E. 17th Street Causeway, Fort Lauderdale, ☎ 954/527-2700, has 361 suites furnished with tropical prints, each with refrigerator, microwave, wetbar and coffee maker. Located a half-mile from Port Everglades, this is a convenient hotel if you're going cruising. The outdoor pool and whirlpool are surrounded by waterfalls and tropical gardens. $$

Estoril Apartments/Motel, 2667 NE 32nd Street, Fort Lauderdale, ☎ 954/563-3840, has 11 units, with refrigerators and microwaves. Choose from an efficiency or one- or two-bedroom unit. Close to the beach, restaurants, shopping, golf and tennis, there's a pool with a BBQ grill. Children under 10 stay free, and owner/hosts Roger and Mary Ambrosio speak English, Spanish and Portuguese. $

Radisson Bahia Mar Beach Resort, 801 Seabreeze Boulevard, Fort Lauderdale, ☎ 954/764-2233, offers 300 guest rooms and suites with scenic views of the Atlantic Ocean or Intracoastal Waterway. Half of the rooms are non-smoking. This is a great location if you'll be boating, fishing or diving out of Bahia Mar Yachting Center. The hotel has a pool, private walkway to Fort Lauderdale Beach, windsurfing, and four lighted tennis courts. Dine at Bahia Mar Bar & Grill or Skipper's Pool Bar. $$-$$$

Hyatt Regency Pier 66, 2301 SE 17th Street Causeway, Fort Lauderdale, ☎ 954/525-6666, is a 388-room, 17-story hotel three miles from downtown Fort Lauderdale. Many rooms have private balconies and overlook either the Atlantic or the pool and garden. Enjoy the hotel's European Health and Beauty Spa.Three swimming pools, two lighted tennis courts, and six restaurants, including the delightful California Café. The revolving Pier Top Lounge has spectacular city and sea views. $$-$$$

Three Suns Motel, 3016 Windamar Street, Fort Lauderdale, ☎ 954/563-7926, has 20 units with refrigerators and microwaves. Some are non-smoking, and you can choose a hotel room, efficiency, suite, one- or two-bedroom unit. Close to boating, shopping, tennis, golf, restaurants and Fort Lauderdale Beach. Children under 17 stay free. Owner/hosts Kerry, Marc, and Peter Biron speak English and French. $-$$

Ft. Lauderdale

Camping

Public Campgrounds in Broward County and Greater Fort Lauderdale:

- **Easterlin Campground,** 1000 NW 38th Street, Oakland Park, ☎ 954/938-0610, has 55 shaded campsites with electricity, picnic tables and grills. Showers, restrooms, ice and soda machine.

- **Quiet Waters Campground,** 6601 N. Powerline Road, Pompano Beach, ☎ 954/360-1315, has 16 campsites with a "rent-a-camp" package: a tent that sleeps up to six people, sleeping pads, picnic tables, grills, coolers, and canoe rentals. Sites are also available for campers with their own tents. Fishing, swimming, and boating on the lake.

■ **T.Y. (Topeekeegee Yugnee) Whispering Pines Campground,** 3300 N. Park Road, Hollywood, ☎ 954/985-1980, has 60 sites for RVs and tents. The 48 RV sites are equipped with electrical outlets, water, grills, picnic tables, and patios. Restrooms have showers and laundry. The Trading Post sells camping supplies, food and film. This oak-shaded park features a swimming lagoon, fishing, boat, and bike rentals, sports equipment rentals and free Friday night movies.

■ **C.B. Smith Lakeside Campground,** 900 Flamingo Road, Pembroke Pines, ☎ 954/437-2650, features 60 RV sites adjacent to a lake, with electricity, water, and sewer hookups. There are also lakeside tent camping sites. Restrooms have showers and a laundry. Fishing, boating, and swimming in the lake. The Park nearby has a swimming beach, water slide, tube ride, boat rentals, fishing, tennis/racquetball, bike rentals, snack bar and miniature golf.

■ **Markham Park Campground,** 16001 W. State Road 84, Sunrise, ☎ 954/389-2000, has 86 campsites, with or without sewer hookup. Restrooms, showers, pool, target range, a paved model airplane field and fishing. A new 56-acre recreational island complex features swimming, tennis, racquetball, boat and bike rentals, picnicking and snack bar.

Camping in the Everglades:

■ **Everglades Holiday Park,** 21940 Griffin Road, Fort Lauderdale, ☎ 954/434-8111 has 100 RV sites which include gas, laundry, showers, restrooms, convenience store, ice and groceries. Full/partial hookups and tent camping sites also available. Campfires allowed in the tent section only. Adjacent to airboat tours, fishing, and boat rentals.

Members of the Florida Association of RV Parks & Campgrounds:

- **Buglewood RV Resort,** 2121 NW 29th Court, Fort Lauderdale, ☎ 800/487-7395, is open year-round. There's a pool, rec hall, billiards, laundry and exercise facilities, 50 amp electric hookups, shuffleboard, and horseshoes. Six miles to beaches.

- **Candlelight Park,** 5731 South SR7, Fort Lauderdale, ☎ 954/791-5023, is a family owned RV park. Bathhouse, clubroom, lake with fishing; near shopping and the beach.

- **Kozy Kampers RV Park,** 3631 W. Commercial Blvd., Fort Lauderdale, ☎ 954/731-8570, has a beach, snack bar, laundry, and fishing. Pets on leashes welcome.

- **Seminole Park,** 3301 North SR7, Hollywood, ☎ 954/987-6961, has 102 full hookups, hot showers, laundry, pay phones, 30 and 50 amp electric hookups, rec hall, shuffleboard, swimming. Adults only November-April.

- **Twin Lakes Travel Park,** 3055 Burris Road, Fort Lauderdale, ☎ 800/327-8182, features six bathhouses, laundry facilities, clubhouse, shuffleboard, bingo, weekly dances, 30 amp electricity, snack bar, and swimming.

- **Yacht Haven Park & Marina,** 2323 SR84, Fort Lauderdale, ☎ 800/581-2322, has 250 sites with 30/50 amp, rec halls, pool with whirlpool, electrical and water hookups, shuffleboard, fishing, boat ramps, laundry facilities, and 24-hour security.

■ Where to Eat

Chinese

 ☆ **Christina Wan's Mandarin House Restaurant,** 2029 Hollywood Blvd., Hollywood, ☎ 954/923-1688, is a friendly family owned restaurant tucked among Hollywood's boutiques. Beautiful floral prints, upholstered booths, white tablecloths, and a serene aquarium create a pleasant atmosphere. Chef's specialties include ginger duck, General Chang's chicken, and stewed prawns. From Hunan beef to Kung Pao chicken, this restaurant will fulfill those Chinese food cravings. They also have an extensive vegetarian menu. $$

Seafood

☆ Dining pierside from **15th Street Fisheries,** 1900 SE 15th Street, Fort Lauderdale, ☎ 954/763-2777, you look out on million-dollar yachts, palm trees, and Ft. Lauderdale's sparkling waterways. Grilled mahi-mahi sandwiches, conch salad, lobster caesar salad, seafood pot pie, crabmeat-stuffed artichoke; all are delicious. Friday is "all you can eat" – buckets of spicy peel-&-eat shrimp and fried clams. The atmosphere is funky nautical. $$

Mediterranean

☆ **H20 Mediterranean Bar and Grill,** 101 South Atlantic Blvd. Fort Lauderdale, ☎ 954/760-7500, specializes in fresh fish. A blue neon sign says "From sea to shining sea," a fish video runs on the overhead TV, and fish mobiles swim over the crowded bar. Chef Angelo Elia creates original dishes with a healthy twist: his antipasto features sun-dried tomatoes, white beans, shrimp, mushrooms, salmon, and eggplant instead of traditional heavy meats and vegetables wallowing in olive oil; his risotto with osso bucco in a light tomato sauce has fresh rosemary. Pink swordfish is fabulous, served with artichoke hearts, asparagus, and red peppers in a sauce made with lemon, white wine, olive oil, and herbs. Don't skip the rich homemade apple tart with cinnamon ice cream. Dine indoors or out along Ft. Lauderdale's famous beach. Great people watching. $$

☆ **California Café Bar & Grill,** Hyatt Pier 66 Hotel, 17th Street Causeway, Fort Lauderdale, ☎ 954/728-3500, boasts one of the best views in the city: floor-to-ceiling windows frame the Intracoastal Waterway as yachts cruise by. A spacious, beautiful restaurant with raspberry and lavender accented walls, California Café serves dishes that taste as good as they look. Start with Dungeness crab cakes, served with spicy black bean salsa and cilantro aioli. Then try salmon Napoleon: tender fish fillets wrapped around a giant grilled portobello mushroom, with mashed potatoes on the side. One of Chef Paul Riso's signature entrées is his macadamia nut-crusted snapper with vodka grapefruit sauce. Best dessert: key lime natilla custard layered with fresh berries and chocolate crisps. $$-$$$

French/Continental

☆ Spend a romantic evening at **Left Bank,** 214 SE 6th Street, Fort Lauderdale, ☎ 954/462-5376, under the spell of owner/chef Jean-Pierre Brehier. Host of the PBS series *Sunshine Cuisine* and regular guest chef on the *Today* show, Chef Brehier is known for his creative light French cuisine. Baby Maine mussels in spinach are prepared with skim milk; pan-seared sea scallops with mango beurre blanc only taste rich. Sesame-crusted rare tuna is enlivened with a tangerine-orange-soy sauce. Many of his signature dishes are low calorie, prepared without butter or cream, so you can indulge in a five-star meal without guilt. Tiramisu brandy sponge cake surrounded by swirls of espresso crème anglaise is divine. $$-$$$

Other Restaurants

Burt and Jack's, Berth 23, Port Everglades, Fort Lauderdale, ☎ 954/522-5225, is a romantic Spanish villa with a piano lounge, overlooking cruise ships docked at Port Everglades. Fresh fish, prime steak specialties. Dinner nightly. Jackets and reservations required. $$

Chart House, 301 SW 3rd Avenue, Fort Lauderdale, ☎ 954/523-0177, overlooks the Performing Arts Center in the city's River Walk district. Steak, seafood, dinner only. $$

Ernie's Bar-B-Que, 1843 S. Federal Highway, Fort Lauderdale, ☎ 954/523-8636, offers casual dining with specialties like conch chowder and barbecue on Bimini bread. Lunch and dinner. $

Evangeline's, 211 S. Atlantic Blvd., Fort Lauderdale, ☎ 954/522-7001, is an oceanfront café with a New Orleans atmosphere. Creole and cajun cuisine, caviar and champagne. Lunch and dinner daily. $$

Rustic Inn Crabhouse, 4331 Ravenswood Road, Fort Lauderdale, ☎ 954/584-1637, is casual and rustic, overlooking the water. Steamed garlic blue crabs are served on newspaper-covered tables as a "do it yourself" feast. Lunch and dinner daily. $

Japanese Village, 716 E. Las Olas Blvd., Fort Lauderdale, ☎ 954/763-8163, features fresh sushi, sashimi and tempura

Ft. Lauderdale

dishes. Lunch and dinner, Monday-Friday; dinner only Saturday-Sunday. $$

Saigon Oriental, 2031 Hollywood Blvd., Hollywood, ☎ 954/923-9256, is a tiny restaurant in a storefront setting, featuring authentic Vietnamese cuisine, such as spicy chicken with lemon grass and broiled shrimp. Lunch and dinner, Monday-Friday; dinner only Saturday-Sunday. $

Zinkler's Bavarian Village, 1401 N. Federal Highway, Hollywood, ☎ 954/922-7321, serves German cuisine, wines and beers. Dinner Monday-Sunday; open at noon on Sunday. $$

Tourism Information

Greater Fort Lauderdale Convention & Visitors Bureau, 1850 Eller Drive, Suite 303, Fort Lauderdale, FL 33316. ☎ 954/765-4466, 800/22SUNNY.

Greater Fort Lauderdale Chamber of Commerce, 512 NE 3rd Avenue, Fort Lauderdale, FL 33301. ☎ 954/462-6000. Web site: www.ftlchamber.com.

🌴 🌴 🌴

Pompano Beach to Deerfield Beach

Driving north from Fort Lauderdale, things calm down. Quiet neighborhoods, oceanfront mansions, and condos are within walking distance of spectacular beaches. County parks offer adventurous recreation, as do fishing charters and scuba diving submerged wrecks. Pompano Beach even hosts a yearly Fishing Rodeo. Nearby towns include Deerfield Beach, Hillsboro Beach, and Coconut Creek.

■ Adventures

On Foot

Hiking

If you enjoy beachwalking, **Hillsboro Beach** is one of Florida's most beautiful beaches. Start at the 2nd Street Fishing Pier at Ocean Boulevard and walk south. The sand is clean and soft, the water warm and crystal clear. Large rocks form peaceful inlets where toddlers build sandcastles. This is a family beach, attracting everyone from teens to doting grandparents. Hillsboro Beach was given a safe city award, so you can feel comfortable here walking the beach at night.

Just west is **Deerfield Island Park,** 1720 Deerfield Island Park, ☎ 954/360-1320, an official Designated Urban Wilderness Area. The park has an 8½-acre mangrove swamp where gopher tortoises, grey foxes, raccoons and armadillos live. The park is on an island surrounded by the Royal Palm Waterway, Hillsboro Canal and the Intracoastal Waterway. On the island you can hike two nature trails: *Coquina Trail* is a half-mile trail through a coastal hardwood hammock, with an observation platform overlooking the Intracoastal Waterway; *Mangrove Trail* runs three-quarters of a mile and includes a 1,600-foot boardwalk through a mangrove wetland. Both trails have free self-guided maps at the park office. The island is accessible only by free park boat, which departs and returns from the Sullivan Park floating boat dock along Riverview Road and Hillsboro Boulevard. Call for the boat schedule.

Fern Forest Nature Center, 201 Lyons Road South, Pompano Beach, ☎ 954/970-0150 is a Designated Urban Wilderness Area with 254 acres of wildlife refuge and hiking trails. Four we recommend are *Cypress Creek* Trail, a half-mile wheelchair-accessible boardwalk through a hardwood hammock; *Prairie Overlook Trail,* a one-mile ground level trail that loops through an open prairie; *Wetlands Wander,* an eighth-of-a-mile trail through a wetland plant community; and *Maple Walk,* a one-third mile primitive trail through a red maple swamp. You might want boots or waterproof shoes for Maple Walk. The park also has a sensory garden, sculptures, a butterfly bridge, and a 20-foot-tall observation platform.

Golf

- The **Carolina Club,** 3011 Rock Island Road, Margate, ☎ 954/753-4000. 18 holes.

- **Crystal Lake Country Club,** 3800 Crystal Lake Drive, Pompano Beach, ☎ 954/943-2902. 36 holes.

- **Deercreek Golf Club,** 2801 Country Club Boulevard, Deerfield Beach, ☎ 954/421-5550. 18 holes.

- **Tam O'Shanter Golf Club,** 1391 NW 45th Street, Pompano Beach, ☎ 954/942-1900. 18 holes.

Tennis

- **Deerfield Beach Tennis Center,** 222 N. Dixie Highway, Deerfield Beach, ☎ 954/480-4422. Lighted courts.

- **Constitution Park,** 2841 W. Hillsboro Blvd., Deerfield Beach, ☎ 954/480-4494.

- **Westside Park,** SW 3rd Avenue, Deerfield Beach, ☎ 954/480-4480. Lighted courts.

On Wheels

A nice area for **road biking** is along A1A paralleling Hillsboro Beach. You can tool around through the quiet neighborhoods or on the A1A sidewalk. Just south is a pleasant ride around the **Pompano Beach Golf Course,** at the corner of Copans Road and US1. **Island Skate,** on A1A, two blocks north of Hillsboro Road, ☎ 954/427-4647, rents bikes by the hour, half-day, overnight or by the week. (They also have in-line skates, surfboards, kayaks and scooters.)

West of Hillsboro Beach, ride in **Tradewinds Park,** 3600 W. Sample Road, Coconut Creek, ☎ 954/968-3880. There's a bike trail around the 18-hole golf course in the eastern section of the park, and you can rent a single or tandem bike in the park for a nominal fee.

On Water

Waterskiing

If waterskiing is your thing, visit **Quiet Waters Park,** 6601 N. Powerline Road, Pompano Beach, ☎ 954/360-1315. A unique overhead cable waterski system called "Ski-Rixen" tows you around the lake as though you were behind a boat. This is an ideal way to practice your waterski techniques before going out on the open water. Canoes, rowboats, or paddleboats may be rented for use in the park's northwest lake, where fishing is also permitted (license required if you are over 16). Other water activities include a swimming beach along the south lake, and a children's water playground.

Scuba Diving

A number of excellent **snorkel and scuba diving sites** are off Deerfield Beach within a mile from shore. Underwater reefs teem with schooling porgies, grunts, parrotfish, angelfish and squid. Strong swimmers can snorkel out to the reefs from hotel beaches, or sign up for scuba diving excursions with professional dive masters.

The artificial reef off the coast has a number of wrecks, including the *Mercedes,* the *Rebel,* and *Cumberland Barge,* which attract big jacks, grouper and barracuda. Don't forget your underwater camera and dive certification card.

Area dive shops:

- **Anchor Scuba, Inc.** 2635 N. Riverside Drive, Pompano Beach, ☎ 954/763-DIVE or 800/374-9792. They specialize in historic shipwreck expeditions, cave diving, and advanced underwater photography.

- **Dixie Divers,** 1645 SE 3rd Court, Deerfield, ☎ 954/420-0009, offers PADI Five-Star dive instruction and certification, as well as daily dive trips.

- **Lighthouse Dive Center,** 2507 N. Ocean Blvd., Pompano Beach, ☎ 954/782-1100, offers dive and snorkel trips/vacation packages.

- **Scuba Network,** 199 North Federal Highway, Deerfield Beach, ☎ 800/949-REEF, offers scuba lessons and daily dives from their 43-foot dive boat, the *Get Down*. They also offer "nonfeeding" shark dives and dive packages to Grand Cayman, Bahamas, Bonaire, and Cozumel.

Fishing

Dozens of boat charters are available in the area. **Helen's Drift Fishing** at Sands Harbor Marina, 101 N. Riverside Drive, Pompano, ☎ 954/941-3209, specializes in family fishing trips. They supply rods, poles, bait, and will clean your catch. Trips go out daily at 8 am, 1 pm and 7 pm.

Sport Fishing, 1755 SE 3rd Court, Deerfield Beach, ☎ 954/360-9343, will help you catch sailfish and marlin on their half-day or full-day trips. They also have trips to the Bahamas if you want to go that far.

Fish 24 hours a day, seven days a week, at **Deerfield Beach Pier,** NE 2nd and Ocean Way, behind the Howard Johnson Hotel. Live bait is available, views of the ocean and beach are spectacular, and it only costs $3 to fish. (Walk the pier for $1.)

If you're in Pompano Beach in May, join the **Pompano Beach Fishing Rodeo,** Southeast Florida's largest saltwater sportfishing tournament. Touted as a "family fun fishing event," the Rodeo awards prizes to family fishing teams, women anglers, junior anglers, and even "small fry" fisherfolk. In recent years 722 registered anglers fished from 220 boats, competing for more than $60,000 in cash and $35,000 in merchandise. Festivities begin Thursday evening with a kickoff party at the Sands Harbor Hotel and Marina, 125 N. Riverside Drive, Pompano Beach, ☎ 954/942-9100. On Friday and Saturday morning, million-dollar yachts parade in Hillsboro Inlet past the historic lighthouse, ready to compete in the Fishing Rodeo. In the afternoons, fish are weighed on two barges moored along the Sands' dock. Some 1,000 lbs. of fish are often reeled in, most of which is donated to area shelters, soup kitchens, and residential homes for the handicapped. On Sunday, awards are presented to winners, along with trophies, checks and prizes. Rodeo weekend is open to the public free of charge.

On Horseback

Enjoy an afternoon of trail rides or English riding lessons at **Tradewinds Stables,** Tradewinds Park, 3600 W. Sample Road, Coconut Creek, ☎ 954/968-3880. The staff gives one-hour guided trail rides through three miles of woods on Saturdays, Sundays and holidays. Rides begin at 9:30 am, 11 am, 2 pm and 3:30 pm. You must make a paid reservation in person the morning of the ride, beginning at 8:30 am. Phone reservations are not accepted.

English Riding lessons are given at Tradewinds Stables Monday through Thursday in the late afternoon. Lessons include one hour of riding and 30 minutes of stable management. Riders must be at least nine years of age or 52" tall to ride. Wear long pants, hard-soled shoes and a riding helmet.

Kids can ride around the Pony Ring on Saturdays, Sundays and holidays from 11 am-3:30 pm. They must be under 52" tall to ride the ponies, and be led by an adult.

Other Adventures

Pompano Harness Track, 1800 SW Third Street, Pompano Beach, ☎ 954/972-2000, is the only harness track in Florida. Pacers and sulky drivers compete November-April. Watch the action from the dining room overlooking the track. Admission.

▪ Sightseeing

In the western area of Tradewinds Park, 3600 W. Sample Road, Coconut Creek, ☎ 954/977-4400, is the unique **Butterfly World.** Stroll among three acres of tropical gardens, where thousands of brilliantly colored butterflies thrive. Waterfalls, fish, birds, orchids, and rose gardens create a delightful habitat. There's also a butterfly farm, a museum/insectarium, gift shop, and plant shop. Enjoy lunch at the outdoor café. Admission.

Ft. Lauderdale

■ Festivals & Events

 Contact the **Deerfield Beach Chamber of Commerce,** ☎ 954/427-1050, or the **Pompano Beach Chamber of Commerce,** ☎ 954/941-2940, for dates and locations of these festivals:

January

Deerfield Beach Art Show

March

Founders Day Parade

April

Pompano Seafood Festival

May

Pompano Beach Fishing Rodeo

June

Mango Festival

October

Broward Country Pioneer Days

November

Deerfest

December

Holiday Boat Parades

■ Where to Stay

Note: Establishments designated as "Superior Small Lodging" are members of a county program designed to promote clean, safe, well-run lodgings. Member lodgings are reviewed and inspected annually, have fewer than 50 rooms and are distinguished by their friendly ambiance and personal service.

☆ **Seabonay Beach Resort,** 1159 Hillsboro Mile, A1A, Hillsboro Beach, ☎ 800/777-1961, is one of our favorite hotels in Southeast Florida. Located on beautiful Hillsboro Beach, the hotel is across the street from the Intracoastal Waterway. Our one-bedroom suite was decorated in restful pastels, with floor-to-ceiling windows and a balcony overlooking the ocean and beach. Our kitchen was stocked with dishes, pans, utensils, microwave, and coffeemaker, so we could dine "at home" after a long day out. The hotel has a heated outdoor swimming pool and backyard lounge chairs with ocean views. Other amenities: children's activity programs and baby sitting, laundry, covered garage parking, and a private boat dock. Snorkel to the reef off the hotel beach, or walk north to the fishing pier. From December through May the fun-loving staff hosts a free barbecue with live music every Thursday afternoon. Restaurants, golf, tennis, boating, diving, and deep-sea fishing are close by. $$

Berkshire Beach Club of Deerfield, 500 North A1A, Deerfield Beach, ☎ 954/428-1000, has 13 units on the Atlantic Ocean. One- and two-bedroom units are available, and children under 13 stay free. A *Superior Small Lodging.* $-$$

Carriage House Resort Motel, 250 South Ocean Blvd., Deerfield Beach, ☎ 800/303-6009, has 30 units close to beach and boardwalk. Choose from a hotel room, efficiency, suite, or one-bedroom unit. A garden patio surrounds the heated pool. Children under seven stay free; English, French and German spoken. A *Superior Small Lodging.* $

Ocean Terrace Suites, 2080 East Hillsboro Blvd., Deerfield Beach, ☎ 954/427-8400, has 31 units, one block from restaurants, shopping and the Fishing Pier. Choose from efficiency, one- , two- , or three-bedroom units, some with private oceanfront balconies. English and Spanish spoken. A *Superior Small Lodging.* $$$

Ft. Lauderdale

Deerfield Beach Hilton, 100 Fairway Drive, Deerfield Beach, ☎ 800/624-3606, features 220 oversized guestrooms with four suites. Grand Ballroom, restaurants, meeting rooms. $$

Jasmin Villa Motel, 801 South Ocean Blvd., Pompano Beach, ☎ 800/941-9939, has 29 units, close to the ocean. Large pool with a barbecue. Choose from a hotel room, efficiency, or one-bedroom unit; children under five stay free. English, Czech-Slovak, German, Hungarian, Polish, and Yugoslav spoken. A *Superior Small Lodging.* $

Ocean Garden Resort, 1508 North Ocean Blvd., Pompano Beach, ☎ 800/315-2542, offers 32 units overlooking the ocean. Choose from hotel room, efficiency or suite; children under 12 stay free. English and French spoken. A *Superior Small Lodging.* $$

Seacastle Resort Inn, 730 North Ocean Blvd., Pompano Beach, ☎ 800/331-4666, has 40 units right on the ocean. Choose from a hotel room or efficiency; children under 12 stay free. Free golf greens fees from April 15-December 15. English, Spanish and French spoken. A *Superior Small Lodging.* $

■ Where to Eat

 ☆ If fresh seafood in a funky nautical setting appeals to you, dine at **The Whale's Rib,** 2031 NE 2nd Street, Deerfield, ☎ 954/421-8880. From fresh lobster salad, to blackened dolphin sandwiches, to baked stuffed shrimp, you won't be disappointed. Homemade soups are wonderful, especially the conch chowder. The raw bar serves fresh oysters, clams, steamed shrimp, and stone crab. Takeout is convenient for a picnic on the beach, just a block away. Very crowded on weekends. $

Brooks, 500 S. Federal Highway, Deerfield Beach, ☎ 954/427-9302, serves four-course dinners in a formal Queen Anne setting. Seafood, dessert soufflés, wines by the glass. Open for dinner from mid-November until mid-May. Closed Mondays in the summer. $$

Cap's Place, Cap's Dock, 2765 NE 28th Court, Lighthouse Point, ☎ 954/941-0418, is an island beach shanty, frequented by FDR and Churchill during World War II. Cap's boat takes diners from the mainland to enjoy fresh broiled seafood and hearts of palm salad. Dinner nightly, open Sunday. $$

Cielito Lindo, 4480 N. Federal Highway, Pompano Beach, ☎ 954/941-8226, serves authentic Mexican cuisine in a "south of the border" setting. Frozen margaritas are a specialty. Lunch and dinner Monday-Saturday; early bird dinner on Sunday. $

Fisherman's Wharf, 222 Pompano Beach Blvd., Pompano Beach, ☎ 954/941-5522 serves seafood on a fishing pier. Dine indoors or out. Live entertainment. Lunch and dinner daily. $

Pelican Pub, 2635 N. Riverside Drive, Pompano Beach, ☎ 954/785-8550, has docking space if you come by boat. An old-fashioned Florida seafood house serving fresh fish delivered by boat. Lunch and dinner daily. $

Viva La Pasta, 1386 S. Federal Highway, Pompano Beach, ☎ 954/946-0963, serves homemade pasta with over 50 different sauces. Dinner Tuesday-Saturday. $

Tourism Information

For further information, contact the **Greater Deerfield Chamber of Commerce,** 1601 East Hillsboro Boulevard, Deerfield Beach, FL 33441-4389. ☎ 954/427-1050.

🌴 🌴 🌴

Ft. Lauderdale

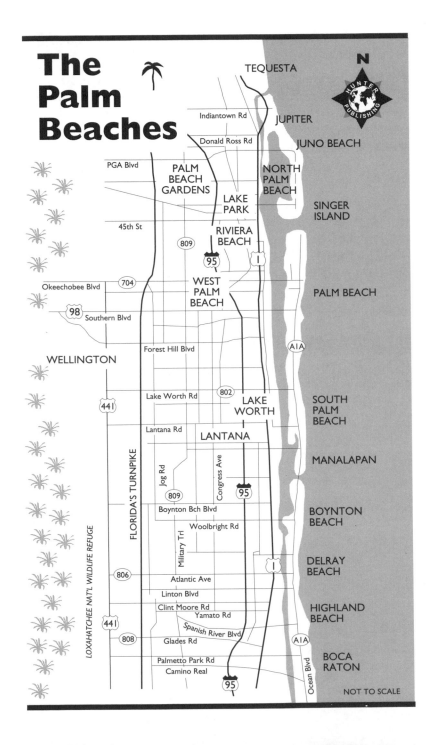

The Palm Beaches

Most tourists are lured to luxury resorts in Boca Raton and Palm Beach, manicured golf courses, and chic Worth Avenue boutiques. But our favorite adventures in this area had nothing to do with resorts or shopping. We photographed wild lions, canoed Florida's only *Wild and Scenic River,* and enjoyed an informative city bike tour. We also went deep-sea fishing, dinner cruising, and turtle watching, and contemplated polo lessons at the famous Palm Beach Polo and Country Club. We never did get to shop legendary Worth Avenue, but then again, our closets are full, aren't yours?

■ Getting Here

Airlines serving **Palm Beach International Airport** include Air Canada, American Airlines/American Eagle, American Trans Air, Bahamasair, Canadian Airlines International, Carnival, Comair, Continental, Delta, Eastwind, Gulfstream International, Laker Airways, Midway, Northwest, Spirit, Trans World, United, USAir.

The airport is located on Turnage Boulevard, adjacent to I-95, 2½ miles west of downtown West Palm Beach and 3½ miles west of Palm Beach. ☎ 561/471-7400. There's a special group of volunteers called "Airport Ambassadors" who welcome travelers at the airport, so feel free to ask them about sightseeing or transportation.

Palm Beach County has four smaller **general aviation airports:** Palm Beach County Park Airport Lantana, 2633 Lantana Road, Lantana, ☎ 561/965-6400; Palm Beach County Glades Airport, 3800 State Road 715, Pahokee, ☎ 561/924-5696; Boca Raton Airport, 3700 Airport Road, Boca Raton, ☎ 561/368-1110; and North County Airport, State Road 710, Palm Beach Gardens, ☎ 561/626-9799.

■ Getting Around

We recommend that you rent a car to travel to the various points of interest in Palm Beach County and the Treasure Coast area.

Most national car rental agencies have facilities near the airport, and offer free transportation to and from their rental offices.

Car Rentals in Palm Beach County

Alamo	☎ 800-327-9633
Avis	☎ 800-331-1212
Budget	☎ 800-527-0700
Dollar	☎ 800-421-6868
Hertz	☎ 800-654-3131
National	☎ 800-227-7368
Thrifty	☎ 800-367-2277
Value	☎ 800-327-2501

Other transportation options include **Yellow Cab Taxi Service,** ☎ 561/689-2222; **Palm Tran Bus Service,** ☎ 561/233-1111 in the northern part of Palm Beach county, ☎ 561/930-1111 in south county; **Greyhound Trailways,** ☎ 800/231-2222; **Carey Limousine Florida, Inc.** ☎ 561/471-5466; and **AMTRAK,** ☎ 800-USA-RAIL.

Boca Raton

Despite miles of sprawling residential developments and shopping malls, Boca Raton has managed to preserve city parks for hiking, fishing, canoeing, and snorkeling. Boca's two miles of beautiful beach makes it easy to enjoy sun bathing, fishing, sailing, and scuba diving. If you feel like splurging, check into luxurious, historic Boca Raton Resort and Club, where the pursuit of pleasure is a major adventure.

🌴 Boca Raton, Delray Beach, Boynton Beach

1. Loxahatchee Nat'l Wildlife Refuge
2. Morikami Museum & Japanese Gardens
3. Royal Palm Polo Sports Club
4. Old School Square
5. Nathan D Rosen Museum Gallery
6. Boca Raton Museum of Art
7. Children's Museum
8. Boca Raton Historical Society
9. Int'l Museum of Cartoon Art
10. Spanish River Park
11. Red Reef Park / Gumbo Limbo Environmental Center
12. Boca Raton Resort & Club

▪ Adventures

On Foot

At **Gumbo Limbo Environmental Center,** Red Reef Park, 1801 North Ocean Boulevard, Boca Raton, ☎ 561/338-1473, loggerhead turtles and baby barracudas swim in a leisurely circle. This unusual nature center features outdoor aquariums, where groupers, snappers, moray eels and stingrays live in large saltwater tanks. At the Touch Tank, kids can pick up hermit crabs and starfish for a closer look.

Botanical adventure lovers will enjoy walking among the center's red, black and white mangroves, bald cypress, silver buttonwood, and sea grape.

In addition to the aquariums and wetlands area, the Visitor Center has unusual exhibits: a staff member will wrap a six-foot Florida kingsnake around your shoulders for a photo. When was the last time you hugged a snake?

The Center conducts turtle walks to natural nesting sites from mid-May through mid-July, Monday through Thursday evenings. Reservations are taken beginning May 1, and tickets cost $3.

At the **Dagger Wing Nature Center,** 11200 Park Access Road, Boca Raton, ☎ 561/488-9953, stroll among endangered wood storks, threatened least terns, and Ruddy Dagger Wing butterflies. The Nature Center has a wetland and hardwood hammock, as well as two 50-acre cypress stands and a marsh.

Photograph wildlife along the 2,000-foot boardwalk, visit butterfly gardens and bat houses. The center has classes in gardening, nature photography, sketching, birding, and building a bat or bird house.

Beachwalking: Boca Area Beaches

- **Red Reef Park,** State Road A1A, Boca Raton, has a lifeguarded beach, children's play area, picnic areas and barbecues. No alcohol permitted.

- **South Beach Park,** State Road A1A at Northeast Fourth Street, Boca Raton, has a lifeguarded beach. No alcohol permitted.

- **South Inlet Park,** State Road A1A south of Boca Inlet, Boca Raton, has 850 feet of lifeguarded beach.

- **Spanish River Park,** North Ocean Boulevard, two miles north of Palmetto Park Road, Boca Raton, has 95 acres of parkland and an 1,850-foot beach. There are five covered shelters, picnic tables, grills, volleyball, restrooms and a two-level, 40-foot-tall observation tower.

- **Atlantic Dunes Park,** State Road A1A, Delray Beach, has a lifeguarded beach. No alcohol permitted.

- **Delray Beach Public Beach,** Ocean Boulevard, Delray Beach, has 7,000 feet of lifeguarded beach. No alcohol permitted.

- **Boynton Beach Municipal Oceanfront Park,** A1A north of East Ocean Avenue, Boynton Beach, has a lifeguarded beach, barbecue and picnic areas, concessions and restrooms.

Golf

The Boca Raton Chamber of Commerce has an extensive list of area golf courses. The American Lung Association "Lung Card" gives discounted greens fees throughout Florida from May-October. Purchase the card by calling ☎ 561/395-4433.

Public Courses

- **Boca Raton Municipal Golf Course,** 8111 Golf Course Road, Boca Raton, ☎ 561/483-6100. 18 holes, par 72; nine-hole par 30 executive course; driving range, putting green. Clubhouse, golf shop, food service, club storage, locker rooms. Golf lessons available.

- **Red Reef Executive Golf Course,** 1111 N. Ocean Boulevard, Boca Raton, ☎ 561/391-5014. Nine-hole par 30 course on the ocean.

- **Southwinds County Golf Course,** 19557 Lyons Road, Boca Raton, ☎ 561/483-1305. 18 holes, par 72.

Tennis

Public Tennis Courts

- **Boca Tierra Park,** 2601 NW 43rd Street, Boca Raton. Two tennis courts.

- **Hidden Lake Park,** NW 4th Avenue, Boca Raton. Two tennis courts.

- **Meadows Park,** 1300 NW Eighth Street, Boca Raton. Two lighted tennis courts. ☎ 561/393-7851.

The Palm Beaches

- **Memorial Park,** 150 Crawford Blvd., Boca Raton. Nine lighted tennis courts. ☎ 561/393-7806.

- **Sand Pine Park,** 300 Newcastle Street, Boca Raton. Two lighted tennis courts.

- **Spanish River Community High School,** NW 51st Street, Boca Raton. Eight lighted tennis courts.

- **University Woodlands Park,** 2501 St. Andrews Blvd., Boca Raton. Two lighted tennis courts.

- **Veterans Park,** Palmetto Road, Boca Raton. Two tennis courts.

On Water

Fishing

 A popular spot for fishing in the Intracoastal Waterway is **Spanish River Park,** 3001 State Road A1A, ☎ 561/393-7810, an award-winning municipal park. Three tunnels under A1A link a natural hammock and wooded preserve with the wide clean beach. There are 10 covered shelters, picnic tables, grills and a 40-foot observation tower with park, ocean, and city views. No fishing license is required here.

If you enjoy dawn or dusk surf fishing, try **Red Reef Park,** 1400 N. State Road A1A, ☎ 561/393-7974. A lighted boardwalk stretches through palmettos, Australian pine, and sea grapes to the mile-long beach. Fishing in designated swimming areas is prohibited from 9-5 pm, so come before or after those times to fish.

Another good park for surf fishing is **South Inlet Park,** A1A, one block south of Camino Real and Boca Inlet, ☎ 561/930-4111. Fish off the beach or from the pier.

Bass fishing is excellent in the **Loxahatchee National Wildlife Refuge,** West End Lox Road, Boca Raton, ☎ 800/683-5873. This 146,000-acre refuge is the northernmost border of the Florida Everglades. Rent a fishing boat or canoe, or take a guided airboat tour.

Snorkeling

Red Reef Park, 1400 N. State Road A1A, ☎ 561/393-7974, has snorkeling right offshore. Reefs teem with parrotfish, blue tang, spray crabs, starlet coral, sea fans, plume worms, and sea urchins. Lifeguards are on duty from 9 am-5 pm. Bring your own snorkel, mask and fins.

Boca Raton has several dive shops offering scuba diving instruction, trips, and dive gear:

- **American Dive Center,** 1888 NW 2nd Avenue, ☎ 561/393-0621, is a PADI Five-Star Center with an indoor heated pool for private and small group instruction. They specialize in night, nitrox, and wreck diving.

- **Boca Seadventures,** 152 NW 20th Street, ☎ 561/391-1474, also offers PADI scuba instruction, as well as marine biology classes. They run local and international dive trips.

- **Dixie Divers,** 8214 Glades Road, Boca West, ☎ 561/477-5388, is a PADI Five-Star shop, offering instruction and dive charters.

- **Force E,** has two locations: 877 E. Palmetto Park Road, Boca Raton East, ☎ 561/368-0555, and 7266 Beracasa Way, Boca Raton West, ☎ 561/395-4407. It offers heated indoor pools for PADI Five-Star instruction.

Canoeing & Kayaking

A canoe trail meanders through mangroves and out along the Intracoastal Waterway at **James A. Rutherford Park,** 600 NE 24th Street, ☎ 561/393-7845. The trail is 5,500 feet long and takes about 40 minutes to navigate. Rent canoes and kayaks at the Park Canoe Livery daily or on weekends. Call first to see if they are open, as the trail is tide-dependent and may be too shallow for canoeing.

On Horseback

Polo

Every year, from December to April, the world's best polo players compete at **Royal Palm Polo Grounds, 6300** Old Clint Moore Road, ☎ 561/994-1876. Players compete from England, Spain, Australia, Mexico, Brazil and the US. March features the $100,000 International Gold Cup. Polo games are held weekdays and Sundays at 1 and 3 pm. Admission.

■ Sightseeing

Museums & Culture

Boca Raton Museum of Art, 801 W. Palmetto Park Road, ☎ 561/392-2500 has a permanent collection of works by Prendergast, Glackens, Rouault, Kuhn and Picasso. Recent acquisitions include works by Nancy Richter, Robert Rauschenberg, and Paul Jenkins. Tour with one of the museum's knowledgeable and enthusiastic docents, or attend their very popular lecture series, "Lunch and Learn." These art seminars feature art experts and lunch at noon; call for schedule. One Saturday each month the museum features tours and storytelling for kids ages five-12. Open Monday-Friday, 10 am-4pm; weekends noon-4 pm. Free.

Children's Museum at Singing Pines, 498 Crawford Boulevard, ☎ 561/368-6875, is a charming historic house where children learn and make new friends. Games, crafts, and dolls from around the world. Open Tuesday-Saturday, noon-4 pm. Admission.

International Museum of Cartoon Art, Mizner Park, 201 Plaza Real, ☎ 561/391-2200, houses over 75,000 cartoons, 100 animated videotapes, and dozens of interactive exhibits. The museum was created by veteran cartoonist and Boca Raton resident Mort Walker, who brought *Beetle Bailey* and *Felix the Cat* to life. Open Tuesday-Saturday, 11 am-5 pm; Sunday noon-5 pm. Admission.

Morikami Park, Museum, and Gardens, 4000 Morikami Park Road, Delray Beach (just north of Boca Raton), ☎ 561/495-0233, offers Japanese culture in a tranquil setting. The complex is on 150 acres of land donated by George Sukeji Morikami, a Japanese farmer who grew pineapples and vegetables here. A variety of exhibits and programs are presented, including the Hatsume Fair, Bonsai Festival and Garden Tour, art shows, films and nature walks. Delicious Japanese lunches are served outdoors at the Cornell Café. Morikami Museum is open daily except Monday from 10 am-5 pm. Closed major holidays. The park and garden are open daily, including holidays, from sunrise to sunset. Museum admission. Free on Sundays, 10 am-noon.

Nathan D. Rosen Museum Gallery, Adolph and Rose Levis JCC, Richard and Carole Siemens Jewish Campus, 9801 Donna Klein Boulevard, ☎ 561/852-3237. The gallery features artists from around the world, a Jewish book fair, and traveling exhibits of Judaica. Call for hours. Free.

Sports Immortals, 6830 North Federal Highway, ☎ 561/997-2575, features the sports memorabilia collection of Joel Platt. Baseballs, paintings, gloves, sports cards, racing helmets, uniforms, and a life-sized figure of Michael Jordan. Open Monday-Friday 10 am-6 pm, Saturday 10 am-5 pm. Admission.

An interesting way to learn about the city is on a tour with **The Boca Raton Historical Society,** 71 North Federal Highway, ☎ 561/395-6766. Society offices are inside Boca's Town Hall, designed by Addison Mizner and restored in 1983. With its striking gold dome and billowing flag, Town Hall is a fascinating place of local history exhibits, arts and crafts. The gift shop sells cards and books. Docents from the society conduct tours of Boca Raton on "Oliver the Trolley," Wednesdays at 9:30 am. Call the Society for reservations. On Tuesdays at 1:30 pm, docents guide visitors through the historic Boca Raton Resort & Club. Learn about architect Addison Mizner's passion for high society life, his real estate accomplishments and failures, and his eccentric style of wearing silk pajamas during the day. Lunch is available at the resort for an additional fee. Since the resort is open to registered guests only, this tour is the only way to visit this magnificent hotel unless you stay here. For tour reservations, call ☎ 561/392-3003. We highly recommend the Historical Society's

The Palm Beaches

knowledgeable and enthusiastic docent, Joan Bream. Ask for her when you make reservations. Fee.

If you're in Boca Raton in early February, tour the Old Floresta neighborhood as part of the **Historical Society's Tour of Homes.** The tour features visits to homes and gardens in Boca's Old Floresta Historic District, designed in 1925 by Addison Mizner. Call for the schedule.

Performing Arts

Contact these venues for their schedule of performances:

- **Boca Ballet Theatre Company,** Royal Palm Plaza, 145 SE Mizner Blvd., ☎ 561/395-6167.

- **Caldwell Theatre Company,** 7873 N. Federal Highway, ☎ 561/241-7432.

- **Florida Philharmonic Orchestra,** 980 N. Federal Highway, ☎ 561/392-7230.

- **Florida Symphonic Pops of Boca Raton,** 100 NE First Avenue, ☎ 561/391-6777.

- **Harid Conservatory,** 2285 Potomac Road, ☎ 561/997-2677.

- **Jan McArt's Royal Palm Dinner Theatre,** 303 SE Mizner Blvd., ☎ 561/392-3755.

- **Little Palm Family Theater,** 2400 NW Boca Raton Blvd., ☎ 561/394-0206.

- **Musicana Supper Club,** 2200 NW Boca Raton Blvd., ☎ 561/361-9704.

- **Temple Beth El Distinguished Artists Series,** 333 SW Fourth Avenue, ☎ 561/391-8900.

- **Zinman Hall,** Adolph and Rose Levis JCC, Richard and Carole Siemens Jewish Campus, 9801 Donna Klein Blvd., ☎ 561/852-3241.

▪ Festivals & Events

January

Fotofusion, Delray Beach, ☎ 561/276-9797.

February

Antique Show, Boca Raton Community Center, 150 NW Crawford Blvd., ☎ 561/393-7806.

Boca Fiesta, same as above.

Juried Art Show, Boca Raton Museum of Art, 801 W. Palmetto Park Road, ☎ 561/392-2500.

Palm Beach National Pro-Am, Delray Beach, ☎ 561/776-0006.

March

Meet Me Downtown Arts & Crafts Show, 1800 N. Dixie Highway, ☎ 561/395-4433.

July

July Fourth Fireworks, Florida Atlantic University, 777 Glades Road, ☎ 561/393-7806.

Wine and All That Jazz, Boca Raton Hotel, 501 E. Camino Real, ☎ 561/395-4433.

July Fourth Fest, ☎ 561/278-0424.

August

Boca Festival Days, various city locations, ☎ 561/395-4433.

Boca Expo, Florida Atlantic University Gym, 777 Glades Road, ☎ 561/395-4433.

October

Halloween Happenings, Mizner Park, ☎ 561/393-7806.

November

Boca Raton City Holiday Tree Lighting, ☎ 561/393-7806.

Harvest Fest, Delray Beach, ☎ 561/278-0424.

The Palm Beaches

December

Holiday Street Parade, 150 NW Crawford Blvd., ☎ 561/393-7806.

Holiday Boat Parade, Intracoastal Waterway, ☎ 561/395-4433.

▪ Where to Stay

☆ **Boca Raton Resort & Club,** 501 East Camino Real, PO Box 5025, Boca Raton, Florida 33431, ☎ 800/327-0101. In 1926, royalty and film stars arrived adorned in furs and diamonds when architect Addison Mizner opened the most expensive inn of its day. Then called The Cloister Inn, the 100-room hotel featured red-coated footmen, Mediterranean architecture, and the six-foot-two, 300-pound Mizner, clad in silk pajamas. The architect sported a monkey on one shoulder, a macaw on the other.

Today the 963-room Boca Raton Resort & Club is favored by moguls and millionaires who bring their families for relaxation and pampering. *Golf Magazine* rated the hotel and its two 18-hole championship courses "one of America's best golf resorts." Similar accolades were bestowed by *Tennis Magazine* for the 34 clay tennis courts. The resort's beautiful Intracoastal Waterway location and 25-slip private marina means you can hop aboard *The Salty Hooker* fishing yacht and be reeling in a sailfish 30 minutes later. Or catch the resort ferry over to the Boca Beach Club for sunbathing and swimming off their private half-mile beach on the Atlantic Ocean.

The resort's five swimming pools are a delight for early morning laps or all day sunning. If you're feeling energetic, sign up for scuba lessons, bike riding, catamaran cruising, volleyball, basketball, racquetball, garden tours, or cooking demos. $$$

Boca Raton DoubleTree Guest Suites, 701 NW 53rd Street, ☎ 800/222-TREE, features 182 suites, each with two TVs, refrigerator, microwave, coffeemaker and wet bar. Amenities include tennis, outdoor heated pool and whirlpool, guest passes to nearby golf courses, and the Scandinavian Fitness Center. $$

Boca Raton Marriott, 5150 Town Center Circle, ☎ 800/392-4600, is in the heart of Boca Center, with 30 boutiques and seven restaurants. The hotel has 256 rooms, continental dining and a piano lounge. Sunday Brunch. $$

Radisson Suite Hotel Boca Raton, 7972 Glades Road, ☎ 800/333-3333, offers 200 spacious suites with TVs, VCR, stereo cassette player, microwave, hair dryer, coffeemaker, and minibar. Complimentary breakfast. There is a heated outdoor pool/whirlpool, lakeside par course jogging trail, and fitness room. Boutiques and restaurants are in the nearby courtyard. $$

Radisson Bridge Resort of Boca Raton, 999 East Camino Real, ☎ 800/333-3333, has 121 rooms and suites with private balconies overlooking the Intracoastal or Atlantic Ocean. Waterfront pool, complimentary health club/saunas. Dining and dancing, live entertainment and Sunday Brunch at Carmen's Restaurant & Lounge at the Top. $$

Ramada, 2901 N. Federal Highway, ☎ 800/2-RAMADA, is a high-rise inn with 95 guest rooms, some non-smoking. Close to Mizner Park and Town Center Mall, the hotel has a restaurant, lounge, pool, jacuzzi, cable TV and laundry. $

Sheraton Boca Raton, 2000 NW 19th Street, ☎ 800/394-STAY is a five-story hotel with 192 rooms and suites four miles from Boca Raton beaches. Fitness center, tennis courts, outdoor pool and tiki bar. $$

Camping

Del-Raton Travel Trailer Park, 2998 S. Federal Highway, Delray Beach, ☎ 561/278-4633, is a year-round adults-only trailer park 1½ miles from the ocean, near malls, restaurants, golf, dog and horse racing. Pay phones, full hookups, 50 amp electricity, laundry and bike trails. No pets.

▪ Where to Eat

☆ **Wildwood Grill,** 551 E. Palmetto Park Road, ☎ 561/391-0000, is a casual restaurant serving wood-grilled chicken, beef and seafood. Specialties include hickory wood-grilled shrimp, seared tuna with sesame seeds, and roast prime rib of beef with gravy and mushrooms. Sides are

The Palm Beaches

unusual: red beans and basmati rice; creamed spinach with jack cheese. Executive Chef Patrick Fagen studied at the Cordon Bleu in France, and is passionate about serving original dishes complemented with his home-grown herbs. He and Chef de Cuisine Georg Kaindl succeed admirably. $-$$

Continental

Angelique, 1840 N. Dixie Highway, ☎ 561/368-7270, serves raviolis stuffed with gorgonzola, sweetbreads with truffles, escargot with herbs and pernod, and marinated pork medallions. $$

Citrus, 4400 N. Federal Highway, ☎ 561/394-0007, may be Florida's first restaurant to serve roasted antelope. Try the spinach bisque soup. Extensive wine list. $$$

French

Café Bouchon, 3011 A14 Yamato Road, ☎ 561/994-4877, is a charming French bistro serving seafood coquille, baby lamb cutlets, and fettucine Bouchon. Apple tatin is a delicious dessert. $$

Tex-Mex

Café Ole, 7860 Glades Road, ☎ 561/852-8063, serves smoked chicken enchilada, chile-dusted fried calamari, and decadent desserts. $

Italian

Culinaria, 7400 N. Federal Highway, ☎ 561/994-4300, is a modern bistro specializing in low-fat flavorful dishes. Try smoked duck and dried bing cherry pizza, or Tuscan bean stew with smoked chicken. $$

Mediterranean

Eilat Café, 7158 N. Bercasa Way, ☎ 561/368-6880, is strictly kosher (no meat or fowl), serving delicious seafood, pastas, and vegetarian dishes. The appetizer sampler of falafel, hummus, tahini, and Turkish salad is enough for a main course. Save room for baklava. $

Tourism Information

Greater Boca Raton Chamber of Commerce, 1800 North Dixie Highway, Boca Raton, 33432-1892, ☎ 561/395-4433.

🌴 🌴 🌴

Palm Beach to Jupiter

Major east-west streets in West Palm Beach include Palm Beach Lakes Boulevard, Banyan Boulevard and Okeechobee Boulevard. Major north-south streets are US1 (Dixie Highway), Olive Avenue, Tamarind, and Australian Avenue. I-95 also runs north-south and is a quick way to get from one end of the county to the other.

Major east-west streets in Palm Beach include Royal Poinciana (A1A), Royal Palm Way and Worth Avenue. Major north-south streets include Cocoanut Row, County Road and Ocean Boulevard.

▪ Adventures

On Foot

John D. MacArthur Beach State Park

If you only have time to visit one park in the Palm Beach area, plan to hike in **John D. MacArthur Beach State Park,** 10900 State Road 703 (A1A), North Palm Beach, ☎ 561/624-6950. This "island in time," is one of the finest examples of subtropical coastal habitat remaining in southeast Florida.

Volunteer naturalists lead 45-minute guided nature walks Wednesday-Sunday at 10 am. This half-mile tour through the park's major habitats – mangrove estuary, hardwood hammock, and beach – is a quick way to get an overview of what's here. You can plan longer hikes on your own.

The Palm Beaches

West Palm Beach & Palm Beach

1. Lion Country Safari
2. Palm Beach Polo & Country Club
3. Coral Sky Amphitheatre
4. Okeeheelee Nature Center
5. Mounts Botanical Garden
6. Palm Beach Kennel Club
7. Raymond F. Kravis Center
   for the Performing Arts
8. Clematis Street / Centennial Fountain
9. Norton Museum of Art
10. Ann Norton Sculpture Gardens
11. Henry Morrison Flagler Museum
12. Hibel Museum of Art
13. Royal Poinciana Playhouse
14. Dreher Park Zoo / South Florida
    Science Museum

We recommend these four walks within the park. Self-guided brochures on each trail are available at the Nature Center.

- *Estuary Low Tide Walk:* Located in a small cove off the northern section of Lake Worth, this area is a mixture of salt and fresh water. At low tide, stop at marker #5 on the left side of the bridge to observe fiddler crabs in the mud flats. At the west end of the boardwalk are oysters. Florida crown conchs and lightning whelks can often be seen on the sandbars. Blue herons, snowy egrets, white ibis, and roseate spoonbills wade the shallows looking for food. Near shore look for puffers, needlefish and mullet.

■ *Wrack Line Walk:* Along the two-mile beach is a line of brown seaweed (sargassum) called the wrack line. Numerous ocean animals are intertwined in the seaweed, such as finger sponge and Portuguese man-of-war. Look for moon and lettered olive seashells, as well as calico scallops and scotch bonnets. If you're lucky you may find the rare paper nautilus. Along the shoreline watch for brown pelicans, terns, sandpipers and gulls. From early May through late August, loggerhead, green, and leatherback turtles nest in this area.

■ *Native Plant Walk:* Stroll along the boardwalk over the cove and into the lovely tropical hardwood hammock. This trail wends through cabbage palm, strangler fig, gumbo limbo trees, mangroves, paradise trees, wild coffee, and moonflower vines.

■ *The Butterfly Garden Trail:* This trail is alive with giant swallowtails, zebra longwings, and gulf butterflies flitting among wild lime, Spanish needle, and firebush plants.

Other walks: In mid-June and mid-July a park ranger leads a walk at 8:30 pm to observe nesting loggerhead turtles. There's also a 30-minute slide presentation on endangered sea turtles. Advance registration is required by calling the William T. Kirby Nature Center at ☎ 561/624-6952. Plan to spend at least an hour at this delightful Center, browsing nature exhibits, displays, and informational videos.

Walks through other gardens and nature centers:

Free guided walks are given at **Mounts Botanical Garden,** 531 North Military Trail, West Palm Beach, ☎ 561/233-1749, on Saturdays at 11 am and Sundays at 2:30 pm. Stroll among tropical and subtropical plants, including fruits, citrus, rose gardens, hibiscus, herbs, and a rain forest. Open Monday-Saturday

The Palm Beaches

North Palm Beach, Palm Beach Gardens, Juno Beach & Jupiter

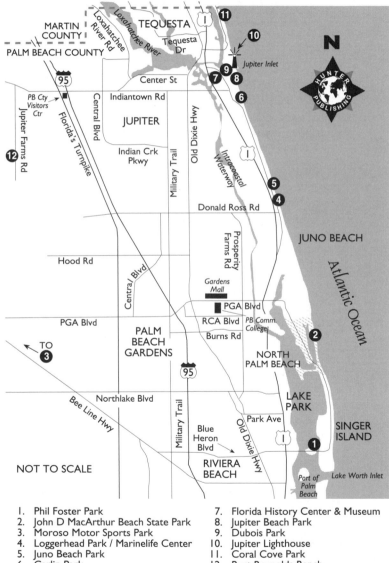

1. Phil Foster Park
2. John D MacArthur Beach State Park
3. Moroso Motor Sports Park
4. Loggerhead Park / Marinelife Center
5. Juno Beach Park
6. Carlin Park
7. Florida History Center & Museum
8. Jupiter Beach Park
9. Dubois Park
10. Jupiter Lighthouse
11. Coral Cove Park
12. Burt Reynolds Ranch

8 am-4:30 pm; Sunday 1 pm-5 pm. Free admission. Visit their Web site at www.mounts.org.

Walk five miles of trails at **Okeeheelee Nature Center,** Forest Hill Blvd., West Palm Beach, ☎ 561/233-1400. The center's 90 acres feature native pine flatwoods and wetlands. The visitor center has hands-on exhibits, and a gift shop. Admission free.

Beachwalking

The Palm Beach area has a number of beaches perfect for long leisurely walks. On any given day teenagers clad in black wetsuits are surfing six-foot waves; teams of bikers speed by in neon windshirts and pointed helmets; executives jog off last night's filet mignon. Here's a guide to recommended beaches:

Lake Worth

- **Lake Worth Municipal Beach,** Ocean Boulevard and Lake Avenue, has a 1,200-foot beach with a pool and lifeguards. There are also picnic areas, grills, a 1,300-foot fishing pier, golf course, shuffleboard, gift shop, and restaurant.

Palm Beach

- **Palm Beach Municipal Beach** on State Road A1A is an undeveloped beach, mostly bulkhead. There is limited parking; no alcohol is permitted.

- **Phipps Ocean Park** on Ocean Boulevard has a 1,300-foot beach with lifeguards. There are picnic and recreation areas, parking. No alcohol.

- **Richard G. Kreusler Park** on State Road A1A has a 450-foot beach with lifeguards.

Juno Beach

- **Juno Beach Park,** 14775 State Road A1A, has a 300-foot guarded beach, showers, and picnic shelters.

- **Loggerhead Park,** US1, has a 900-foot beach, nature trail, Marinelife Center, picnic area, bike path, four tennis courts and a kid's play area.

The Palm Beaches

Jupiter

- **Carlin Park,** on State Road A1A, has 3,000 feet of rocky beach, hiking trails, and a fitness trail. Lifeguards, restrooms, ample parking, restaurant, and covered picnic areas.

- **Coral Cove Park** on State Road A1A, Jupiter Island has a 600-foot beach, with rock formations and Intracoastal Waterway frontage. Lifeguards are on duty.

- **Dubois Park,** 19075 Dubois Road, has a beach located along Jupiter Inlet, with lifeguards on weekends and holidays. There are shaded picnic areas, a wading area for children, and restrooms.

- **Jupiter Beach Park,** Beach Drive, south of Jupiter Inlet, has a 1,700-foot lifeguarded beach with a fishing jetty.

A Major Climb

If you have lots of energy, climb to the top of **Jupiter Lighthouse,** on Captain Armour's Way, US1 and Beach Road in Jupiter, ☎ 561/747-8380. Designed

by General Mead (later commander of the Union forces at Gettysburg), the lighthouse was completed in 1860 and has been in continuous operation since. It is listed on the National Register of Historic Places. The Jupiter Lighthouse Museum houses local artifacts and memorabilia from the lighthouse and Old Fort Jupiter. The museum is open Sunday-Wednesday, 10 am-4 pm. Visitors must be at least 48 inches tall to climb the lighthouse. Guided tours are also available. Admission.

The historic Jupiter Lighthouse.

Turtle-Watching in Juno Beach

Crusty, a 20-year-old loggerhead turtle, arrived at the Marinelife Center with his flipper nearly severed by monofilament fishing line. Two baby loggerheads were dying in a park sink when a volunteer brought them here for treatment.

These turtles are now alive and well at the **Marinelife Center of Juno Beach,** 14200 US Highway One, Loggerhead Park, Juno Beach, ☎ 561/627-8280 (Web site www.marinelife.org/), a non-profit research/education organization. Thanks to the expertise of the center's volunteers, many of the turtles are rehabilitated and released back into the wild. Those that can't be released are provided with lifetime homes.

In June and July, the center offers weekly beach walks to watch green turtles and loggerheads lay their eggs. Call for reservations. From January through May, it sponsors a Winter Lecture Series, featuring talks like "A Photographic Look at the Coral Reefs of Palm Beach County" and "The Mysterious Lives of Sharks Revealed." Call for the current schedule.

The Center Gift Shop has a delightful selection of fish jewelry, marine notecards, turtle T-shirts, stuffed animals, and children's nature books. The center is open Tues-Sat, 10 am-4 pm, Sunday noon-3 pm. Free, but donations are appreciated.

Golf

With over 145 golf courses, Palm Beach boasts more than any other US county. What they all have in common are perfect fairways and lush greens.

These courses are par 72 unless otherwise noted, and are public or semi-private.

- **Boynton Beach Municipal Golf Course,** 8020 Jog Road, Boynton Beach, ☎ 561/969-2200. Par 71.

- **Cypress Creek Country Club,** 9400 Military Trail, Boynton Beach, ☎ 561/732-4202.

- **Westchester Golf and Country Club,** 12250 Westchester Club Drive, Boynton Beach, ☎ 561/734-6300. Par 3.

- **Lake Worth Municipal Golf Course,** One Seventh Avenue North, Lake Worth, ☎ 561/582-9713. Par 70.

The Palm Beaches

- **Lacuna Golf Club,** 6400 Grand Lacuna Blvd., Lake Worth, ☎ 561/433-3006. Par 71.

- **Lucerne Lakes Golf Course,** 144 Lucerne Lakes, Lake Worth, ☎ 561/967-6810.

- **North Palm Beach Country Club,** 940 US Highway One, North Palm Beach, ☎ 561/626-4344.

- **Palm Beach Gardens Golf Club,** 11401 Northlake Blvd., Palm Beach Gardens, ☎ 561/775-2556.

- **Palm Beach Par 3 Golf Course,** 2345 S. Ocean Blvd., Palm Beach, ☎ 561/582-4462. Par 54.

- **Royal Palm Beach Golf and Country Club,** 900 Royal Palm Beach Blvd., Royal Palm Beach, ☎ 561/793-0875.

- **Binks Forest Country Club,** 400 Binks Forest Drive, Wellington, ☎ 561/795-0595.

- **Emerald Dunes,** 4653 Okeechobee Blvd, West Palm Beach, ☎ 561/684-4653.

- **Golf and Sports Center of the Palm Beaches,** West Palm Beach, ☎ 561/683-4544. Par 54.

- **Lone Pine Golf Club,** 6251 N. Military Trail, West Palm Beach, ☎ 561/842-0480. Par 62.

- **Okeeheelee Golf Course,** 1200 Country Club Way, West Palm Beach, ☎ 561/964-4653.

- **Turtle Bay Golf Club,** Century Village, 2751 Golf Club Circle, West Palm Beach, ☎ 561/686-0948. Par 61.

- **West Palm Beach Country Club,** 7001 Parker Avenue, West Palm Beach, ☎ 561/582-2019.

- **Indian Creek Golf Club,** 1800 Central Blvd., Jupiter, ☎ 561/747-6262.

- **Jupiter Dunes Golf Club,** 401 N. Highway A1A, Jupiter, ☎ 561/746-6654. Par 54.

Tennis

- **Boynton Beach Tennis Center,** 3111 S. Congress Avenue, Boynton Beach, ☎ 561/734-8556.

- **Palm Beach Community College,** 4200 Congress Avenue, Lake Worth, ☎ 561/434-9004.

- **North Palm Beach Tennis Club,** 951 US Highway 1 , North Palm Beach, ☎ 561/626-6515.

- **Seaview Courts,** 348 Seaview Avenue, Palm Beach, ☎ 561/655-1188.

- **PGA National Health & Racquet Club,** 600 Avenue of Champions, Palm Beach Gardens, ☎ 561/627-4444. Semi-private; 19 courts.

- **Gaines Park Tennis Center,** 1501 Australian Avenue, West Palm Beach, ☎ 561/659-0735.

- **Howard Park Tennis Center,** 901 Lake Avenue, West Palm Beach, ☎ 561/833-7100.

- **Phipps Park,** 4301 S. Dixie Hwy., West Palm Beach, ☎ 561/835-7045.

- **Carlin Park,** 400 S. Ocean Drive, Jupiter, ☎ 561-964-4420. Public; six courts.

- **Jupiter Bay Racquet Club,** 353 S. US Highway 1, Jupiter, ☎ 561-744-9424. Semi-private; seven courts.

- **Jupiter Community Park,** 3377 Church Street, Jupiter, ☎ 561-746-5134. Public; six courts.

- **Jupiter Ocean and Racquet Club,** 1605 S. US Highway 1, Jupiter, ☎ 561-747-1500. Semi-private; 13 courts.

- **Loggerhead Park,** 1111 Ocean Drive, Juno Beach, ☎ 561-964-4420. Public; four courts. Pavilion.

- **North Palm Beach Country Club,** 951 US Highway 1, North Palm Beach, ☎ 561-626-6515. Public; 12 courts.

- **Palm Beach Gardens Tennis Courts,** 10500 N. Military Trail, Palm Beach Gardens, ☎ 561-775-8277. Public; 10 courts.

On Wheels

Biking

 Did you know Palm Beach has serene Chinese and Japanese Gardens? Do you know which is the town's most expensive mansion? Which hotel hosts croquet matches on their front lawn?

Brian Marozzi, creator and owner of **Palm Beach Tours,** will guide you around beautiful Palm Beach by bike, sharing historic anecdotes and hilarious gossip about his favorite town. You'll ride along the Intracoastal Waterway on famous Lake Trail, past mansions of the rich and famous, luxe neighborhoods, posh hotels, hidden gardens, art museums, and historic churches.

Palm Beach Tours also has a two-passenger wicker bicycle, reminiscent of the turn-of-the-century Palm Beach Chariot, with a pedaling driver who will take visitors to local attractions and restaurants.

In addition to biking, the company offers historical, botanical, museum, antiques, and shopping tours. Call for details and schedules. **Palm Beach Tours, Inc.,** 301 Clematis Street, Suite 3000, West Palm Beach, ☎ 561/835-8922 or 888/868-TOUR.

Bike on Your Own

To bike on your own, several rental shops provide bikes and city trail maps:

- **Palm Beach Bicycle Trail Shop,** 223 Sunrise Avenue, Palm Beach, ☎ 561/659-4583.

- **Back Trails Rider,** 10965 N. Military Trail, Palm Beach Gardens, ☎ 561/694-6866.

- **Wheels of Wellington,** 13889 Wellington Trace, Wellington, ☎ 561/795-3038.

Lion Country Safari

The sign says it all: "Rhinos have right of way" at **Lion Country Safari,** Southern Boulevard West, West Palm Beach, ☎ 561/793-1084; Web site www.lioncountrysafari.com. The nation's first "drive-through cageless zoo" has been open since

1967, but it's still a thrill getting close to rhinos, gibbons, giraffes, elephants, lions, zebras, and chimpanzees. Passing Lake Dakaru, Australian emu cross slowly in front of your car. Masai cattle and Asian water buffalo graze in the fields nearby. Lions roll upside down like honey-colored kittens, snoozing in the sun after devouring 10 lbs. of meat. African elephants splash in their pool after dining on 200 lbs. of hay. The largest private collection of chimps in North America lives here, often visited by chimpanzee expert Dr. Jane Goodall, who calls this exhibit "the finest natural display of wild chimpanzees in the world outside Africa."

The adjacent **Safari World Amusement Park** is fun for kids, featuring exotic birds and primates, a carousel, mini-golf, and a paddleboat tour around Lake Shanalee. There's also a newborn animal nursery, a petting zoo, and a reptile park with crocodiles, alligators, snakes and lizards. With admission to Lion Country Safari, the amusement park is free.

❋ Snapshot

Meet Rusty Harr, Curator of the Preserve, Lion Country Safari, West Palm Beach.

SS: What's a day like with all these wild animals?

RH: My job is to make sure the animals are healthy and taken care of. There's always something new going on; babies are born year round. When a baby giraffe or rhino comes along that's pretty spectacular...

SS: Does it ever get dangerous?

RH: During breeding season we have rhino fights and the males forget about everything. They don't notice cars or even other animals so you have to watch your car! Even our own trucks get dented if we aren't careful.

SS: What's the best way to have an adventure at Lion Country Safari?

RH: Observe the preserve at different times. Animals migrate through the preserve, eat, sleep, and play, according to the time of day. You can see these different activities if you drive through more than once. Who knows what adventure you'll experience? Remember, they are wild and there are no cages here!

The Palm Beaches

A mother and baby rhino at Lion Country Safari.

On Water

Boating & Fishing

 The ocean, Intracoastal Waterway, and Palm Beach County's many lakes and canals provide endless opportunities for boating and fishing. Because Palm Beach County is closer to the Gulf Stream than any other US shoreline, it's possible to reel in a wide variety of fish within a mile or two of shore. Sailboats, powerboats or canoes can be rented at area parks and marinas, listed below.

Boat Rentals

- **Club Nautico Powerboat Rentals,** PGA Blvd, Palm Beach Gardens, ☎ 561/744-5752 (boats for cruising, fishing, waterskiing, diving).

- **Harbor Point Marina,** 2225 Monet Drive, North Palm Beach, ☎ 561/622-6890.

- **Old Port Cove Marina,** 112 Lake Shore Drive, North Palm Beach, ☎ 561/626-1760.

- **PGA Marina,** 2385 PGA Blvd. Palm Beach Gardens, ☎ 561/622-9191.

- **Palm Harbor Marina,** 400 N. Flagler Drive, West Palm Beach, ☎ 561/655-4757.

- **Palm Beach Yacht Club & Marina,** 800 N. Flagler Drive, West Palm Beach, ☎ 561/655-1944.

- **Sailfish Marina,** 98 Lake Drive, Palm Beach Shores, ☎ 561/844-1724.

Fishing Guides & Charters

- **Adventure Floatplane,** 2011 N. Flagler Drive, Palm Beach, ☎ 561/832-3770.

- **B-Love Fleet Drift Fishing,** 314 Ocean Avenue, Lantana, ☎ 561/588-7612.

- **Baby Grand Sport Fishing Charter,** 98 Lake Drive, Palm Beach Shores, ☎ 561/881-3881.

- **Blue Water Sport Fishing,** 1095 N. Highway A1A, ☎ 561/743-6942.

- **CUDA Palm Beach Sport Fishing Charters,** Palm Beach, ☎ 561/832-1350.

- **Fish Palm Beach,** 1958 Anderson Lane, West Palm Beach, ☎ 561/433-0307.

- **Lill's Charters,** 2063 Shady Lane, North Palm Beach, ☎ 561/624-6387.

 TIP *Palm Beach County has compiled a handy "Fish Finder Kit," containing information on artificial reefs, boat ramps, marinas, fish camps, charters, tournament schedules and tides. To order the Kit: write the **West Palm Beach Fishing Club,** c/o Fish Finder, PO Box 468, West Palm Beach, FL. 33402. Happy angling!*

Cruising

Hop aboard a "cruise to nowhere" and enjoy dining, dancing, gambling and musical entertainment.

The Palm Beaches

The *Viking Princess* **Casino Cruises,** ☎ 800/841-7447, set sail daily from the Port of Palm Beach. Cruises include meals, live entertainment, sportsbook betting. Craps, blackjack, slots, roulette, and Caribbean stud poker are in the on-board casino. Choose from Funshine Cruises (Mon, Wed, Fri, Sat 10 am-4 pm), Moonlight Magic Cruises (Mon, Tues, Wed, Thurs 7:30 pm-Midnight), Party Cruises (Fri/Sat 7:30 pm-1 am) or Brunch Cruises (Sundays 11 am-5 pm). Group, Senior and Children's rates available. Cruise free anytime within your birthday month.

Star of Palm Beach **Cruises,** ☎ 561/848-STAR, cruise the Intracoastal Waterway along Palm Beach's famous mansions. Dinner cruises include cocktails, dinner, dancing, and live entertainment. There are also lunch, sightseeing, and sunset party cruises.

Water taxis are a fun, economical way to sightsee the Palm Beach area. Narrated Intracoastal Waterway tours. Departures daily from **Sailfish Marina** on Singer Island, ☎ 561/930-8294; and from **Panama Hattie's** restaurant, PGA Blvd and Intracoastal Waterway, ☎ 561/243-0686.

Canoeing

The **Loxahatchee River** is a mysterious Jules Verne *Lost World* of 600-year-old cypress trees, alligators, owls, and hardwood canopies mirrored in tea-colored water. Exploring Florida's only Wild and Scenic River in a canoe or kayak is exhilarating and easy with **Canoe Outfitters,** at Palm Beach County's Riverbend Park, Indiantown Road (SR706), about one mile west of I-95, Jupiter, ☎ 561/746-7053.

Few people know the river like owner Eric Bailey, who grew up in the area. Since 1980, he and wife Sandy have guided enjoyable trips on one of the state's most beautiful rivers. On weekends you'll meet their daughters, who are usually doing homework and selling Girl Scout cookies.

Trip One takes five-six hours of paddling over eight miles and wends through a cypress canopy, past Trapper Nelson's historic home, and into a mangrove estuary. Trip Two takes two hours of paddling time, making a round trip to Masten Dam.

You'll see a variety of wildlife on both trips, as well as tropical vegetation. Reserve a guide or paddle on your own. Canoe and kayak lessons are also available by reservation. If you're feeling *really* adventurous, ask the Baileys about their wilderness trips to Alaska, Baffin Island, Northwest Territories of Canada, Yukon Territories, and Costa Rica.

✳ **Snapshot**

Meet Eric Bailey, Owner, Canoe Outfitters, Jupiter.

SS: Eric, how did you create a business on the Loxahatchee River?

EB: I grew up in West Palm Beach and have been running Canoe Outfitters on this river for over 16 years. I love it here. On the water you'll see otters; on the river banks, deer, hogs, possums and raccoons. We have owls, eagles, osprey, blue herons, woodpeckers, alligators, snakes and a ton of turtles!

SS: What kind of plant life grows along the river?

EB: Prehistoric leather ferns, cypress, mahogany, hickory, oak, maple.

SS: What attracts people to this river?

EB: They enjoy seeing the outdoors, being social. Families love it. The Loxahatchee is the only federally designated Wild and Scenic River in Florida. Fortunately the people in this state realize they have a gem and made sure this beautiful river wouldn't become condominiums.

SS: What does Loxahatchee mean?

EB: It's a Seminole word meaning "creek of turtles" and it sure lives up to its name.

SS: What are some of the benefits of canoeing?

EB: When I'm stressed out, I get in a canoe or kayak and just let the river carry me to a quiet spot. I sit there for however long it feels good, and when I come back, I'm a whole different person. I recommend everyone try it, either for an hour or the whole day. I give lessons on the weekdays for beginners.

The Palm Beaches

Scuba Diving & Snorkeling

Palm Beach County has good diving and snorkeling, with comfortable water temperatures almost year-round, except for January and February. (If you're a real diehard and want to dive during those months, wear a full-body wetsuit.) One mile north-east of the Palm Beach Inlet are three **shipwrecks:** the *PC1170* (at 90 feet), the *Amaryllis* (at 90 feet), and the *Mizpah,* a 180-foot patrol boat (at 90 feet). All were sunk to form an artificial reef, now home to grunts, jacks, barracuda, turtles, and moray eels.

Less than a mile east of the Breakers Hotel is **Breakers Reef,** an underwater garden of flower coral, gorgonians, sea fans, sponges, porkfish and spadefish at 40-60 feet.

At **Palm Beach Reef,** about 5,000 yards north of Breakers Reef, check out the 1965 vintage Rolls Royce Silver Shadow. Underwater at 80 feet it still looks classy.

John D. MacArthur Beach State Park, 10900 State Road 703, A1A, North Palm Beach, ☎ 561/624-6952 offers guided snorkeling tours the first and third Saturdays in June, July and August. The offshore limestone reef teems with angelfish, porkfish, lobsters and sea turtles. Bring your own gear, mask, fins and snorkel. Reserve through the Nature Center.

Dive Shops

- **Aquaventure Dive Scuba Center,** 409 Lake Avenue, Lake Worth, ☎ 561/582-0877.

- **Atlantic Underwater,** 901 Cracker St., West Palm Beach, ☎ 561/686-7066.

- **Dixie Divers,** 1401 South Military Trail, West Palm Beach, ☎ 561/969-6688.

- **Ocean Sports Scuba Center,** 1736 S. Congress Avenue, West Palm Beach, ☎ 561/641-1144.

- **Palm Beach Marine Institute,** 13425 Ellison Wilson Road, Juno Beach, ☎ 561/624-6941.

- **Scuba Club,** 4708 Poinsettia Avenue, West Palm Beach, ☎ 561/844-2466.

- **Seascape Scuba Charters,** 130 First Way, West Palm Beach, ☎ 561/691-5808.

- **Seafari Dive and Surf, Inc.,** 75. E. Indiantown Road, Suite 603, Jupiter, ☎ 561/747-6115.

Waterskiing

Take a waterski lesson or just enjoy the sport at **Mike Siepel's Barefoot International** in Lantana. Equipment is supplied. ☎ 561/964-3346.

Windsurfing

Mangonia Park, Australian Avenue north of 26th Street in West Palm Beach, is a popular lake for windsurfing and sailing. No motors or engines are allowed.

Fountain Fun

The dancing waters of **Centennial Fountain** at the downtown West Palm Beach Library, 100 Clematis Street, ☎ 561/835-7042, are a cooling treat for kids and adults alike. The water erupts in varying heights in a random computer-generated pattern, which kids love trying to catch. There's a lifeguard and public restrooms, so bring your suit and suntan lotion. The fountain is usually on from 7 am-10 pm daily. Afterwards, curl up in the air-conditioned library for a nice summer read.

In the Air

 At the **Lantana Airport,** 2633 Lantana Road, Lantana, enjoy riding in a **biplane, vintage plane, or helicopter.** During the winter and spring they offer two-passenger **glider rides.** For reservations, ☎ 561/965-9101.

On Horseback

 Palm Beach Polo and Country Club, 11809 Polo Club Road, West Palm Beach, ☎ 561/798-7000, is often called the "Wimbledon of Polo." Every season, international superstars ride the finest thoroughbreds in fast-paced high goal tournaments. Competition takes place on 11 fields, enjoyed by spectators in a tiered 5,000-seat stadium.

The Sunday Polo Season runs from January through May, featuring the Challenge and Sterling Cup League, Gold Cup of the Americas, US Open Polo Championship & Handicap, the World Cup, and Southern Silver Cup League. Tickets to the 3:30 pm matches are inexpensive, available by reservation Mon-Sat. 8:30 am-4:30 pm at ☎ 561/793-1440. Dress is sports chic.

If you want to learn the "sport of kings" yourself, call the club for a schedule of polo classes. See our interview with Calixto Garcia-Velez, Director of Polo Operations, for more information.

✸ Snapshot

Meet Calixto Garcia-Velez, Director of Polo Operations, Palm Beach Polo & Country Club.

SS: How can a first-time visitor to the Polo Club learn to play?

CV: We have a polo school that runs year-round. We start you off just riding to see your skills. Then we match you to a certain type of horse and give personalized instruction for two or three days. If all goes well, you participate in two practice games. That would be a typical week's program.

SS: Do men and women take separate classes?

CV: There's no difference between males and females when learning to play polo. Husbands and wives can be in the same class.

SS: Cali, for someone who has never seen a polo game, can you give us some rules?

CV: If you've never seen it before, it's a little difficult to comprehend. There are four players on each team, each player in a different position. One and two are mainly offensive players, three and four, mainly defensive. The field is 300 yards long by 165 yards wide. The object is to score more goals than the other team. Kind of like hockey on horseback. Very fast, quite exciting, and it can be dangerous. You're out in the sunshine, the grass is green, the wind is in your face. It's exhilarating to be out there, whether you're a spectator or a polo player.

SS: What attracted you to polo?

CV: My family was in ranching and I used to show hunter/jumpers in New York. But I liked the physical contact and the excitement of polo. I played other sports in high school and college, but once polo gets in your blood, that's it! They say the only two ways you ever quit playing polo are you die or run out of money.

SS: How did you become affiliated with Palm Beach Polo Club?

CV: I played here as a professional for most of my life, then quit to run a family business in Mexico. I came back here in 1996 and they offered me this job. It's a great combination because I play polo, which I love, and also help organize and grow the club. We have more teams here now than ever from America, England, Pakistan, Germany. It's played in many foreign countries as well – Africa, Poland, Czechoslovakia, France, Spain, Germany, Switzerland.

SS: Does the Club supply horses and polo equipment?

CV: You can come here tomorrow and buy everything you need to play polo in about 30 minutes. You can rent a horse an hour later, and be out on the field. We're a turnkey operation. Enroll in our school and a week later you'll be playing in a game. If you like competition and adventure, with a touch of danger, you should definitely try polo. There's speed, physical contact, the outdoor life, and fit, healthy people. You'll rub elbows with some of the most gifted athletes in the world, many from Fortune 500 companies.

Other Adventures

Auto Racing

Moroso Motorsports, Beeline Highway, Palm Beach Gardens, ☎ 561/622-1400, offers drag racing, stock car racing, and mudbogging year round. From mid-October through April, enroll at the Skip Barber Racing School: in eight days you'll complete lap requirements, take a car control school program, and compete in a weekend race.

Baseball

Catch the **Montreal Expos** and **St. Louis Cardinals** in March for Spring Training at the new **Roger Dean Stadium,** 4751 Main Street, Jupiter, ☎ 561/775-1818. The $275 million, 7,000-seat stadium is a state-of-the-art facility. To get here, take I-95 to the Donald Ross Road exit in Jupiter, head east to Central Blvd., and follow the signs.

Croquet

In Palm Beach County, **croquet** is taken very seriously. Of the 250 US clubs, 16 are located here. The United States Croquet Association, the sport's governing body, is located at the **Palm Beach Polo & Country Club,** where the Croquet National Championship is played every year. Call ☎ 561/753-9141 for tournament schedule.

The Palm Beaches

Dog Racing

Greyhounds race at speeds up to 40 mph at the **Palm Beach Kennel Club,** 1111 N. Congress Avenue, West Palm Beach, ☎ 561/683-2222. Hosting the sixth largest spectator sport in America, the club offers year-round matinees and evening races, with legal betting and seasonal dining.

Trap & Skeet

The **Palm Beach Trap and Skeet Club,** West Palm Beach, features American trap and skeet, sport clay stand, five-stand sporting clay, and a new Olympic bunker trap on 100 acres. Open Wednesday, Saturday and Sunday. Call ☎ 561/793-8787.

■ Sightseeing

Callery-Judge Grove, 4001 Seminole Pratt Whitney Road, Loxahatchee, ☎ 561/793-1676, features tours through their citrus groves and packing house to see how Indian River grapefruit and Florida's tangerines are picked and shipped to supermarkets worldwide. Sample their orange juice and take home a free bag of fresh citrus.

Burt Reynolds fans will enjoy a day at the 160-acre **Burt Reynolds Ranch,** 16133 Jupiter Farms Road, Jupiter, ☎ 561/746-0393. Tour *Smokey & the Bandit's* "Gator Motel," and *B.L. Stryker's* log cabin on the lake. Burt even has a treehouse. Call ahead for tours.

Dreher Park Zoo, West Palm Beach, ☎ 561/533-0887, is home to more than 400 animals from 100 different native and exotic species. They have the nation's only outdoor exhibit of Goeldi monkeys, along with a children's petting zoo and reptile exhibit.

Hallpatee Seminole Village at Knollwood Groves, Lake Worth, ☎ 561/734-4800, features authentic displays of native Seminole Indian culture. Alligator wrestling shows, airboat rides, and guided Everglades tours.

Ragtops Motor Cars, West Palm Beach, ☎ 561/655-2836, displays ragtops vintage automobiles valued over one million dollars. Soda bar and gift shop in a unique multi-level facility.

Rapids Water Park, West Palm Beach, ☎ 561/848-6272, is fun for kids, with four gigantic waterslides, a Big Surf wave pool, 18-hole mini-golf course, rainforest, waterfalls and a Jacuzzi. Open March-September.

Museums & Culture

 Ann Norton Sculpture Gardens, 253 Barcelona Road, West Palm Beach, ☎ 561/832-5328, features Ann Norton's sculptures on 3½ acres of gardens.

Armory Art Center, 1703 S. Lake Avenue, West Palm Beach, ☎ 561/832-1776, is a historic art deco building featuring exhibits of works by living Florida artists. The studio art school offers classes and workshops for all ages.

Henry Morrison Flagler Museum, Whitehall Way and Cocoanut Row, Palm Beach, ☎ 561/655-2833, is a marble mansion built in 1901 by Henry Flagler, partner in Standard Oil and developer of the Florida East Coast Railroad. A luxury hotel from 1925 to 1959, the house opened as a museum in 1960. Many of the original Victorian furnishings are here, as is "The Rambler," an 1886 railroad car built for Flagler's personal use, which recently underwent extensive renovation.

Hibel Museum of Art, 150 Royal Poinciana Plaza, Palm Beach, ☎ 561/833-6870, is dedicated to the work of American artist Edna Hibel, featuring her paintings, drawings, lithographs, porcelains, and sculpture. On the second Sunday in November through April, the Museum presents free Promenade Concerts.

Florida History Center & Museum, 805 North US1, Jupiter, ☎ 561/747-6639, has artifacts from early pioneers, prehistoric Indians, tools, Spanish silver coins, maps and a photo archive. The History Center also gives guided tours of "The Historic Triangle," which includes the Jupiter Lighthouse Museum, DuBois Pioneer House, and the History Center's museum. Open Tuesday-Friday 10 am-5 pm, Saturday and Sunday 1-5 pm. Admission.

Norton Museum of Art, 1451 S. Olive Avenue, West Palm Beach, ☎ 561/832-5194, has a permanent collection of French Impressionist and post-impressionist Chinese art. Traveling exhibitions are also presented. A delightful gift shop and outdoor garden.

Society of the Four Arts, Four Arts Plaza, Palm Beach, ☎ 561/655-7226, is a cultural complex with a museum, theater, library, auditorium, and gardens. New art exhibits are shown in the gallery every month. Open Dec-April.

South Florida Science Museum, 4801 Dreher Trail North, West Palm Beach, ☎ 561/832-1988, features hands-on science exhibits, the largest public use telescope in South Florida, and the South Florida Aquarium, with marine life from South Florida and the Caribbean. The Aldrin Planetarium, Gibson Observatory, Native Plant Center, Light and Sight Hall, and Science Theatre are here as well.

Lighthouse Gallery & School of Art, 373 Tequesta Drive, Tequesta, ☎ 561/746-3101, features monthly art exhibits, lectures, workshops, and classes throughout the year. Call for hours.

Performing Arts

Coral Sky Amphitheatre, 601-7 Sansbury's Way, West Palm Beach, ☎ 800/759-4624, www.coralsky.com, is the new Sony Music/Blockbuster theatre with top musical groups and acts.

Quest Theatre Institute, 444 24th Street, West Palm Beach, ☎ 561/832-9796, is an African-American-owned multicultural professional theater offering original and classic works.

The Raymond F. Kravis Center for the Performing Arts, 701 Okeechobee Boulevard, West Palm Beach, ☎ 800/KRAVIS-1, has a 2,200-seat main concert hall, a 300-seat theater, rehearsal hall and a 1,100-seat amphitheater under the stars. Classical, country, contemporary and cutting edge entertainment. See their calendar of events and order tickets on-line at www.kravis.org/.

Royal Poinciana Playhouse, 303 SE Mizner Boulevard, Palm Beach, ☎ 561/659-3310, billed as "the most glamorous theatre in the country," features top stars in Broadway and off-Broadway hits and concerts.

Entertainment

 The hottest new cultural, retail and entertainment district in West Palm Beach is **Clematis Street.** Beautifully restored buildings are now home to some 30 restaurants, 50 shops, galleries and clubs. You'll enjoy daytime Brown Bag Concerts, a Saturday morning Farmer's Market, and Thursday evening Clematis by Night events. Every Thursday from 5:30-9 pm, there's live music – everything from reggae to jazz to rock and roll – and food stands offering pizza, Cuban cuisine, seafood and soul food. Parking is free after 5pm in the Banyan Street garage, the library parking lot and along Clematis Street. For a special events schedule, call ☎ 561/659-8007; Web site www.clematisbynight.com. Clematis Street is off Flagler Drive, between Banyan Boulevard and Datura Street, in West Palm Beach.

■ Festivals & Events

January

Pre-Royal Palm Skeet Tournament, West Palm Beach, ☎ 561/793-8787.

South Florida Fair/O'Canada Exposition, West Palm Beach, ☎ 561/793-0333.

Laura Hart Invitational Croquet Tournament, Wellington, ☎ 561/753-9141.

$25,000 He's My Man Royal Palm Classic, West Palm Beach, ☎ 561/683-2222.

February

Palm Beach Seafood Fest, West Palm Beach, ☎ 561/832-6397.

Palm Beach Tropical Flower Show, West Palm Beach, ☎ 561/655-5522.

ArtiGras, annual art festival, PGA Blvd. At the Gardens Maill, Palm Beach Gardens, ☎ 561/433-9000, ext. Code 1234. Admission.

March

Taste of Tropics, West Palm Beach, ☎ 561/233-1759,
Samuel Stayman Memorial Pro-Am Bridge Tournament, West Palm Beach, ☎ 561/689-7700.

Blowing Rocks Music Festival, Jupiter, ☎ 561/747-2022.

Artfest by the Sea, annual arts festival, Loggerhead Park along A1A in Juno Beach, ☎ 561/746-7111.

April

West Palm Beach Italian Fest, West Palm Beach, ☎ 561/832-6397.

PGA Seniors' Championship, Palm Beach Gardens, ☎ 561/622-GOLF.

SunFest, music and arts festival, West Palm Beach, ☎ 561/659-5980.

May

Pioneer Days Festival, West Palm Beach, ☎ 561/793-0333.

$5,000 Bud Light Iron Dog Triathalon Final, West Palm Beach, ☎ 561/683-2222.

Marinelife Center Turtle Time Festival, Juno Beach, ☎ 561/627-8280.

June

Sun-N-Fun, West Palm Beach, ☎ 561/968-7808.

Tropical Fruit Fest, West Palm Beach, ☎ 561/233-1759.

July

Fourth on Flagler, West Palm Beach, ☎ 561/659-8004.

October

Oktoberfest, Lantana, ☎ 561/967-6464.

Taste of Tropics, West Palm Beach, ☎ 561/233-1759.

Seafare, seafood and local history festival, Jupiter, ☎ 561/747-6639. A benefit for the Florida History Museum.

November

Annual Florida Heritage Festival, West Palm Beach, ☎ 561/832-6397.

Hoffman's Chocolates Annual Holiday Wonderland, Greenacres, ☎ 561/967-2213.

Lighthouse Gallery Annual Fine Art Festival, Carlin Park in Jupiter, ☎ 561/746-3101.

December

Winter Fantasy on the Waterway, Intracoastal Waterway, ☎ 561/395-4433.

Art Week, West Palm Beach, ☎ 561/832-1776.

▪ Where to Stay

Palm Beach

The Breakers, One S. County Road, Palm Beach, ☎ 800/833-3141, has 572 oceanfront guestrooms on the beach. Golf, tennis, health club, pool, children's pool, entertainment, kids club/activities. There's an on-site currency exchange and 60 languages are spoken. $$$

The Chesterfield Hotel and Suites, 363 Cocoanut Row, Palm Beach ☎ 800/243-7871, is a small boutique hotel with 53 rooms and suites. Two blocks from Worth Avenue, and three blocks from the beach, the hotel has a heated pool and spa with private cabanas. Fine dining, afternoon tea, and nightly entertainment. $$

The Colony Hotel, 155 Hammond Ave, Palm Beach, ☎ 800/521-5525, has 91 rooms just a half-block from the beach. Golf and tennis are nearby, as is Worth Avenue. The hotel has a heated pool, welcome champagne cocktail, restaurant, lounge. French and Spanish are spoken. $$$

Four Seasons Resort Palm Beach, 2800 South Ocean Blvd., Palm Beach, ☎ 800/432-2335, features 210 rooms in a luxury beachfront resort. The hotel has a pool, tennis courts, health club, jacuzzi, full service spa, two restaurants, and entertainment. French, Italian, Spanish and German are spoken. $$$

The Palm Beaches

Palm Beach Resort & Beach Club, 3031 South Ocean Blvd., Palm Beach, ☎ 561/586-8898, has 29 one- and two-bedroom suites, across the street from the beach. The hotel has a pool, and there is a golf course nearby. $$

Plaza Inn, A Bed & Breakfast Hotel, 215 Brazilian Avenue, Palm Beach, ☎ 800/233-2632, has 50 rooms with refrigerators. Located one block from the beach, the hotel has a heated pool, tennis courts and is near a golf course. A full home-cooked breakfast is served each morning. French and Spanish are spoken. $-$$

Palm Beach Gardens

PGA National Resort & Spa, 400 Avenue of Champions, Palm Beach Gardens, ☎ 800/633-9150 is a luxury hotel with 339 rooms and enough restaurants for every day of your vacation: Crab Catcher (seafood), Arezzo (Italian), Ta-kil-ya (Mexican), Citrus Tree (salads), and Oasis (poolside sandwiches). The hotel has five 18-hole golf courses, a beach, a 26-acre sailing lake, nine pools, five croquet lawns, 19 tennis courts, health/racquet club, and a European spa. Spanish and French are spoken. $$-$$$

Palm Beach Shores

Sailfish Marina & Resort, 98 Lake Drive, Palm Beach Shores, ☎ 800/446-4577, has 15 rooms. Amenities include a pool, Thursday craft shows, outdoor restaurant, sightseeing tours, dockage, water taxi, and the beach nearby. The hotel hosts Florida's Big Game Sportfishing Charter Boats. Scandinavian and German spoken. $-$$

Singer Island

Bellatrix Resort, 1000 East Blue Heron Blvd., Singer Island, ☎ 561/845-8222, has 14 rooms with kitchenettes and is three blocks from the beach. Pool and dock. $

Days Inn Oceanfront Resort, 2700 North Ocean Drive, Singer Island, ☎ 561/848-0999, has 165 rooms on the beach. There's a heated pool, Jacuzzi, tiki bar, shuffleboard and beach volleyball. $-$$

West Palm Beach

Courtyard by Marriot, 600 Northpoint Parkway, West Palm Beach, ☎ 561/640-9000, has 149 rooms with coffee makers and cable TV. The hotel has a pool and jacuzzi. Spanish is spoken. $

Hibiscus House Bed and Breakfast, 501 30th Street, West Palm Beach, ☎ 800/203-4927, is a 1920's Florida house with six rooms. They serve a full breakfast daily, as well as cocktails. There's a heated pool and shuttle service to town and the airport. $-$$

Palm Beach Polo & Country Club, 11199 Polo Club Road, West Palm Beach, ☎ 561/798-7000, has 65 rooms with kitchenettes. The Club features 10 polo fields, an equestrian center, six pools, golf courses, 24 tennis courts, three spas, watersports and a health club. Spanish, French and German are spoken. $$-$$$

West Palm Beach Bed & Breakfast, 419 32nd Street, West Palm Beach, ☎ 561/848-4064, is a Key West-style guest house offering four poolside cottages with kitchenettes. Near the beach, the hotel has a pool, complimentary tropical breakfast buffet, and shuttle service to town and the airport. Golf course nearby. $

Juno Beach & Jupiter

The Hampton Inn, 13801 US1, Juno Beach, ☎ 561/626-9090, has a variety of rooms, including a king deluxe with sink, microwave, refrigerator and jacuzzis; or a king study with sofa sitting area. Two blocks from the beach, the hotel offers free local phone calls and a complimentary deluxe continental breakfast. $-$$

The Best Western Intracoastal Inn, 810 US1, Jupiter, ☎ 561/575-2936, has 53 rooms. The hotel is close to beaches, fine restaurants and shopping; and has a pool, whirlpool and a pier overlooking the Intracoastal Waterway. $

Jupiter Bay Rentals and Sales, US1 south of Indiantown Road, ☎ 800/749-1949, offers furnished one- and two-bedroom condos available for rent by the month, the season, or the year. There are two heated swimming pools, nine tennis courts and a half-mile walking trail. Clubhouse, restaurant and bar. $-$$

Jupiter Beach Resort, 5 North A1A, Jupiter, ☎ 800/228-8810, is a secluded oceanfront resort. Rooms have private balconies, minibars, cotton robes, in-room coffee makers, and complimentary morning newspapers. Amenities include a heated outdoor pool, lighted tennis court, bike rentals, shopping, and two restaurants. $$

Jupiter Reef Club, 1600 S. Ocean Drive, Jupiter, ☎ 561/747-7788, features 31 villas with ocean views. Villas have kitchens, washer/dryers, phones, two TVs and air-conditioning. The club is on the beach, and has a heated pool, hot tub, a patio, BBQ area and a shaded gazebo. $$

Wellesley Inn, 34 Fisherman's Wharf, Jupiter, ☎ 561/575-7201, has a suburban location near upscale restaurants and shops, one mile from the beach. The Inn offers a complimentary breakfast, outdoor heated pool, laundry, in-room coffee maker, and free Showtime movies. Children under 18 stay free with parents. $-$$

Camping

Lion Country Safari KOA, PO Box 16066, West Palm Beach, ☎ 800/354-5524, is next to Lion Country Safari Park, and close to fishing, beaches, boating, golf and shopping. Amenities include cable TV, grocery stores, laundry, rec hall, bike rentals, hiking trails, shuffleboard, horseshoes, pool, and volleyball.

Palm Beach Traveler Park, 6159 Lawrence Road, Lantana, ☎ 561/967-3139, is an adult camping park with a rec hall, shuffleboard, horseshoes, pot luck meals, bingo. Amenities include pay phones, full hookups, 30 amp electricity, laundry. No pets.

Juno Beach RV Park, 900 Juno Ocean Walk, Juno Beach, 561-622-7500, is a short walk to the beach, shops and dining. Amenities include groceries, RV supplies, LP gas in the adjoining plaza. The park has a heated pool, jacuzzi, winter activity program, fishing, golf, horseshoes, playground and shuffleboard.

▪ Where to Eat

Mediterranean

Casablanca Café Americain, 101 North County Road, Palm Beach, ☎ 561/655-1115, has an intimate setting with panoramic views. Specialties include roasted Long Island duckling, Greek moussakka, onion-crusted snapper, and low fat/low cholesterol entrées. $$-$$$

Janeiro Restaurant and Wine Bar, 191 Bradley Place, Palm Beach, ☎ 561/659-5223, serves pecan-crusted Chilean salmon, fricassee of escargot, gazpacho, and grilled shiitake mushrooms. Live entertainment from a piano, sax and drum trio. $$$

American

264 The Grill, 264 South County Road, Palm Beach, ☎ 561/833-6444, is a casual neighborhood spot located in a land-mark Mizner building. The Grill specializes in prime beef, fresh seafood, veal, pastas and great burgers. Lobster and stone crabs are served in season. $$

The Breakers, One South County Road, Palm Beach, ☎ 800/833-3141 or 561/655-6611, combines elegant surround-ings with spectacular ocean views. Breakfast, lunch and dinner are served daily; Sunday Brunch is very special, with caviar, omelette and seafood buffets, and some 40 dessert choices. $$

Captain Charlie's Reef Grill, 12846 US Highway One, in Beach Plaza, Juno Beach, ☎ 561-624-9924. A favorite with lo-cals (be prepared to wait), this friendly, casual place features fresh seafood at reasonable prices, as well as a great wine list. The cuisine is "Floribbean," a creative fusion of Caribbean, New American, Cuban, and Asian flavors. Try conch fritters with star-fruit jam and hot pepper reduction sauce; fettucine with rock shrimp, clams, roasted peppers and gorgonzola cheese; or peppered tuna medallions with blueberry teriyaki. There are delicious beef and pork entrées as well. For dessert, try home-made Caribbean cobbler with crème anglaise. Their new place, *3 Doors Up* (the name and location), is good for a lighter meal or to share an appetizer while you wait for a table at the Reef. A fun touch: the cooks communicate between the two kitchens with two-way radios. $-$$

The Palm Beaches

Ke'e Grill, 14020 US1, Juno Beach, ☎ 561/776-1167, features fresh seafood in upscale, white-tablecloth surroundings. Enjoy the bronzed swordfish, basted and grilled with a soy-sesame glaze, or maple mustard barbecued salmon. Meat lovers will be happy with the certified Black Angus steaks, and there are pasta dishes as well. It's a popular place, so be prepared to wait, but you can sit at the bar and be mesmerized by the flaming torches outside. $$

Lazy Loggerhead Café, 601 South A1A at Carlin Park beach in Jupiter, ☎ 561/747-1134, is a great place for a casual breakfast or lunch. Everything is prepared to order using fresh ingredients, and portions are huge. Burn off those calories with a brisk walk on the beach after your meal. $

The Raindancer Steak House, 2300 Palm Beach Lakes Blvd., West Palm Beach, ☎ 561/684-2810, is a casual restaurant serving sirloin, thick-cut filet mignon, and pork chops, with a salad bar and moderately priced wine list. $$

The River House, 2373 PGA Blvd., Palm Beach Gardens, ☎ 561/694-1188, has a casual Key West atmosphere with magnificent views of the Intracoastal. Fresh seafood, poultry, steaks and a salad bar. Docking facilities available. $$

Ruth's Chris Steak House, 661 US Highway One, North Palm Beach, ☎ 561/863-0660, is known as "Home of Serious Steaks." Serving aged US Prime beef broiled to order, as well as seafood, vegetable dishes, and home-made desserts. $$$

Sugar Cane Island Bistro, 353 US Highway One, Jupiter, ☎ 561/743-4177, features fresh local fish, organic greens, pastas, tropical fruits, and home-baked pastries. Wed-Sun. $$

Ta-Boo, 221 Worth Avenue, Palm Beach, ☎ 561/835-3500, is an upscale American Bistro and Bar, serving prime rib, steaks, seafood, pasta, pizza and salads. Sunday Brunch is from 11:30 am-3 pm. Dancing on Friday and Saturday nights. $$

Waterway Café, PGA Blvd. and the Intracoastal, Palm Beach Gardens, ☎ 561/694-1700, is a casual family place, featuring fresh seafood, pasta, salads, brick oven gourmet pizza, steak and chicken entrées. $$

Tex-Mex

Rosalita's Tex-Mex Grill, 5949 S. Congress Avenue at Lantana Road, Atlantis, ☎ 561/964-5747, serves *carne asada,* swordfish fajitas, *arroz con pollo,* and a wide variety of vegetarian dishes. $

Italian

No Anchovies, 1901 Palm Beach Lakes Blvd., West Palm Beach, ☎ 561/684-0040 is a neighborhood pastaria, serving vegetarian pizza, fettuccine primavera, linguine posilippo, scampi livornese, and veal piccata. Pizzas are baked in their woodburning oven. They have a second restaurant at 2650 PGA Boulevard, Palm Beach Gardens, ☎ 561/622-7855. $$

Tourism Information

Palm Beach County Convention and Visitors Bureau, 1555 Palm Beach Lakes Boulevard, Suite 204, West Palm Beach, 33401. ☎ 561/471-3995. Visit their Web site at www. palmbeachfl.com.

Northern Palm Beach County Chamber of Commerce, 1983 PGA Blvd, #104, Palm Beach Gardens, FL 33408, ☎ 561/694-2300; fax 561/694-0126. Web site www.npbchamber.com.

Jupiter Tequesta Juno Beach Chamber of Commerce (JTJB), 800 N US Highway One, Jupiter, FL 33477. ☎ 561/746-7111, 800/616-7402; fax 561/746-7715. Web site: www.jupiterfl.org.

❦ ❦ ❦

The Palm Beaches

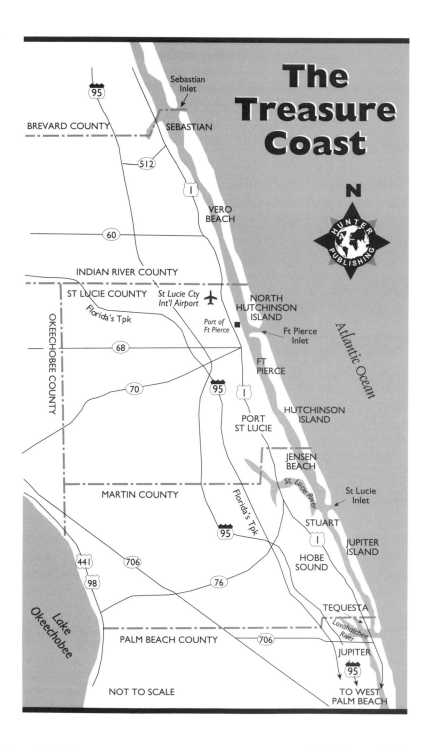

The Treasure Coast

T he Treasure Coast encompasses Florida's southeast towns from Tequesta to Sebastian, including Martin, St. Lucie, and Indian River counties. The name "Treasure Coast" refers to the one million dollars in Spanish coins, jewelry, bullion, and ingots recovered in the late 1950s and early 1960s by Sebastian resident Kip Wagner. Historians say the booty came from 10 ships of the 1715 Spanish Plate Fleet, which sank in a hurricane. The fleet was carrying $14 million worth of gold, silver, emeralds, pearls and trade goods from the Orient. Think of what's still under the sea.

Diving for treasure off the Treasure Coast is still a major event each spring. If you have the time, money and skill, go for the gold. If not, there are plenty of other Treasure Coast adventures to keep you busy: deep-sea fishing, sailing, kayaking, scuba diving, hot air ballooning, hiking, and turtle watching, to name a few.

Hobe Sound to Ft. Pierce

■ Adventures

On Foot

Blowing Rocks Preserve, 574 South Beach Road, Hobe Sound, ☎ 561/744-6668, is a beautiful 73-acre coastal barrier island preserve where you can watch sea turtles hatch, enjoy nature walks, and photograph a variety of birds. Bounded by the Atlantic Ocean and Intracoastal Water-

Hobe Sound, 🌴 Stuart, Jensen Beach

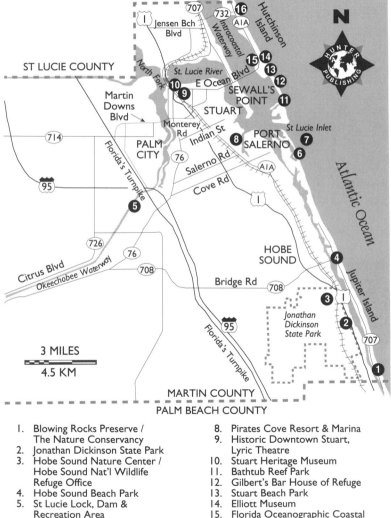

1. Blowing Rocks Preserve / The Nature Conservancy
2. Jonathan Dickinson State Park
3. Hobe Sound Nature Center / Hobe Sound Nat'l Wildlife Refuge Office
4. Hobe Sound Beach Park
5. St Lucie Lock, Dam & Recreation Area
6. St Lucie Inlet State Preserve
7. St Lucie Inlet State Preserve Reef
8. Pirates Cove Resort & Marina
9. Historic Downtown Stuart, Lyric Theatre
10. Stuart Heritage Museum
11. Bathtub Reef Park
12. Gilbert's Bar House of Refuge
13. Stuart Beach Park
14. Elliott Museum
15. Florida Oceanographic Coastal Science Center
16. Jensen Beach Park

way, this diverse preserve is owned and managed by The Nature Conservancy.

The preserve features the largest Anastasia limestone outcropping on the Atlantic Coast. Four distinct native plant communities thrive here: shifting oceanfront dune, coastal strand, interior mangrove wetlands, and tropical hardwood hammock.

From April through September, sea turtles crawl ashore at night to deposit their eggs in the warm sand. Green, leatherback, and loggerhead turtles nest at the preserve, all listed as endangered or threatened species. Volunteers assist with the sea turtle conservation program, which includes sea turtle rescue, and offer guided turtle walks. Call for reservations to participate.

October through May, volunteers lead nature walks on Sundays at 11 am and Thursdays at 2 pm. There are also nature photography walks with photo journalist Helen Longest-Slaughter, and star-gazing walks with Charlie Fredrickson of the Astronomical Society of Palm Beach. Call for schedules.

Birders will see brown pelicans, double-crested cormorants, snowy egrets, black-bellied plovers, sanderlings, laughing gulls, mourning doves, pileated woodpeckers, Carolina wrens, and boat-tailed grackles.

The preserve's **Hawley Education Center** houses a CD-interactive program and exhibits on the Indian River Lagoon's biological importance. The preserve is open 9 am-5 pm daily.

Jonathan Dickinson State Park, 16450 SE Federal Highway (US1), Hobe Sound, ☎ 561/546-2771, has four scenic nature trails. Home to bald eagles, scrub jays, Florida sandhill cranes, and gopher tortoises, 20% of this 10,284-acre park is coastal sand pine scrub, a biological community so rare it is designated "globally imperiled." Trails through the scrub are located off the entrance station parking lot and at Hobe Mountain.

Birders will spot great egrets, little blue herons, yellow-crowned night herons, white ibis, black and turkey vultures, mourning doves, screech owls, nighthawks, red-bellied woodpeckers, and blue-gray gnatcatchers. Nature programs and guided tours are offered throughout the year; call the park for a schedule.

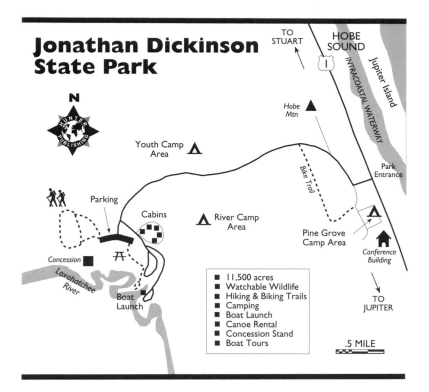

Hiking, nature observation, and photography are popular at
Hobe Sound National Wildlife Refuge, 13640 US1, Hobe
Sound, ☎ 561/546-2067. This 968-acre refuge includes 3½ miles
of beach, sand dunes, and mangroves on Jupiter Island, and a
sand pine scrub forest along the Intracoastal Waterway. The
refuge is a nesting area for leatherback, green and loggerhead
sea turtles, who produce over 500,000 hatchlings during most
years. Also living in this refuge are brown pelicans, wood storks,
ospreys, whitetailed deer, raccoon, fox, bobcat, indigo snakes,
scrub lizards, and gopher tortoises. The Hobe Sound Nature
Center sponsors nature lectures, guided walks, slide and video
programs, and sea turtle walks during June and July, by reservation. The refuge is open daily from sunrise to sunset; the Nature Center is open Monday-Friday 9-11 am and 1-3 pm.

Enjoy a guided boardwalk tour through a coastal hardwood
hammock and a mangrove forest at the **Florida Oceano-**

graphic Society's Coastal Science Center, 890 NE Ocean Boulevard, Hutchinson Island, Stuart, ☎ 561/225-0505. Walk among 50-year-old live oaks, wild coffee trees, prehistoric leather ferns, and delicate butterfly orchids. Guided walks are Wednesday and Saturday at 10 am and 2 pm; or enjoy the boardwalk on your own anytime. Inside the Frances Langford Visitor Center are aquariums of snook, tarpon, French angelfish, spiny lobsters and sea horses from the Indian River Lagoon. On the wall is Mrs. Langford's fish collection, including a 374-pound blue marlin, a 750-pound bluefin tuna, and a sharp-toothed barracuda. (We want to meet this dynamo fisherwoman!) The Center is open Monday-Saturday 10 am-5 pm.

Two other parks we enjoyed: the **St. Lucie Inlet Preserve,** with a 3,300-foot boardwalk meandering through thick forests of live oak, paradise trees, and ferns. This preserve is only accessible by private watercraft or a several-mile walk from a parking area south of the preserve. St. Lucie Inlet is at the north end of Jupiter Island, open 8 am-sunset, year-round. ☎ 561/744-7603.

Ft. Pierce Inlet State Recreation Area, 905 Shorewinds Drive, Fort Pierce, ☎ 561/468-3985, has the mile-long Marsh Rabbit Run Trail on Jack Island Preserve. Or stroll the Buttonwood Trail through black mangroves, buttonwood trees, and land crab nests. To experience a seaside hardwood hammock, walk the trail on the south side of the inlet. You'll be among beautiful live oaks, cabbage palms, sea grapes and strangler figs. To learn more about the history and biology of this inlet, call for the schedule of guided ranger walks. During WWII, it was the birthplace and training ground for US Navy Frogmen, forerunners of today's Navy Seals.

Heathcote Botanical Gardens, 210 Savannah Road, Fort Pierce, ☎ 561/464-4672 is a 3½-acre garden of tropical flowers, native and exotic foliage, and Japanese gardens. Open year-round Tuesday-Saturday, 9 am-5 pm. From November through April they are also open on Sunday from 1-5 pm.

Enjoy a sea turtle slide presentation, then walk the beach where they nest at the **Florida Power and Light** facility, 6501 S. A1A, South Hutchinson Island, ☎ 800/334-5483. Reservations are taken in May for the June-August turtle observation walks. FPL also has an Energy Encounter, with hands-on displays

🌴 Hutchinson Island, Port St. Lucie & Ft. Pierce

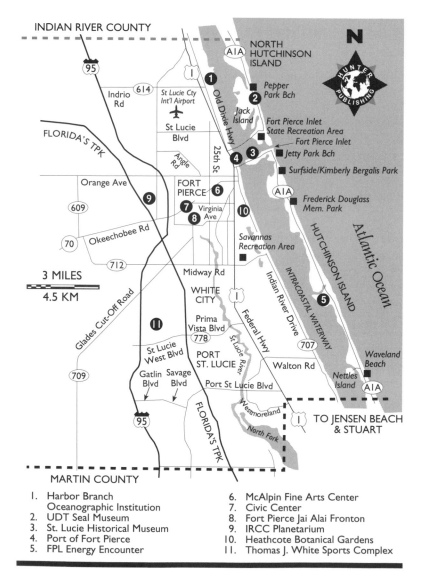

1. Harbor Branch
   Oceanographic Institution
2. UDT Seal Museum
3. St. Lucie Historical Museum
4. Port of Fort Pierce
5. FPL Energy Encounter
6. McAlpin Fine Arts Center
7. Civic Center
8. Fort Pierce Jai Alai Fronton
9. IRCC Planetarium
10. Heathcote Botanical Gardens
11. Thomas J. White Sports Complex

about nuclear power and the environment. Open 10 am-4 pm, Monday-Friday; free.

During winter months watch wild manatees basking in warm waters across from the **Fort Pierce Utilities Authority Power Plant.** The observation tower and education center are open free to the public. Located at Orange Avenue and Indian River Drive, Fort Pierce, ☎ 561/466-1600. Open November 1-April 15, Tuesday-Sunday 10 am-5 pm.

Savannas Recreation Area, 1400 E. Midway Road, Fort Pierce, ☎ 561/464-7855 is a 550-acre park within a freshwater marsh, stretching from St. Lucie County to Martin County. The park is nice for fishing, hiking and picnics. Rent canoes and fishing boats, climb the observation tower, and visit a petting farm. Open 8 am-9 pm daily.

St. Lucie Lock, Dam and Recreation Area has boat ramps, fishing, a nature trail, camping area, a playground, restrooms, showers, grills, beaches and phone. Watch the highest lift lock (13 feet) on the Okeechobee Waterway. Open 6 am-9 pm, daily. The area is located west of Port Salerno at the north end of Locks Road, off SR 76, southwest of I-95. ☎ 561/221-3349.

A Photo Safari

"You think you're in the middle of a dream. Just you and a big, hungry Florida 'gator. Nothing between you and him but water, grass, croaking frogs. You look skyward and the only living creature is an osprey soaring in the wild blue yonder. It isn't a dream. You're on a photo safari."

Those are the enticing words of award-winning photographer Harry Bittle, who leads **wildlife photo safaris** for serious amateur photographers. Harry guides photographers to remote areas in search of alligators, exotic birds, bald eagles, panthers, deer, and turkeys. Bring your 500mm lens and comfortable walking shoes.

Trips are customized to your interests, and include a gourmet sandwich lunch and soft drinks. Nature lovers who just want to bring binoculars are welcome too. Call Harry Bittle at 1795 SW Diana Terrace, Stuart, ☎ 561/220-8161.

Golf

Martin & St. Lucie Counties:

▪ **The Championship Club at Summerfield,** 3400 SE Summerfield Way, Stuart, ☎ 561-283-1500. Public; 18 holes.

▪ **Cobblestone Country Club,** 10644 Whooping Crane Way, Palm City, ☎ 561-597-4501. Semi-private; 18 holes.

▪ **Cutter Sound Golf and Yacht Club,** 2363 SW Carriage Hill Terrace, Palm City, ☎ 561-221-1822. Semi-private; 18 holes.

▪ **Golden Bear Country Club at Hammock Creek,** 2400 Golden Bear Way, Palm City, ☎ 561-220-2599. Semi-private; 18 holes.

▪ **Heritage Ridge Golf Club,** 6510 SE Heritage Blvd. Hobe Sound, ☎ 561-546-2800. Semi-private; 18 holes.

▪ **Indianwood,** 14574 SE Rake Drive, Indiantown, ☎ 561-597-3794. Semi-private; 18 holes.

▪ **Lost Lake Golf Club,** 8300 SE Fazio Drive, Hobe Sound, ☎ 561-220-6666. Semi-private; 18 holes.

▪ **Martin County Golf and Country Club,** 2000 SE St. Lucie Blvd., Stuart, ☎ 561-287-3747. Public; two 18-hole courses.

▪ **Pine Lakes Golf Club,** 1827 N. Pine Lake Drive, Stuart, ☎ 561-692-0346. Semi-private; 18 holes.

▪ **76 Golf World,** 6801 S. Kanner Highway, Stuart, ☎ 561-220-7676. Public; 18 holes. Driving range, miniature golf, snack bar.

▪ **Ballantrae Golf and Yacht Club,** 3325 SE Ballantrae Blvd., Port St. Lucie, ☎ 561-337-5315. Semi-private; 18 holes.

▪ **Club Med Sandpiper,** 3500 SE Morningside Blvd. Port St. Lucie, ☎ 561-335-4400. Semi-private; two 18-hole courses and one nine-hole course.

- **Fairwinds Golf Course,** 4400 Fairwinds Drive, Ft. Pierce, ☎ 561-462-4653. Public; 18 holes.

- **Gator Trace Golf and Country Club,** 4302 Gator Trace Drive, Ft. Pierce, ☎ 561-464-0407. Semi-private; 18 holes.

- **Indian Hills Golf and Country Club,** 1600 S. Third Street, Ft. Pierce, ☎ 561-464-7108. Semi-private; 18 holes.

- **PGA Golf Club at The Reserve,** 1916 Perfect Drive, Port St. Lucie, ☎ 800-800-4653. Semi-private; two 18-hole courses.

- **St. Lucie West Country Club,** 951 SW Country Club Drive, Port St. Lucie, ☎ 561-340-1911. Semi-private; 18 holes.

- **Savanna Club Golf Course,** 3492 Crabapple Road, Port St. Lucie, ☎ 561-879-1316. Semi-private; 18 holes.

- **Wilderness Golf Course,** 2550 SE Westmoreland, Port St. Lucie, ☎ 561-337-3511. Public; nine holes.

- **Dodger Pines Country Club,** 4600 26th Street, Vero Beach, ☎ 561-569-4400. Semi-private; 18 holes.

- **Dodgertown Golf Club,** 4201 26th Street, Vero Beach, ☎ 561-569-4800. Semi-private; nine holes.

- **Hawk's Nest Golf Club,** 6005 Old Dixie Highway, Vero Beach, ☎ 561-569-9402. Private; 18 holes.

- **Sandridge Golf Club,** 5300 73rd Street, Vero Beach, ☎ 561-770-5000. Public; two 18-hole courses.

- **Sebastian Municipal Golf Club,** 101 E. Airport Drive, Sebastian, ☎ 561-589-6800. Public; 18 holes.

- **Vista Plantation,** 48 Plantation Drive, Vero Beach, ☎ 561-569-2223. Public; 18 holes.

- **Vista Royale Golf and Country Club,** 100 Woodland Drive, Vero Beach, ☎ 561-562-8110. Public; three nine-hole courses.

Tennis

Martin and St. Lucie Counties:

- **Falkenburg Tennis Club,** 400 NW Baker Rd., Stuart, ☎ 561-692-9088. Semi-private; 12 courts.

- **Heritage Oaks Racquet Club,** 18000 SE Heritage Dr., Tequesta, ☎ 561-746-6650. Private; six courts.

- **Joseph V. Reed Park,** 9004 Hercules Dr., Hobe Sound, ☎ 561-221-1418. Public; four courts.

- **Langford Park,** 2369 NE Dixie Highway, Jensen Beach, ☎ 561-334-1954. Public; four courts.

- **North River Shores Tennis Club,** 2393 N.W. Britt Road, Stuart, ☎ 561-692-0266. Semi-private; seven courts.

- **Sailfish Park,** Georgia Avenue and E. Ocean Blvd., Stuart, ☎ 561-288-5335. Public; four courts.

- **Tequesta Park,** 2280 County Line Road, Tequesta, ☎ 561-575-6240. Public; four courts.

- **Lakewood Park,** 6102 Kings Highway, Fort Pierce, ☎ 561-462-1521. Public; four courts.

- **Lawnwood Recreation Complex,** 1302 Virginia Avenue, Fort Pierce, ☎ 561-462-1521. Public; 10 courts.

- **Whispering Pines Park,** 900 S.W. Darwin Blvd., Port St. Lucie ☎ 561-878-2277. Public; four courts.

On & In the Water

Swimming

 Martin and St. Lucie counties are blessed with some of the most stunning beaches in the US. Here's where to find sun, sand and surf:

Martin County Beaches, South to North:

- **Hobe Sound Beach Park,** intersection of Bridge Road (SR 707) and Beach Road, Jupiter Island, has

314 feet of beach, 90 parking spaces, showers, bathrooms, a lifeguard tower and picnic area.

▪ **Bathtub Reef Beach Park,** at the south end of Hutchinson Island, north of St. Lucie Inlet, has 1,080 feet of beach, 288 parking spaces, showers, bathrooms, an observation area and two lifeguard towers. A river boardwalk on the west side of MacArthur Boulevard leads to the Indian River. When the tide is out, the area inside the reef is a perfect wading pool for small tots. This a good snorkeling reef as well.

▪ **Chastain Beach Access,** just north of Bathtub Reef Park on MacArthur Boulevard, Stuart, has 80 feet of beach with large beach rocks, and 30 parking spaces, The submerged rocks offshore create good surfing waves.

▪ **Stuart Beach Park,** on MacArthur Boulevard, off State Road A1A in Stuart, has 1,160 feet of beach, 429 parking spaces, concession stand, showers, bathroom, two basketball courts, one volleyball court, two lifeguard towers and picnic spots. Lots of teenagers hang out here and it's jammed with families on the weekends.

▪ **Tiger Shores,** a small, secluded area a quarter-mile north of Stuart Beach off State Road A1A, has 100 feet of beach and 32 parking spaces. Good for shore fishing.

▪ **Bob Graham Beach,** just south of Jensen Beach Causeway on State Road A1A, has 2,358 feet of beach and 67 parking spaces.

▪ **Jensen Beach/Sea Turtle Beach Park,** on State Road 707A and State Road A1A in Jensen Beach, has 2,540 feet of beach, bathrooms, showers, sheltered picnic tables, two volleyball courts, two lifeguard towers, a concession stand, and 450 parking spaces.

St. Lucie County Beaches, South to North:

▪ **Waveland Beach,** on State Road A1A just north of the Jensen Beach Causeway, has 325 feet of beach, 100 parking spaces, bathrooms, showers, a boardwalk, picnic areas, concession stand and a lifeguard tower.

■ **Frederick Douglass Memorial Park,** four miles south of the Fort Pierce Inlet on State Road A1A, has 1,000 feet of beach, 175 parking spaces, bathrooms, showers and picnic spots. Good seashelling here, and horseback riding is permitted.

■ **Surfside Park,** on State Road A1A one mile south of the Fort Pierce Inlet, has 585 feet of beach, 100 parking spaces, bathrooms and picnic spots. A boardwalk leads to **Kimberly Bergalis Park,** with 600 feet of beach, 100 parking spaces, bathrooms, showers and picnic spots.

■ **South Jetty Park/Seaway Drive Access,** on the south side of Fort Pierce Inlet at the end of Seaway Drive, has 180 feet of beaches, 60 parking spaces, a fishing pier, picnic spots, bathrooms, showers, one lifeguard tower. Good windsurfing and fishing here.

■ **Fort Pierce Inlet State Recreation Area/North Jetty Park,** on State Road A1A in Fort Pierce, has 2,200 feet of beach on the north shore of the inlet, bathrooms, showers, picnic tables, one lifeguard tower. Excellent surfing.

■ **Pepper Park Beach,** on State Road A1A, two miles south of the Indian River county line, one mile north of the Fort Pierce Inlet, has 1996 feet of beach, 300 parking spaces, two tennis courts, one basketball court, picnic spots, bathrooms, and showers. Docks across the islands allow access by boaters from the river.

Boating & Fishing

"It is still dark. With visions of leaping sailfish dancing in your head, you step aboard, preparing for the adventure of a lifetime, sailfishing Gulfstream waters. Fifteen minutes, 20 minutes, then click, the left outrigger has been hit. You grab the rod and wait... one... two... three... arching back, you set the hook. Rod bent, the reel being stripped of line, you sit back into the fighting chair. Ready for the adventure of a lifetime."

These are the words of veteran sportsfisherman Gary Guertin, General Manager of **Pirates Cove Resort and Marina,** 4307 SE Bayview Street, Stuart, ☎ 800/332-1414. For decades the Treasure Coast has provided the perfect habitat for marlin, sailfish, dolphin, wahoo, kingfish, tuna, cobia. Presidents, CEOs, celebrities, and offshore anglers journey from around the world to match wits with mighty Atlantic Ocean gamefish.

Pirates Cove Resort and Marina

The full-service marina at Pirates Cove Resort features the Pirates Cove Charter Fleet, located in the heart of "Sailfish Alley." Stop by to chat with the various captains, any of whom will have you out fishing in 45 minutes. Fully licensed charters include open day boats or enclosed salon boats, available for half-day or full-day fishing.

Pirates Cove Bait and Tackle Shop at the marina does rod and reel repairs and line winding; they also sell offshore/inshore tackle, clothing, gifts, sundries, ice, beer, wine, soft drinks, and snacks.

Each year Mr. Guertin and Pirates Cove Resort and Marina host two world-class fishing tournaments. The August "Summer Slam" focuses on catch-and-release fishing for dolphin, wahoo, and kingfish, awarding over $10,000 in cash and prizes to winners. In December, the "Sailfish Classic," also a catch-and-release event, opens the official Sailfish Tournament Season in South Florida. Anglers from around the US compete for over $20,000 in cash and prizes to reel in these sportfish.

Here's a partial listing of Pirates Cove Marina sportfishing charter boats:

- ***Big Katuna,*** a 42-foot Bertram, offers sportfishing, sightseeing, sunset cruises, and excursions to the Bahamas. Enjoy cuisine prepared by Captain Wally Reynolds, USCGL. Full- or half-day charters include crew, bait, all tackle. Reservations, ☎ 561/546-7169.

- ***Uncle T,*** a 47-foot Sportfishing charter powered by twin turbocharged diesel engines, is equipped with a state-of-the-art electronics package. It sleeps six, and there is a galley with dinette area, hot and cold water, microwave, refrigerator, color TV, stereo, air conditioning, heat, and full head. Day, overnight, custom and Bahama charters available. Reservations with Captain Steven Castellini, ☎ 561/287-7379.

■ **Oodles Sportfishing** has a 44-foot Custom Sportfish with GPS, Loran, color scope fishfinder, and temperature graph. Full- or half-day charters with USCG Captain Pat Silver. Reservations, ☎ 561/283-3697.

■ *Agitator,* a 51-foot Golden Egg Harbor sportfisherman with Tuna Tower, has twin G.M. diesels, 48-mile radar, two Lorans, VHF single side band, depth finders, and auto-pilot, spacious air-conditioned accommodations, and two full heads. Full- and half-day rates, special occasion and evening cruises, parties, food and beverage provisions on request. Reservations with USCG Captains Mort Rappaport or Paul Aikens, ☎ 561/221-0328.

■ *Safari I,* US Coast Guard inspected, has ship-to-shore radio, radar, Loran, fishfinders, and large enclosed salon. Deep-sea fishing trips are offered from 8:30 am-1 pm, 1:30-6 pm, and nights. Reservations at ☎ 561/334-4411. Free tackle and bait.

■ *No Alibi* is a sportfishing boat that carries up to six passengers and is equipped with a full safety package and up-to-date electronics. Amenities include a dinette area with hot/cold water, microwave, refrigerator, color TV, stereo, enclosed head. Charter includes ice, bait, tackle and a full line of Penn & Shamano rods and reels. They offer trolling and live bait for deep-sea fishing, bottom and wreck fishing. Reservations with Captain Rich Humphreys at ☎ 561/223-0956.

Contact Pirate's Cove Resort and Marina for their complete roster of deep-sea fishing charter boats.

Saltwater Guides

If you have your own boat and/or just want to hire a saltwater fishing guide, here's a resource list.

- **Breakwater Charters,** Fort Pierce, ☎ 561/464-6243.

- **Emerald Lady Sport Fishing Charters,** ☎ 561/468-0566.

- **Got-M-On Charters,** Stuart, ☎ 561/286-3638.

- *Happy Hooker* **Charter Boat,** Fort Pierce, ☎ 561/489-2180.

- **Harbortown Charter Fleet,** Fort Pierce, ☎ 561/466-0947.

- **Holliday,** Stuart (ask for Mike), ☎ 561/229-1565.

- **Indian River Plantation,** Stuart, ☎ 561/225-6989.

- **Pirates Cove Marina,** Manatee Pocket, Stuart, ☎ 561/287-2500.

- **Sailfish Bait & Tackle,** ☎ 561/221-9456.

- **Shafer,** Fort Pierce (ask for Chip), ☎ 561/465-4638.

- **Tyler Grove Fishing Charters,** Fort Pierce, ☎ 561/569-7037.

- **U and I Charter,** Fort Pierce, ☎ 561/466-5876.

Fishing - River, Inlet, Flats, Refuge

Inlet Lagoon Guide Service will take you fishing in the St. Lucie and the Indian River Lagoon for snook, tarpon, sea trout and redfish aboard a 17-foot Linesider. Reservations with USCG Captains Dustin Boorman and Craig Boorman at ☎ 561/287-2613; 2513 SE St. Lucie Blvd., Stuart.

Enjoy a day on the Indian River or St. Lucie River aboard *The Good Tern,* a 17-foot Parker, fishing for trout, snook, pompano or sheepshead. Bait and tackle supplied. Reservations with Captain Dick Reed at ☎ 561/546-8034; 8164 SE Croft Circle, B-7, Hobe Sound.

Fish for snook, trout, redfish, tarpon aboard *Reel Job,* with FFF Certified Flycasting Instructor USCG Captain Warren Gorall. Fly and light tackle specialist. Florida Keys tarpon trips are also available. ☎ 561/288-3996.

Saltwater fishing on the beach and along the Intracoastal Waterway is available at Hobe Sound National Wildlife Refuge, at the north end of Beach Road on Jupiter Island, ☎ 561/546-2067. Only rods and reels or poles are permitted; state fishing license required.

Fishing Clubs

- **Stuart Sailfish Club,** ☎ 561/286-9373.
- **Stuart Rod & Reel Club,** ☎ 561/878-0475.
- **Fort Pierce Sportfishing Club,** ☎ 561/461-6909.
- **Treasure Coast Bassmasters,** ☎ 561/335-5746.

Freshwater Guides

- **Joe Kubik,** Fort Pierce, ☎ 561/231-3813.

Pleasure Boating & Cruising

Climb aboard *The Pirate's Lady* at Pirates Cove Resort and Marina, 4307 SE Bayview Street, Stuart, ☎ 561/545-3355. Choose from three cruises: Ecological Exploration is a narrated two-hour tour in the Indian River Lagoon to Jupiter Island's Peck's Lake. The Historical Tour is a narrated two-hour exploration, sailing to historic downtown Stuart and back. Their 1½-hour Sunset Cruise travels along Martin County's beautiful waterways at sunset. USCG licensed, the boat carries up to 49 passengers and is also available for private charters and special events. Beer, wine, soda, juices, and snacks are available on all cruises.

Keep a lookout for porpoises, manatees, pelicans, blue herons, and egrets aboard the *Island Princess,* departing from Indian River Plantation Beach Resort, 555 NE Ocean Blvd., Stuart, ☎ 561/225-2100. Choose a Nature Cruise, Indian River/St. Lucie River Cruise, Jupiter Island/Lunch Cruise, or Sunset Cruise.

Full-service cash bar; lunches and dinners available on request. Private charters are available.

Cruise the St. Lucie River aboard *Belle Carol,* a 60-passenger paddlewheel riverboat, 1927 NW Azalea Street, Stuart, ☎ 561/692-0475. Scenic cruises depart Tuesday, Thursday, Friday, Saturday and Sunday, and feature narration on local history and river lore.

Explore the Loxahatchee, Florida's only federal and state designated Wild and Scenic River aboard the *Loxahatchee Queen II,* at Jonathan Dickinson State Park, 16450 SE Federal Highway, Hobe Sound, ☎ 800/746-1466. A park-trained Coast Guard licensed captain shares information on the river's history and wildlife. Alligators, manatees, bald eagles, and raccoons live in this area. The boat docks at a unique historical site, Trapper Nelson's – former home of the river "wild man" who moved here in 1936. Tour Trapper Nelson's log cabins, a Seminole Indian "chickee" (shelter made of palmetto fronds), a small wildlife zoo, and tropical gardens. Call for tour times.

Photograph dolphins and manatees in the St. Lucie River North Fork aboard the schooner *Amanda,* a re-creation of an 1830 Essex pinky, or pink stern. Built in 1965 in Boston, the Amanda participated in the Statue of Liberty Op Sail in 1986 and in the Delaware River's Mosholu Cup three times, winning the prestigious trophy in 1988. Today she cruises the St. Lucie River year-round, offering morning, afternoon and sunset cruises. Tropical fruit, cheese and crackers, vegetables/dips, and drinks are served on board. Sail with USCG licensed Captain Bob Schultz, 414 N. River Drive, Stuart, ☎ 561/692-0517.

Boat Rentals

- **Treasure Coast Boat Club** rents fishing, cruising and jet boats at 54 NW Federal Highway, Stuart, ☎ 561/692-3505. The inboard and outboard boats are 19 feet and larger, and all have Bimini tops.

- Rent a pontoon, bowrider, jet skis, tubes and water skiing equipment at **Jupiter Hills Lighthouse Marina,** 18261 SW Federal Highway, Tequesta, ☎ 561/744-0727.

- **Big Bob's Waverunners,** 3545 NE Indian River Drive, Jensen Beach Causeway, ☎ 561/225-2266 rents waverunners, sailboats, offshore fishing boats, water-ski boats, tubes, boogie boards, and pontoon party boats for half-hour, one-hour, four-hour and eight-hour time frames.

- **Rosemeyer's Boat Rental, Inc.,** 3281 NE Indian River Drive, Jensen Beach, ☎ 561/334-1000 rents 27-foot luxury pontoon boats, 22-foot cruise/sportfish boats, 20 ski boat runabouts, bowriders, and Yamaha waverunners. Water skis and fishing equipment are free with boat rentals. Fishing guides available.

Bait Shops

There are hundreds of bait shops along the Treasure Coast, but we found the folks at **Brackish Jack's Bait & Tackle** especially helpful. Besides bait and tackle, they sell beer, cigarettes, soda, ice, snacks, live shrimp, mullet, and pinfish. Ask for the free pocket-sized Tide Table, which lists times of morning and afternoon high and low tides. The mini-guide also lists legal lengths for various fish, how to gauge their weight, and fish seasons. Very handy. 3805 NE Indian River Drive, Jensen Beach, ☎ 561/225-FISH.

Sailing

Chapman School of Seamanship

Always wanted to immerse yourself in sailing? Contact **Chapman School of Seamanship,** 4343 SE St. Lucie Blvd., Stuart 34997, ☎ 800/225-2841. They offer short courses and tutorials in boat handling, charting, navigation, and electronics for individuals, couples, and small groups.

Founded by the late Glen D. Castle and Charles F. Chapman, editor of Motor Boating & Sailing, and author of the boater's bible, *Chapman Piloting, Seamanship & Small Boat Handling,* the school has been in operation for over 30 years.

The school's main focus is preparing mariners for professional employment in the field, through the Professional Mariner Training course. In 12 intensive weeks students learn navigation rules, charting, coastal/offshore navigation, electronics, seamanship and safety, engines, and a variety of other subjects.

Recreational boaters can take the American Sailing Association Certification Program, or a six-day offshore sailing course, or 12-hour evening courses in powerboat handling and marine electronics. For a complete schedule of courses, call or write Chapman School of Seamanship.

US Sailing Center of Martin County

The **US Sailing Center of Martin County**, 3101 NW Causeway Blvd., PO Box 1417, Jensen Beach, 34958, ☎ 516/334-8085, is a non-profit organization that introduces children and adults to the sport of sailing and racing. They also organize local, regional, national and international sailboat regattas, and facilitate training of Olympic-class sailors.

In the past few years, more than 500 children ages five-18 have learned to sail and race at this center, using donated fleets of Optimists, Lasers, 420s and Flying Scots. The curriculum includes boating safety, seamanship, sportsmanship, navigation and preparation for competitions.

Major regattas have been hosted by the center, including the Vanguard 15 Midwinter Championships, Club 420 Midwinters, Pineapple Cup Regatta, and the Women's Open. The center also serves as a training facility for US Sailing Instructor Certification courses.

Kayaking

Paddling pristine St. Lucie Inlet State Park is pure serenity. Great blue herons, egrets, cormorants and ospreys flap across your bow. Red-clawed crabs scuttle in shallow water onto mangrove roots. Snook, jack, and redfish feed on mullet, as stingrays glide beneath the water's surface. Best of all, there's no traffic, no construction, and no people, except other kayakers.

Bordered on the northern end by the St. Lucie Inlet, and by adjoining federal land to the south, the 928-acre St. Lucie State Park is a barrier island with a maze of twisting and turning mangrove creeks. Accessible only by boat, the park's bays and side passages have names like *Hole in the Wall, Mosquito Ditch,* and *End of the World.* Out in this watery wilderness it truly feels like the end of the world.

If you put in at Cove Road, you can paddle three miles to *End of the World* in a leisurely hour and a half. Hop out on a beautiful deserted beach. Next to the beach boardwalk is a picnic pavilion, toilets, showers, and a solar-powered water desalinization plant.

Cove Kayak Center, 400 NE Ocean, Stuart, ☎ 561/334-0300 makes a day of kayaking simple: they bring kayaks to various launch sites in the preserve and along the St. Lucie River, guide you through the mangroves, point out wildlife, share delightful anecdotes, and at the end of a wonderful day transport the kayaks back to their Center. They also run tours from Sandsprit Park to the Spoil Islands and have offer paddles. Ask for Bernie DeHart or Ron Russell.

☀ Snapshot

Meet Bernie DeHart, Cove Kayak Center, Stuart.

SS: What got you into kayaking, Bernie?

BD: I've lived here a number of years and used to keep my kayak tied to a palm tree along the water. I became addicted to the sport, so I had to start my own business to share this place with other kayakers.

SS: What's special about kayaking here?

BD: We have friendly water: it's warm and only several inches deep, and that opens the sport to anyone. Here in Martin County, the wildlife viewing is spectacular. We have the St. Lucie Preserve and the Hobe Sound National Wildlife Refuge, huge natural areas that are protected. Mangroves are filled with ibis, os-preys, and kingfishers. We may spot an eagle if we're lucky. In the water we often see pufferfish, redfish, hermit crabs walking around in shells, live whelks, sandollars and horseshoe crabs. So much life!

SS: What do you love about kayaking?

BD: How close you get to wildlife! I paddled by a night heron with magnificent colors and I was eight feet away. He just sat there. Manatees feeding on the grass come up under my boat at night. They lift me up and put me down again. They're such gentle slow-moving creatures, and you can get very close to them. This is a very special place, and kayaking is absolutely the best way to see it.

To rent a kayak for your own explorations, visit **Tropical Visions** at their waterfront headquarters in historic downtown Stuart, 600 W 1st Street, ☎ 561/223-2097.

Canoeing

Paddle the Loxahatchee River underneath a canopy of cypress trees as schools of fish dart underneath your canoe. **Jonathan Dickinson State Park** rents canoes by the hour at the park's concession stand, 16450 SW Federal Highway, Hobe Sound, ☎ 800/746-1466.

Scuba Diving

Some people live their dreams. Captain Barry Ross, of **Blue Dolphin Charters,** quit his Chicago corporate job, sold his home, and bought a live-aboard dive boat in Florida. Today he happily guides all levels of divers on shallow reef dives, wreck dives, deep dives, spear fishing, and underwater photo courses. His 42-foot Thomas Kedge Keel Trawler, *Pirate's Gold,* takes out six divers per trip to see coral reefs, big fish and shipwrecks. See the **snapshot** of Captain Ross on the next page.

Departing from Pirates Cove Resort and Marina at 4307 SE Bayview Street in Stuart, as well as other locations, Captain Ross will show you wrecks like the *Rankin, Deep Tug, Amazon, Muliphen, Halsey, Esso Bonaire,* the Cave, and other world-class dive sites for advanced divers. Blue Dolphin Charters also offers private or group recreational and technical instruction, as well as Bahama trips. For reservations, ☎ 561/220-6931.

Reef Research Team

If you're an experienced diver and will be residing in the Treasure Coast area for six months or more, consider this: the **Palm Beach County Reef Research Team** wants YOU. You'll receive six months of specialized training in collecting and recording data for underwater mapping, biological sampling, scientific methodology and population studies.

To become a member of the Reef Research Team you must be a member of the Florida Oceanographic Society and the Reef Research Dive Team. You must also be a certified open water diver, with an Advanced Open Water certification license.

Current projects of the Reef Research Team include: mapping and surveying for future artificial reef sites, research on alternate air sources in conjunction with Diver's Alert Network, production of an informational video on Martin County Artificial Reef Sites, and assisting in the coordination of Florida's annual "coastal reef clean-up."

Sounds like a lot of time underwater for a good cause. If you're interested in joining The Reef Research Team, contact the **Florida Oceanographic Society,** 890 NW Ocean Blvd. Hutchinson Island, ☎ 561/225-0505.

❋ Snapshot

Meet Captain Barry Ross, owner Blue Dolphin Charters, Stuart.

SS: Barry, what kind of dive adventures does your company offer?

BR: This area is known for its abundance of WWII ships and merchant marine vessels, sunk during the war or recently as artificial reef projects. Diving onto a 500-ft. ship once used in the invasion of Guadalcanal is an experience. It's in 70-130 feet of water!

SS: That's a lot deeper than most sport divers attempt.

BR: Well the world of tech diving is for divers that want more excitement, going below the recreational diver limit of 130 feet. These divers want to see ships like the *Muliphen* at 187 feet, 13 miles southeast of Ft. Pierce harbor. That's a full-day dive – two hours to the location, an hour getting ready, 30 minutes of diving, and an hour of decompression.

SS: Why go to these great depths?

BR: You'll see bigger fish, seven to 15 feet long, or even a 60-foot whale shark. Looking at these ship wrecks, physically landing on the deck itself, or cruising along like a submarine is fun. Taking underwater video, photographs or hunting for 30-lb. groupers is my idea of a good dive day.

SS: What kind of training do you provide?

BR: One of the prerequisites for deep-water technical diving is to be an advanced Open Water Diver; we can provide that kind of training. We also enjoy taking divers on the more shallow eight- to 45-foot dives, to see fish or go lobster hunting. Either way, diving is my favorite adventure.

Dive Shops

Here's a partial list of area dive shops:

- **Marine Connection,** 2911 North US1, Ft. Pierce, ☎ 561/465-6460.

- **South East Diving Institute,** 1717 South US1, Ft. Pierce, ☎ 800/456-2188.

- **Deep Six of Fort Pierce,** 2323 South Federal Hwy., Ft. Pierce, ☎ 561/465-4114.

- **Dixie Divers of Ft. Pierce,** 1717 South US1, Ft. Pierce, ☎ 561/461-4488.

- **Blue Planet Dive & Surf,** 1317-B NW St. Lucie West Blvd., Port St. Lucie, ☎ 561/871-9122.

- **Dixie Divers of Stuart,** 1839 S. Federal Hwy., Stuart, ☎ 800/456-2088.

- **Deep Divers Unlimited,** 6083 SE Federal Hwy., Stuart, ☎ 561/286-0078.

- **Adventure Scuba,** 150 North US1, Tequesta, ☎ 561/746-1555.

In the Air

 If your idea of fun is rolling upside down in a Zlin 2421 aerobatic plane at 150 mph, then this will be your kind of adventure. Michael Towner, president of **Thrill of a Lifetime Flights,** offers custom-tailored flights you'll never forget. Instructor Andre Gutsch specializes in acrobatic maneuvers with names like hammerhead, roll, loop and inverted flight. "People who love rollercoasters love these rides," he says. Gutsch says most people don't get air sick, but he'll give you a bag just in case. He'll also give you a parachute... just in case. (Only kidding.) If you're seeking extreme excitement, give them a call. Located at the Stuart Airport, **Flight Training International,** 2501 SW Aviation Way, Suite F, Stuart, ☎ 561/221-0838.

Few activities are as relaxing as ballooning, so why not try it? Captain Mark Chapdelain will pilot you in his colorful balloon over Florida's picturesque coastline. Enjoy champagne after the flight, and take home a complimentary T-shirt and certificate of flight. Don't forget your camera. **Balloons Over Florida,** 4124 NE Skyline Drive, Jensen Beach; ☎ 561/334-9393, 800/887-2965.

❋ Snapshot

Meet Mark Chapdelain, President, Balloons Over Florida, Stuart.

SS: For someone who's never tried it, what is ballooning like?

MC: It's a marvelous feeling. A monstrous bag of air grows from the ground, becoming 55 feet wide and seven stories tall. You won't even know we've lifted off, it's so smooth. We talk to people on the ground as we fly. It's so calm you can lay a handkerchief on the balloon basket and it won't blow away.

SS: What do you see from the air?

MC: Wild boar, deer, alligators, occasionally manatees if we're flying over the Intracoastal or the north and south forks of the St. Lucie River. We stay at 50 feet or less, so people can feel like they can touch the ground or water, flying right through the treetops. We saw a raccoon staring up into the balloon. Too bad nobody had a camera!

SS: What got you into ballooning?

MC: I bought a balloon and got training in the sport. Then people started asking how they could buy a ride, so I got a commercial pilot's license and found out how beautiful this area is for ballooning. We charge $150 per person for a one-hour ride. The whole event takes three hours, with champagne at the end and a certificate of first flight and a T-shirt.

SS: What's been the most unexpected event during a flight?

MC: Well a gentleman asked his girlfriend to marry him, which shocked her. I think she said yes, fearing he might throw her out of the basket if she refused. We were all surprised, but they were both happy at the end.

SS: What about people who are afraid of heights?

MC: In 550 flights, no one has ever wanted to come back down!

Other Adventures

Baseball

Catch the **New York Mets** during March Spring Training at Thomas J. White Stadium, 525 NW Peacock Blvd., Port St. Lucie, ☎ 561/871-2115.

Jai-Alai

According to the *Guiness Book of World Records,* jai-alai is the fastest sport in the world. See the speeding pelota (ball) at **Ft. Pierce Jai-Alai,** Kings Highway and I-95, Ft. Pierce, ☎ 800/ Jai-Alai. If you're new to the sport, a program explains the game, introduces the players, and outlines possible bets. Comfortable theater-style seating is right on top of the action and dining is available at the Courtside Club. For horse and dog racing enthusiasts, closed-circuit satellite broadcasts are presented during the year for wagering.

▪ Sightseeing

Tour one of the premier ocean research facilities at **Harbor Branch Oceanographic Institution,** 5600 Old Dixie Highway, Ft. Pierce, ☎ 561/465-2400. This non-profit organization conducts research and education in marine sciences and ocean engineering. Models of submersible craft are on display, as are aquariums with indigenous sea creatures. Research vessels, aquaculture facilities, and labs are also open to visitors. Courses, special activities, films, and a lecture series are offered. The Visitor Center has touch-screen kiosks and a film highlighting the research programs. Open Monday-Saturday 10 am-4 pm. Tours are led at 10 am, noon, and 2 pm. Admission.

Find out why the town of Stuart became "Sailfish Capital of the World" and why pineapples were Stuart's major industry in the 1880's. The Stuart area branch of the American Association of University Women (AAUW) has created an excellent self-guided walking tour of **Historic Stuart** that includes an 1890 schoolhouse, a 1926 hotel, original homes, and the town's first general store. Victorian-style lanterns, a restored post office arcade, and an old fashioned gazebo are part of the newly revived downtown district. Write the AAUW for their free informative brochure at PO Box 95-3292, Stuart 34995, or call ☎ 561/286-2848.

Museums & Culture

 St. Lucie County Historical Museum, 414 Seaway Drive, Fort Pierce, ☎ 561/462-1795 has exhibits on local history, Spanish Treasure ships, Seminole Indian camps, a restored Florida home, and a 1919 fire engine.

Stuart Heritage Museum, 161 SW Flagler Avenue, Stuart, ☎ 561/220-4600 displays artifacts on the history of Martin County, focusing on Stuart's earliest families. Open for tours on Saturdays 10 am-4 pm; other times by special appointment. Free.

If you enjoy vintage autos, don't miss **The Elliott Museum,** 825 NE Ocean Blvd., Hutchinson Island, ☎ 561/225-1961. Inventor Sterling Elliott's car collection documents the auto's evolution, and features treasures like a 1909 Hupmobile, a 1902 Stanley Steamer, a 1922 Rolls Royce Silver Ghost, and a 1932 Austin. Other exhibits include a hand-carved circus, an 1800s country store, and turn-of-the-century wedding gowns. Open 11 am-4 pm daily. Admission.

About two miles south of the Elliott Museum on Hutchinson Island is **Gilbert's Bar House of Refuge,** a lifesaving station for shipwrecked sailors built in 1875. The oldest standing structure in Martin County, the National Historic Landmark museum is the last remaining US Coast Guard Lifesaving Station on Florida's east coast. Some of the marine artifacts and maritime exhibits date back to the 16th century. Open daily, 10 am-4 pm. Admission. 301 SE MacArthur Blvd., Hutchinson Island, Stuart, ☎ 561/225-1875. Note: The House of Refuge is scheduled to close for renovations, but as of press time no date had been set. Call to make sure they are open before planning a visit.

Birthplace of the US Navy Frogmen, the **UDT Seal Museum** is the only museum in the world dedicated solely to Underwater Demolition Teams and their successors, Sea Air Land commandos of the US Navy. Hours of operation vary, so call first. 3300 North A1A, North Hutchinson Island, Fort Pierce, ☎ 561/462-3597.

Theater & Performing Arts

- **The Barn Theatre,** 2400 SE Ocean Blvd, Stuart, ☎ 561/287-4884.

- **Case and Company Center for the Arts,** 333 Tressler Drive, Suite E, Stuart, ☎ 561/287-1194.

- **Indian River Community College Fine Arts Series,** 3209 Virginia Ave, Ft. Pierce, ☎ 561/878-1388.

- **Lyric Theatre,** Flagler Avenue, Stuart, ☎ 561/220-1942.

- **St. Lucie Community Theatre's Readers' Theatre,** 629 Weatherbee Road, Ft. Pierce, ☎ 561/465-0366.

- **St. Lucie County Civic Center,** 25th & Virginia Ave, Ft. Pierce, ☎ 561/468-1526.

- **Treasure Coast Concert Association.** 3065 Pruitt Road, Port St. Lucie, ☎ 561/335-2310.

- **Treasure Coast Opera Society,** St. Lucie County Civic Center, 1309 Indiana Avenue, Ft. Pierce, ☎ 561/465-6204.

▪ Festivals & Events

January

Book Mania, Downtown Stuart, ☎ 561/221-1403.

Annual "On the Green" Art Festival, Fort Pierce, ☎ 561/468-3253.

Stuart Boat Show, Northside Marina, Stuart, ☎ 561/283-3999.

February

St. Lucie County Annual Home Show, Fort Pierce, ☎ 561/465-7560.

Chocolate Festival, Stuart, ☎ 561/223-8822.

Martin County Fair, Stuart, ☎ 561/220-FAIR.

March

ArtsFest, Stuart, ☎ 561/287-6676.

St. Patrick's Day Celebration, Stuart, ☎ 561/283-0541.

April

A Taste of Martin County, various locations, ☎ 561/287-1088.

Secret Gardens Tour, various locations, Stuart, ☎ 561/287-1088.

May

Memorial Day Celebration, Port St. Lucie, ☎ 561/878-2277.

Sailfish Powerboat Races, Jensen Beach Causeway, ☎ 561/287-1088.

June

Juried Art Show, Stuart, ☎ 561/287-6676.

July

Red, White, and Boom Celebration, Fort Pierce, ☎ 561/462-1522.

Fireworks Displays, Port St. Lucie, ☎ 561/287-1088; Stuart, ☎ 561/286-2848.

August

Dancin' in the Streets, Stuart, ☎ 561/286-2848.

Annual YMCA/Benihana Celebrity Chef Cookoff, Sewall's Point, ☎ 561/284-4444.

September

Cattleman's Dance, Fort Pierce, ☎ 561/462-1530.

October

Harvest Moon Stroll, Heathcote Botanical Gardens, Fort Pierce, ☎ 561/464-4672.

Annual Pumpkin Decorating Festival, Port St. Lucie, ☎ 561/878-2277.

Rainbow Festival, Port St. Lucie, ☎ 561/595-9999.

November

River Dayz Festival, Stuart, ☎ 561/221-0346.

Annual Pineapple Festival, Jensen Beach, ☎ 561/334-3444.

Annual Scottish Festival, Fort Pierce, ☎ 561/461-7607.

Annual Martin County Boat and Fishing Show, Martin County Fairgrounds, ☎ 561/287-1088.

December

Christmas Boat Parade, Stuart, ☎ 561/283-3999.

Christmas Parades, downtown Stuart, Hobe Sound, Port St. Lucie, Fort Pierce, ☎ 561/287-1088.

Christmas Caroling, Elliott Museum, Hutchinson Island, ☎ 561/225-1961.

■ Where to Stay

☆ **Pirates Cove Resort and Marina,** 4307 SE Bayview Street, Stuart, 34997, ☎ 800/332-1414, is boating and fishing heaven. Imagine rolling out of bed, eating a sumptuous breakfast at Pirates Loft Restaurant, and leaving the dock for a day of deep-sea fishing, all before dawn. The resort's private marina is equipped with 43 slips for boats up to 80 feet. Guests can arrive by water via the Intracoastal Waterway, which connects to the ocean 1½ miles away. Docking facilities include cable TV hook-ups, telephone service, water, electricity, laundry, showers, fuel, and a full-service bait, tackle and gift shop. Or arrive by car, settle into one of the 50 spacious comfortable rooms, and charter a sportfishing boat at the marina.

General Manager Gary Guertin is a congenial host who greets his guests on a first-name basis. In any given hour Gary is trading fish stories, recommending the best local beach, suggesting a popular museum exhibit, and asking how you enjoyed last night's fresh grilled wahoo. It's a friendly, low-key place.

If you're not into fishing, you'll still enjoy the heated fresh water pool, touring by bike or trolley, or just watching comical pelicans fighting over the fish snacks brought back by deep-sea charters. $$-$$$

☆ **Holiday Inn Oceanside Jensen Beach,** 3793 NE Ocean Boulevard, Jensen Beach, 34957, ☎ 561/225-3000 (in Florida,

☎ 800/992-4747), is on one of the prettiest beaches in the area. Stroll along the ocean for miles, watching pelicans and sandpipers; or toss in a line from shore and catch your own bluefish. The 178 guest rooms have private balconies; suites have wet bars, refrigerators, and coffee makers. Amenities include a heated oceanfront pool, complimentary tennis for day/night play (and a resident tennis pro for lessons), a health/fitness center, massage, and a table tennis/video game room. Currents Café Oceanfront Restaurant is sunny and pleasant with ocean views, serving a variety of American dishes. The lounge has a daily happy hour and live entertainment Wednesday-Saturday. The hotel is near area attractions, golf courses, sports, cruise boats, and theater. $-$$

Jensen Beach

Courtyard Marriott Hutchinson Island, 10978 S. Ocean Drive, Jensen Beach, ☎ 561/229-1000, features rooms with Atlantic Ocean or Intracoastal Waterway views. The hotel is on the beach, with a heated pool and exercise facility. Golf and tennis are nearby, golf packages are available. Free coffee and HBO/Disney Channel. A breakfast buffet is served in the roof top dining room. $

Island Beach Resort, 9800 S. Ocean Drive, Hutchinson Island, Jensen Beach, ☎ 800/642-5630, has spacious one- and two-bedroom apartments, with full ocean views, kitchens and balconies. The hotel has a heated pool, BBQ area, tiki bar. On site is a restaurant, lounge and nightly entertainment. $

Stuart

The Indian River Plantation Marriott, 555 NE Ocean Blvd., Stuart, ☎ 561/225-3700, reservations 800-775-5936, offers a variety of hotel rooms, suites and villas on 200 tropical acres. Nested between the Atlantic Ocean and the Intracoastal Waterway, the hotel has three golf courses, ocean beaches, a tennis club, full-service marina, four swimming pools, a full-time activities department, and seven restaurants and lounges. $$$

Camping

Jonathan Dickinson State Park, 16450 SE Federal Highway, Hobe Sound, ☎ 561/546-2771, has the Pine Grove camping area with 90 campsites. Amenities include restrooms, phones, an outdoor amphitheater, and car parking. The park's River Camp area is along the Loxahatchee River, close to canoe rentals, fishing, nature walks, picnic area, and private cabins. The concession sells snacks, groceries and souvenirs. Boat tours available.

Huckleberry Finn RV Resort, 7601 SW Lost River Road, Stuart, ☎ 561/220-0909, is a new campsite, convenient to the ocean, beaches, state parks, golf, boating, fishing, Cracker Barrel and McDonald's restaurants. Amenities include boat ramp, canoe and boat rentals, swimming pool.

Nettles Island, 9801 S. Ocean Drive, Jensen Beach, ☎ 561/229-1300, is an RV camping resort on an island, with ocean access. Amenities include a boat ramp, grocery store, laundry, rec hall, fishing, mini-golf, swimming pool, and tennis courts.

Road Runner Travel Resort, 5500 St. Lucie Blvd., Ft. Pierce, ☎ 800/833-7108, has 450 full hookups in a 38-acre Florida hammock. Amenities include tennis courts, picnic area, convenience store, and a seasonal restaurant. Four miles from the ocean, beaches and fishing.

■ Where to Eat

☆ **Luna,** 49 Flagler Avenue, Stuart, ☎ 561/288-0550, is a casual Italian restaurant in historic downtown Stuart. After a leisurely stroll through the area's antique shops, galleries, bookstores, and gift shops, relax over delicious homemade pizza baked in a stone hearth oven. A wide variety of veal dishes are served, as well as chicken, pastas, and salads. Friendly service. Lunch and dinner seven days. $

☆ **Pirates Loft Restaurant,** Pirates Cove Resort and Marina, 4307 SE Bayview Street, Port Salerno, Stuart, ☎ 561/287-2500, has two separate dining rooms with pleasant marina views. Begin with an appetizer of jumbo shrimp, oysters, or crabcakes, but save room for the succulent fresh fish – mako shark, pompano, tuna, wahoo, dolphin or grouper. Chicken, baby back ribs, and tender prime rib are also on the menu. If you can't make it for lunch or dinner, drop by at sunset for cocktails at the outdoor bar. Live entertainment and dancing in the evenings. A comfortable fun spot with the biggest fish tales in town. Lunch and dinner seven days. $$

American

Flagler Grill, 47 SW Flagler Avenue in downtown Stuart, ☎ 561/221-9517, features skillfully prepared New American cuisine and a great wine list. The lively upscale ambiance is part of Stuart's renovated historic downtown area. $$

Seafood

Conchy Joe's Seafood Restaurant and Bar, 3945 NE Indian River Drive, Jensen Beach, ☎ 561/334-1130, is a rambling 1930's Florida style roadhouse, adorned with gator hides and boars' heads. They specialize in Florida and Bahamian seafood dishes, as well as shrimp, crabs and lobster. Legendary rum punches. Reggae/calypso bands perform Wednesday-Sunday evenings. Lunch and dinner seven days. $

Fish Tales, 5042 SE Federal Highway, Stuart, ☎ 561/288-5011, features fresh fish caught daily, and entrées like shrimp Francaise, grouper parmesan, and a trio of stuffed grouper, dolphin, and salmon. They serve filet mignon and roasted lamb chops as well. Dinners only, from 5 pm. $-$$

French

The French Garden, 2875 East Ocean Blvd., Stuart, ☎ 561/223-0015, showcases the talents of chef/owner Gilles Cassiani who was trained in Nice. Provence-style cuisine includes grilled lamb chops, duck breast, and Grand Marnier soufflé with raspberry sauce. Lunch Tuesday-Friday, noon-2 pm; dinner Mon-Sat from 5:30 pm. $$

British

The **Jolly Sailor Pub,** 1 SW Osceola Street, Stuart, ☎ 561/221-1111, is owned by Bob Davis, who spent 27 years in the British merchant Navy, including 10 years aboard the *QE II.* In historic downtown Stuart, the nautical decor is fun, with lots of teak and ship models. Try the fish & chips, shepherd's pie, whole Dover sole, or bangers & mash. Cold beer on tap. Lunch and dinner seven days. $

Tourism Information

Hobe Sound Chamber of Commerce, 8779 E. Bridge Rd, PO Box 1507, Hobe Sound, FL 33475, ☎ 561/546-4724.

The Stuart/Martin County Chamber of Commerce, 1650 South Kanner Highway, Stuart, FL 34994. ☎ 561/287-1088.

Jensen Beach Chamber of Commerce, 1910 NW Jensen Beach Blvd., Jensen Beach, FL 34957. ☎ 561/334-3444.

St. Lucie County Tourist Development Council, 2300 Virginia Avenue, Fort Pierce, FL 34982. ☎ 800/344-TGIF.

Online Info: **www.stuartfla.com/** and **www.flmainstreet. com/jensenbeach/** are two town sites on the Web.

🌴 🌴 🌴

🌴 Vero Beach & Sebastian

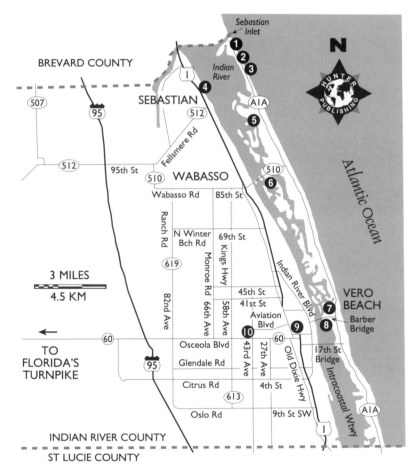

1. Sebastian Inlet State Recreation Area
2. McLarty Treasure Museum
3. McLarty Visitors Center & Park
4. Mel Fisher's Treasure Museum
5. Windsor Polo & Equestrian Center
6. Environmental Learning Center
7. Vero Beach Municipal Marina
8. Center for the Arts
9. Heritage Center/Citrus Museum
10. Dodgertown

Vero Beach & Sebastian

Continuing north on The Treasure Coast are more adventures in Sebastian and Vero Beach, including surfing, scuba diving, boating, fishing, polo matches, birding, and dolphin watching.

■ Adventures

On Foot

Hiking/Birding

Hike the ⅝-mile nature trail at **Sebastian Inlet State Recreation Area,** 9700 South Highway A1A, Melbourne, ☎ 561/984-4852. The trail meanders through a palm oak hammock and mangrove forest. This park has a cross section of biological habitats, including open water, beach, dune, coastal strand, maritime hammock, and mangrove swamp, which attracts a variety of birds. You'll see northern gannet, brown pelican, double-crested cormorant, anhinga, great blue heron, great egret, white ibis, wood stork, mottled duck, osprey, willet and royal tern. There are also two Folkssport Association 10K trails.

Golf

- **Sebastian Municipal Golf Course,** 101 East Airport Drive, Sebastian, ☎ 561/589-6800. 18 holes, par 72.

- **Sandridge Golf Club,** King's Highway, a few miles south of Sebastian, ☎ 561/770-5000. Two 18-hole, par 72 courses, one championship level.

- **Aquarina Country Club,** State Road A1A, Sebastian, ☎ 561/728-0600. 18 holes; par 62.

- **The Habitat at Valkaria,** 3591 Fairgreen St, Valkaria, across the Sebastian River, ☎ 561/952-4588. 18 holes.

- **Whisper Lakes,** 2550 53rd St, Vero Beach, ☎ 561/567-3321. 18 holes; par 54.

- **Summit View Golf Club,** west of US1 in Grant, ☎ 561/951-2009. 18 holes; par 58.

Miniature Golf

- **Safari Golf N' Games,** Oslo Road, Vero Beach, ☎ 561/562-6492. 36 holes with waterfalls and jungles.

Tennis

- **Grand Harbor Tennis Club,** 1001 Harbor Drive, Vero Beach, ☎ 561/778-9100. Eight courts, four are lighted.

- **The Jungle Club Sports Complex,** 1060 Sixth Avenue, Vero Beach, ☎ 561/567-1400. Two lighted tennis courts.

- **Meadowood Golf and Tennis Club,** 9425 Meadowood Drive, Fort Pierce, ☎ 561/466-4116. Five courts, three are lighted.

- **Riomar Bay Yacht Club,** 2345 State Road A1A, Vero Beach, ☎ 561/231-4686. Seven courts, two lighted.

- **Riverside Park Tennis and Racquetball Complex,** Riverside Park, Vero Beach, ☎ 561/231-4787. 10 courts, six lighted.

- **Sea Oaks Tennis Club,** 1480 Winding Oaks Circle, Vero Beach, ☎ 561/231-3102. 16 courts, seven lighted.

- **West Side Racquet Club,** 4291 Fifth Place SW, Vero Beach, ☎ 561/562-7660. Eight courts, four lighted.

On Water

Surfing

The 578-acre **Sebastian Inlet State Recreation Area,** 9700 South A1A, Melbourne, ☎ 561/984-4852, is known throughout Florida for excellent surfing. Part of a barrier island divided by a man-made inlet, the park stretches from the Atlantic Ocean to the Indian River. Three miles of beach attracts swimmers and surfers who compete in several national surfing tournaments held here yearly. The best season for surfing is September-May, when the waves swell high from low-pressure systems and cold fronts. In the winter you'll definitely want a wetsuit! A variety of surfboards are available at local shops, some of which offer surfboard and bodyboard rentals. A few of them are listed below.

- **Deep Six Watersports,** 416 Miracle Mile Way, Vero Beach, ☎ 561/951-1804.

- **The Greenroom Surf Shop,** 8789 US1, Wabasso, ☎ 561/388-5908.

- **Inner Rhythm Surf and Sport,** 2001 14th Avenue, Vero Beach, ☎ 561/778-9038.

- **Eastern Surfing Association,** Treasure Coast District, 1571 Third Avenue, Vero Beach, 32960.

- If you want to take surfing lessons with a local pro, call Lou Maresca at **Surf School,** ☎ 561/231-1044.

Fishing

The jetties, surf, and shoreline at **Sebastian Inlet State Recreation Area,** 9700 South A1A, Melbourne, ☎ 561/984-4852, are good spots for snook, redfish, tarpon, black drum and Spanish mackerel fishing. The recreation area's bait shop provides rods, reels and live/frozen bait.

Indian River County ocean beaches are excellent for fishing. Light tackle from six-10 lbs. used in summer will attract snooks, jacks, ladyfish, moonfish, sheepshead, whiting and small barracuda. In the fall, migrations bring baitfish close to the beaches and sturdy rods and big plugs or natural bait is needed. Expect to catch large redfish, tarpon, king mackerel, big snook, sharks and bluefish.

The **Sebastian River** is home to tarpon, snook, jacks, ladyfish, gars, largemouth bass and black drum. Boat launch facilities are at Sand Point Marina, just off US1, and Dale Wimbrow Park off Roseland Road.

Sign up for fly tying and casting lessons, or pick up a new rod and reel, at **The Back Country Fly Shop,** 2855 Ocean Drive, Vero Beach, ☎ 561/231-9894.

✳ Snapshot

Meet Terry O'Toole, Park Ranger, Sebastian Inlet State Park, Sebastian.

SS: Why is this park special for surfing?

TT: We have some of the nicest waves on the east coast of Florida, with monster holes that create waves up to eight feet high, which surfers love. September/October is when the waves are biggest. We have surfing contests year-round; the Association of Surfing Professionals and the National Scholastic Surfing Association host contests here.

SS: What's adventurous about surfing?

TT: Being out in the water! You gotta get wet to enjoy it. It can be cold in January and February, around 63°, so wear a wetsuit. Besides wild and crazy surfers, we have dolphins and birds feeding on baitfish. Sometimes snook, redfish and tarpon come shooting through the waves: you might want to get out of the water when they come through.

SS: Do people surf here at night?

TT: Nobody surfs at night if they have any common sense. You could get in more trouble than it's worth.

SS: Any advice for first-time surfers, Terry?

TT: Get out there and have fun. Wax your board and go for a *Surfin' Safari,* just like the Beach Boys said.

Boating

Vero Beach Municipal Marina, on the east side of the Indian River north of the Barber Bridge, ☎ 561/231-2819, is a busy boating center. More than 3,000 boats dock here every year, some for charter, others are private. The marina is a good lodging facility for boaters, and a clearinghouse for local boating and marine information.

Boaters can head for the Atlantic Ocean, into the Indian River, or Sebastian River. Powerboats, sailboats, airboats, kayaks and canoes are available for rent. The Intracoastal Waterway is the main thoroughfare for boats on the Indian River, with Sebastian and Fort Pierce inlets providing ocean access.

Boat Rentals:

- **Bally Hoo Boat Rentals,** 12 Royal Palm Blvd, Vero Beach, ☎ 561/562-7924. Fishing and pontoon rentals from 12-28 feet.

- **Honest John's Fish Camp and Boat Rentals,** 750 Mullet Creek Rd., Melbourne Beach, ☎ 561/727-2923.

- **Indian River Marine Sales and Rentals,** 3435 Aviation Blvd., Vero Beach, ☎ 561/569-5757. Canoes, kayaks, instruction, tours.

- **Treasure Coast Pontoon Rentals,** 118 SE 11th Street, Vero Beach, ☎ 561/567-0571.

- **Captain Hiram's Watercraft Rentals,** 1606 Indian River Drive, Sebastian, ☎ 561/589-5560. Waverunners, jet boats, pontoon boats.

- **Sebastian Water Sports, Inc.,** 412 Indian River Drive, Sebastian, ☎ 561/388-5688.

Pleasure Cruising

The Lady Dolphin

Swimming in groups of two and four, grey Atlantic bottlenose dolphins undulate gracefully alongside our boat. Surfacing to breathe, they seem to smile at the wall of cameras pointed their way. "There!" screams one passenger, leaping from her seat. "Quick Don, get the camera!" She's so excited, I'm worried she might fall overboard. If you've only seen dolphins at aquariums or marine parks, this is a delightful way to meet them in the wild. Climb aboard the *Lady Dolphin,* a paddlewheel sightseeing boat for a leisurely two-hour dolphin-watching cruise. No matter how many episodes of Flipper you've seen, it's a still a big thrill when wild dolphins swim by.

Another interesting aspect of the cruise is along Pelican Island National Wildlife Refuge, a protected island home to white and brown pelicans, egrets, herons, and cormorants. Listed on the National Register of Historic Places and a National Historic Landmark, the island was established by Teddy Roosevelt in 1903 as America's first wildlife refuge.

"We couldn't have picked a better nature tour, could we?" a New York matron asks her daughter, who is too busy snapping dolphin and bird photos to answer.

The *Lady Dolphin,* 1200 Indian River Drive, Sebastian, ☎ 561/589-4422; e-mail LadyDolphin@indian-river.fl.us; Web site www.ladydolphin.com. Cruises leave mornings and afternoons, Wednesday, Friday, Saturday, and Sunday.

Other Cruises

The *Vero Princess* runs year-round from the north side of the Barber Bridge in Vero Beach, ☎ 561/231-7374. Daily cruise offerings include a dolphin cruise from 10:30 am-12:30 pm; a manatee cruise from 1:30 pm-3:30 pm; and a sunset cruise from 4 pm-dusk. Shuttle service is available from participating beach resorts for all three cruises.

River Queen cruises the shallow waters of the Indian River Lagoon and Sebastian River daily year round. They offer a 10 am Manatee or Dolphin Watch in the Indian River Lagoon; a 1 pm Sebastian River Jungle Cruise; and a 4:30 pm Pelican Island Refuge Cruise. There are also scheduled Moonlight Cruises and private charters available. 1606 Indian River Drive, Sebastian, ☎ 561/589-6161.

Kayaking

Steve Cox, owner of **Adventure Kayaking Tours,** 3435 Aviation Blvd., Vero Beach, ☎ 800/554-1938, offers weekly kayak classes. In three hours, you'll learn basic skills and boat handling in a beautiful river or lake setting. If you're already a kayaker or canoeist, Steve leads different kayak adventures: searching for manatees on the North Fork of the Sebastian River; observing bird life around Pelican Island National Wildlife Refuge; paddling the shoreline and marshes of Blue Cypress Lake; or touring and picnicking at Trapper Nelson's Cabin in Jonathan Dickinson State Park.

To rent a kayak or canoe for your own adventures, check out **Indian River Marine Sales,** 3435 Aviation Boulevard, Vero Beach, ☎ 800/881-7403.

Diving

Vero Beach has excellent **beach diving,** especially in summer when water temperatures are in the high 70s and visibility reaches 50 feet. From Sebastian Inlet south to Fort Pierce, the reef begins near the beach and reaches out 200 feet offshore. Look for *Boiler Wreck,* a 200-foot steel ship that sank April 30, 1894. You can see a section of the ship protruding from the water's surface, as she is only 15-20 feet down. The wreck is off the end of State Road 60 East, 150 yards east of the Ocean Grill Restaurant.

One mile south of the Sebastian Inlet Bridge is *El Capitana,* one of the 10 treasure galleons that were shipwrecked onto the reefs in 1715. Hundred of ballast stones and several cannons are found on this reef, which starts 20 feet offshore.

Area beaches that permit diving include Wabasso Beach, Indian River Shores, Tracking Station, Jaycee and Conn Way Beaches, and Humiston Beach.

Unless you are an experienced scuba diver, it's best to go out with a PADI or NAUI divemaster who knows the area. Scuba with area dive shops, such as **Dixie Divers,** 1833 US1, Vero Beach, ☎ 561/770-1188. They offer a three-day certification course, guided scuba and snorkel trips, and a full line of dive gear for rent.

In the Air

Banners say it all: "A Gravity Powered Adventure." "We'll change your altitude, at Florida's most beautiful Drop Zone." At **Skydive Sebastian,** 40 W. Airport Drive, Sebastian, ☎ 800/399-JUMP, novice skydivers learn freefall and canopy control skills through a seven-level program. If you're short on time, sign up for tandem skydive. After a half-hour of instruction, you and your instructor freefall together, starting two miles above Sebastian.

You'll receive instruction in parachute control, steering, and landing, all of which will come in very handy after you exit the aircraft. For an extra charge, skydive instructors will videotape your jump. Reservations required; open seven days, 8 am-sunset.

Other Adventures

Pack a picnic and spend Sunday afternoon at **Windsor Polo & Equestrian Center,** eight miles north of Vero Beach on Route A1A, ☎ 561/589-9800. Local residents compete with out of town teams in a variety of events: the Devon Cup, American Red Cross Polo Challenge Cup, and Vero Beach Rotary Challenge Cup, to name a few. Matches are open to the public and begin at 2 pm. Bleacher seating is available, as are delicious barbecued chicken and beef sandwiches. Admission.

In March, catch the **LA Dodgers** in spring baseball training at Holman Stadium, Dodgertown, 4101 26th Street, Vero Beach. Call ☎ 561/569-6858 for tickets and information.

■ Sightseeing

Museums & Culture

Visit the **Indian River Citrus Museum and Heritage Center**, 2140 14th Avenue (corner of 14th Avenue and 21st Street) in downtown Vero Beach, to learn about the pioneers who established one of the most successful citrus regions in the world. The gift shop sells cookbooks and orange blossom perfume. ☎ 561/770-2263. Open Tuesday-Friday, 10 am-4 pm.

The **McLarty Treasure Museum,** Sebastian Inlet State Recreation Area, 9700 South A1A in Melbourne, exhibits treasure from a 1715 Spanish shipwreck, and has exhibits on the Ais Indians, earliest inhabitants of this area. There's a continuous showing of *Treasure: What Dreams Are Made Of,* a film on contemporary treasure salvaging. Open daily 10 am-4:30 pm. ☎ 561/589-2147. Admission.

There's even more booty at **Mel Fisher's Treasure Museum,** 1322 US1 in Sebastian. Browse through treasure, artifacts and jewelry from the Spanish *Atocha,* the *Santa Margarita,* and the *Henrietta Mare.* Museum staff members are still uncovering treasure from the 1715 Plate Fleet found near Sebastian. Open Monday-Saturday, 10 am-5 pm; Sundays, noon-5 pm. Admission. ☎ 561/589-9875.

The **Environmental Learning Center**, 255 Live Oak Drive, Wabasso Island, Vero Beach, is a hands-on, 51-acre center where kids learn about wetlands, mangroves, butterflies, and native gardens. ☎ 561/589-5050.

Find out who brought the first oranges to Florida, and which state produces more grapefruit than the rest of the world combined, at **Hale Indian River Groves**, Wabasso, ☎ 800/289-4253. Tour Steve and Polly Hale's citrus groves, then shop their fruitstand to ship home orchard fresh oranges and grapefruit. Ask for their orange dessert pie recipe. Free glasses of cold orange and grapefruit juice are refreshing. Headquarters and packing house are at 9250 US1 in Wabasso; other locations are at 580 S. US1 and 615 Beachland Boulevard, both in Vero Beach.

One of the largest arts facilities on Florida's Treasure Coast is **Center for the Arts**, 3001 Riverside Park Drive, Vero Beach, ☎ 561/231-0707. From landscapes to portraits, pre-Columbian pottery to post modern sculpture, the center hosts a wide variety of year round exhibitions. There are classes, concerts, seminars, artist workshops, a film series, gift shop, and the Ecclestone Library. The Museum is open daily from 10 am-4:30 pm; Tuesday evenings they stay open until 8 pm. The Center is closed on Mondays during the summer.

■ Where to Stay

☆ **Disney's Vero Beach Resort**. This luxurious oceanfront property, 9250 Island Terrace, Vero Beach 32963, ☎ 800/359-8000, is a good choice for families traveling with young children. The hotel offers the "2DC-Disney Discovery Club," a program for kids from ages three-14, where they tour the Indian River Lagoon by canoe, visit a working cattle ranch, or retrace footsteps of early Florida explorers. The resort is spacious and light, designed to look like a turn-of-the-century grand hotel, with rocking chairs and back porches. The 115 rooms are colorfully decorated, and feature balconies, coffee makers, and refrigerators. Adjacent to the main inn are 60 vacation villas with kitchens. Resort amenities include a nine-hole miniature golf course, croquet lawns, swimming pool with slide, tennis and basketball, a general store and two restaurants. The wide hotel beach invites strolling. **$$**

Sleep on the ocean at **Palm Court Resort Hotel** (formerly Days Hotel Vero Beach Resort), 3244 Ocean Drive, Vero Beach, ☎ 800/245-3297. The hotel has 109 guest rooms, some nonsmoking, all with cable TV and in-room movies. There's a heated outdoor swimming pool, windsurfing, catamaran, and jet ski rentals nearby. The Palm Court French restaurant serves breakfast, lunch and dinner. The hotel is within walking distance to Vero Beach boutiques and galleries. **$$**

The Driftwood Resort, 3150 Ocean Drive, Vero Beach, ☎ 561/231-0550, is an oceanfront resort built from ocean-washed timbers set among tropical landscaping. Villas are one- or two-bedroom kitchenettes, with air conditioning and TV. Hotel amenities include pools, Jacuzzis, grills, poolside dining at Waldo's Open Air Deck, or indoors at The Driftwood Inn. A National Registry of Historic Places resort. **$-$$**

Captain Hiram's Islander Resort, 3101 Ocean Drive, Vero Beach, ☎ 800/952-5886, offers 16 guestrooms close to Vero Beach. Rooms have refrigerators, cable TV and Caribbean decor. Amenities includes an outdoor pool, a library, chess/backgammon sets, and bicycles. **$**

Here's a budget motel 10 minutes from Dodgertown spring training games: **Aquarius Oceanfront Resort,** 1526 Ocean Drive, Vero Beach, ☎ 561/231-5218 has oceanfront rooms with double beds, balconies and kitchenettes. The motel has a pool, picnic tables, grill and shuffleboard. Walking distance to restaurants. **$**

The Captain's Quarters, 1606 Indian River Drive, Sebastian, ☎ 561/589-4345, features rooms on the scenic Indian River. Private balconies, cable TV, refrigerators. The hotel is adjacent to Captain Hiram's restaurant/bar/marina. Convenient for fishing, river cruises, boat/jet ski rentals. **$**

Camping

Indian River County has 55 spoil islands ideal for **primitive camping.** There's no water or electricity, and the islands are accessible only by private boat. Write or call for the Dept. of Environmental Protection brochure, *Spoil Islands of the Indian River Lagoon, Indian River County,* at 1000 Buffer Preserve Drive, Fellsmere, 32961, ☎ 561/953-5004.

Long Point Park, north of Sebastian Inlet off State Road A1A, ☎ 561/952-4532, offers 170 campsites, some primitive, others with water, electricity and sewers. Amenities include restrooms, showers, laundry, boat launch and a pool.

Middleton's Fish Camp, Blue Cypress Lake, 18 miles west of Interstate 95 on State Road 60, ☎ 561/778-0150, has small cabins and primitive campsites along canals. Restrooms and water available.

Sebastian Inlet State Park, State Road A1A, Sebastian, ☎ 561/589-9659, has 51 campsites with electricity and water. The campground is near Sebastian Inlet and the beach. Reservations are taken up to 60 days and recommended in winter months.

▪ Where to Eat

☆ **Ellie's,** 41 Royal Palm Boulevard, Vero Beach, 32960, ☎ 561/ 778-2600. It's difficult deciding which is more beautiful: the ambiance of this restaurant, the food presentation, or the sleek, well-dressed crowd. Wall murals are a jungle of leopards, monkeys and hummingbirds; hurricane lanterns add a soft glow. It's clear everyone has gathered to savor owner/chef Mark Gottwald's brilliant original cuisine. Begin with cold smoked beef and wild mushrooms, then enjoy an entrée of crispy salmon with Cabernet sauce and Niçoise vegetables, or fresh cavatelli with cured tomato and black truffles. Desserts are decadent and worth every calorie. The extensive wine list features American and French reds and whites; we enjoyed the 1994 Ferrari-Carano Chardonnay. Open for dinner Wednesday-through Sunday, 5:30-9:30 pm during the winter season. Reservations recommended. $$

☆ **The Black Pearl,** 2855 Ocean Drive, Vero Beach, ☎ 561/234-4426. Owner/Chef Ian Greenwood darts among tables conversing with his guests, at this festive restaurant with crimson walls and black Art Deco sculptures. Stunning bird of paradise flower arrangements add to the color palette. Start with steamed mussels in white wine – a heavenly dish with lots of garlic. Try the chef's signature dish of onion-crusted grouper with citrus caramel glaze; or chicken breast stuffed with cheese and spinach, wrapped in phyllo pastry. Finish with homemade strawberry ice cream or the rich apple tart. Dinner is served seven days from 6-10 pm. $$

Camelia's, 3103 Cardinal Drive, Vero Beach, ☎ 561/234-3966, has three dining rooms colorfully decorated in floral prints and local paintings. Try the "oysters Fellini" appetizer, broiled in nut butter with roasted peppers and pancetta. Entrées include fish, veal, chicken or pasta; their fresh basil sauce is made from vine-ripened tomatoes. $$

Tangos Creative American Cuisine, 925 Bougainvillea Lane, Vero Beach, ☎ 561/231-1550, is a European bistro-style restaurant, serving prime meats, fresh seafood and pasta, homemade breads and specialty beers/wines. Owner/Chef Ben Tench uses the best of native Florida ingredients. Dine outdoors on the patio, or inside among pots of colorful flowers. $$

Tourism Information

Indian River County Chamber of Commerce, 1216 21st Street, Vero Beach, 32960, ☎ 561/567-3491. Web site http://vero-beach.fl.us/chamber/.

Sebastian River Area Chamber of Commerce, 700 Main Street, Sebastian, FL 32958, ☎ 561/589-5969. Web site http://sebastian.fl.us/chamber/.

🌴 🌴 🌴

Index

Adventures: Boca Raton, 153-158; Coral Gables and Coconut Grove, 47-52; Fort Lauderdale, 124-130; Hobe Sound to Ft. Pierce, 197-221; Key Biscayne, 65-70; Miami Beach, 91-100; North Miami Beach, 106-109; Palm Beach to Jupiter, 165-184; Pompano Beach to Deerfield Beach, 141-145; South Dade, 33-40; Vero Beach and Sebastian, 231-238
Ah-Tha-Thi-Ki Museum, 131
Air activities, 22; Balloons Over Florida, 219-220; Hollywood, 118-119; Lantana Airport, 181; Miami Beach, 96-97; SkyDive Miami, 38, 39; Skydive Sebastian, 237-238; Stuart, 219-220; Weeks Air Museum, 40-41

Baseball: 81, 238, 183, 221, 183
Basketball, Miami, 82
Bay Harbor, map, 111
Beachwalking, see on Foot
Biking, see on Wheels
Biltmore Hotel, 51, 53, 60
Birdwatching, 17; Hobe Sound, 197, 199; Sebastian Inlet, 231
Biscayne National Park, 35-38
Blowing Rocks Preserve, 197, 199
Boating: Coral Gables and Coconut Grove, 50-51; Davie, 121-122; Fort Lauderdale, 125-130; Hobe Sound to Fort Pierce, 208-217; Hollywood, 116-117; Key Biscayne, 68; Miami, 80; Miami Beach, 94-95; Miami cruises, 79; North Miami Beach, 108; Palm Beach, 176, 177; Palm Beach cruises, 177-178; Sebastian cruises, 235-236; South Dade, 35-36, 38; Vero Beach, 234-235
Boca Raton, 152-165; adventures, 153-158; camping, 163; festivals and events, 161-162; map, 153; Resort, 162; sightseeing, 158-160; where to eat, 163-164; where to stay, 162-163
Butterfly World, 145

Camping: Boca Raton, 163; Everglades, 136; Fort Lauderdale, 135-137; Hobe Sound to Fort Pierce, 227; Indian River County, 240-241; Miami, 88; Palm Beaches, 192; South Dade, 36, 43-45
Canoeing: Boca Raton, 157; Hobe Sound, 217; Hollywood, 117; Palm Beach, 178-179; South Dade, 35-36
Cape Florida Lighthouse, 65-66
Cape Florida Recreation Area, 67-70
Chekika Recreation Area, 33
Climate, 13-14
Coral Gables and Coconut Grove, 47-63; adventures, 47-52; festivals and events, 57-60; getting here, 47; maps, 49, 55; sightseeing, 52-57; where to eat, 62-63; where to stay, 60-61
Cruises, see Boating

Davie, adventures, 120-124
Deerfield Island Park, 141
Delray Beach, map, 153
Diving: Deerfield Beach, 143-144; Fort Lauderdale, 126; Key Biscayne, 69; Miami Beach, 94-95; North Miami Beach, 108-109; Palm Beach, 179-180; Reef Research Team, 217-218; South Dade, 37-38; Stuart, 217-219; Vero Beach, 237
Dog racing: Hollywood, 120; Miami, 82; Palm Beach, 184
Dolphins, 213, 236

Entertainment: Boca Raton, 160; Fort Lauderdale, 132; Hobe Sound to Fort Pierce, 223; Miami, 83-84; Palm Beaches, 186-187
Everglades Trail, 33-34

Fairchild Tropical Garden, 47-48
Festivals and events: Boca Raton, 161-162; Coral Gables and Coconut Grove, 57-60; Fort Lauderdale, 132-134; Hobe Sound to Fort Pierce, 223-225; Key Biscayne, 72-73; Miami, 83-86; Miami Beach, 100-101; Palm Beaches,

187-189; Pompano Beach/Deerfield Beach, 146; South Dade, 42
Fishing, 21; Boca Raton, 156; Davie, 121-122; Fort Lauderdale, 128; Hobe Sound to Fort Pierce, 208-217; Hollywood, 116-117; Indian River County, 233-234; Key Biscayne, 69; Miami, 81; Miami Beach, 94-95; North Miami Beach, 107-108; Palm Beach, 176-177; Pompano Beach to Deerfield Beach, 144; Sebastian Inlet, 233; South Dade, 36-37
Flamingo Gardens, 120-121
Florida: climate, 13-14; flora and fauna, 14-17; geography, 11-12; geology, 3-4; history, 3-11; map, x; wetlands, 12
Florida Oceanographic Society, 200-201, 218
On foot, 19-20; Boca Raton, 153-156; Coral Gables and Coconut Grove, 47-48; Davie, 120-121; Fort Lauderdale, 124-125; Hobe Sound to Fort Pierce, 197-206; Hollywood, 114; Key Biscayne, 65-67; Miami, 76-78; Miami Beach, 91-92; North Miami Beach, 106; Palm Beach to Jupiter, 165-173; Pompano Beach to Deerfield Beach, 141-142; South Dade, 33-34
Football, Miami, 81-82
Fort Lauderdale, 113-149; adventures, 124-130; camping, 135-137; festivals and events, 132-134; getting around, 113-114; getting here, 113; map, 115; sightseeing, 129-132; where to eat, 137-140; where to stay, 134-135
Fort Pierce: botanical gardens, 201; golf, 205; map, 202; Oceanographic Institution, 221; sightseeing, 221, 222; swimming, 208; tennis, 206
Fort Pierce Inlet Recreation Area, 201
Glass-bottom boats, 36
Golf: Boca Raton, 155; Fort Lauderdale, 125; Key Biscayne, 66; Margate, 142; Martin County, 204-205; Miami, 76, 78; Miami Beach, 91; North Miami Beach, 106; Palm Beach, 171-172; Pompano Beach, 142; St. Lucie County, 204-205; Sebastian, 231-

232; South Dade, 34; Vero Beach, 205, 232
Gumbo Limbo Environmental Center, Boca Raton, 153-154

Hallpatee Seminole Village, 184
Harbor Branch Oceanographic Institution, 221
Heathcote Botanical Gardens, 201
Hiking, see on Foot
Hillsboro Beach, 141, 147
Hobe Sound to Ft. Pierce, 197-229; adventures, 197-221; camping, 227; entertainment, 223; festivals and events, 223-225; maps, 198, 202; sightseeing, 221-223; where to eat, 227-229; where to stay, 225-226
Hollywood, adventures, 114-120
Holocaust Memorial, 98
Homestead: auto racing, 40; biking, 35; Biscayne National Park, 35-38; where to eat, 45-46
Horse racing: Hollywood, 120; Miami, 82; Pompano Beach, 145
Horses: Coconut Creek, 145; Coral Gables, 52; Davie Rodeo, 124; Palm Beach Polo and Country Club, 181-183; Royal Palm Polo Grounds, 158
Hurricanes, 13, 14
Hutchinson Island: map, 202; swimming, 207

Information sources, 24-27
In-line skating: Key Biscayne, 68; Miami Beach, 93-94; Pompano Beach, 142

Jai-alai: Fort Pierce, 221; Hollywood, 120; Miami, 82
Jensen Beach: where to eat, 228; where to stay, 225-226
Jet skiing: Miami, 80; North Miami Beach, 109
John U. Lloyd Beach Recreation Area, 114
Jonathan Dickinson State Park, 199; camping, 227; canoeing, 217; excursions, 213; map, 200
Juno Beach: camping, 192; on foot, 169; map, 168; turtle watching, 171; where to eat, 193-194; where to stay, 191

Jupiter: on Foot, 170; golf, 172; lighthouse, 170; Roger Dean Stadium, 183; tennis, 173; where to eat, 194; where to stay, 191

Kayaking: Boca Raton, 157; Hollywood, 117-118; North Miami Beach, 108; St. Lucie Inlet, 215-216; Stuart, 216-217; Vero Beach, 236-237
Kendall: biking, 35; where to eat, 45-46; where to stay, 43
Key Biscayne, 64-75; adventures, 65-70; festivals and events, 72-73; getting here, 65; map, 64; sightseeing, 71-72; where to eat, 74-75; where to stay, 73

Lake Worth, 169, 171-172, 173
Lantana: air sports, 181; camping, 192; waterskiing, 181
Lighthouses: Cape Florida, 65-66; Jupiter, 170
Lion Country Safari, 174-175, 192
Loxahatchee River, 178-179, 213, 217
Loxahatchee Wildlife Refuge, 156

MacArthur Beach State Park, North Palm Beach, 165-167, 169-173, 180
Manatees, 15, 35, 203, 213, 236
Matheson Hammock County Park, 48
Miami, 28-112; adventures, 76-82; camping, 88; Downtown and Greater, 75-89; entertainment, 83-84; festivals and events, 84-86; getting around, 29-32; getting here, 29; maps, 28, 77; safety, 31; Seaquarium, 71-72; sightseeing, 82-83; sports arenas, 81-82; where to eat, 88-89; where to stay, 86-87
Miami Beach, 89-105; adventures, 91-100; festivals and events, 100-101; getting here, 90-91; maps, 90, 111; sightseeing, 98-100; where to eat, 104-105; where to stay, 102-103
Monastery, Ancient Spanish, 109
Monkey Jungle, 41
Morikami Park, 159
Mounts Botanical Garden, 167
Museums, see Sightseeing

Nature centers/trails: Boca Raton, 153-154; Butterfly World, 145; Davie, 120-121; Deerfield Island Park, 141; Everglades Trail, 33-34; Florida Oceanographic Society, 200-201; Fort Lauderdale, 124-125; Fort Pierce, 201; Harbor Branch Oceanographic Institution, 221-223; Hobe Sound, 197, 199; Hollywood, 116, 117; Pompano Beach, 141-142; St. Lucie Inlet Preserve, 201; Sebastian Inlet, 231; Vero Beach, 239; West Palm Beach, 169; wildlife photo safaris, 203
North Miami, where to stay, 87
North Miami Beach, 105-112; adventures, 106-109; map, 111; shopping, 109; sightseeing, 109; where to eat, 112; where to stay, 109-110
North Palm Beach: MacArthur Beach State Park, 165-167, 169-173, 180; where to eat, 194

Palm Beach: croquet, 183; on Foot, 169-173; golf, 171-172; map, 166; polo, 181-183; tennis, 173; on water, 176-181; on Wheels, 174-175; where to eat, 193; where to stay, 189-90
Palm Beaches, 150-195; adventures, 165-184; camping, 192; entertainment, 186-187; festivals and events, 187-189; getting around, 151-152; getting here, 151; map, 150; sightseeing, 184-187; where to eat, 193-195; where to stay, 189-192
Palm Beach to Jupiter, 165-195; maps, 166, 168
Parrot Jungle and Gardens, 54
Photo safaris, 174-175, 203
Polo: Boca Raton, 158; Palm Beach, 181-183; Vero Beach, 238
Pompano Beach to Deerfield Beach, 140-149; adventures, 141-145; festivals and events, 146; sightseeing, 145; where to eat, 148-149; where to stay, 147-148
Port St. Lucie: golf, 204-205

Reef Research Diving Team, 217-218

Safaris, photo, 174-175, 203
Safety tips: biking, 20-21; on Foot, 19-20; personal, 31; on water, 22
Sailing, see Boating
St. Lucie Inlet Preserve, 201, 215-216
St. Lucie Lock, Dam and Recreation Area, 203
St. Lucie River, 213
Scuba, see Diving
Sebastian, 230-242; adventures, 231-238; camping, 240-241; cruising, 235-236; golf, 205; map, 230; sightseeing, 238-239; skydiving, 237-238; where to stay, 240
Sebastian Inlet Recreation Area, 231, 233-234, 238, 241
Shooting, trap and skeet, 184
Sightseeing: Boca Raton, 158-160; Coconut Grove, 54-57; Coral Gables, 52-54; Fort Lauderdale, 129-132; Fort Pierce, 221, 222; Key Biscayne, 71-72; Miami, 82-83; Miami Beach, 98-100; North Miami Beach, 109; Palm Beaches, 184-187; South Dade, 40-41; Stuart, 221-222; Vero Beach and Sebastian, 238-239
Singer Island, where to stay, 190
Snakes, 16
Snorkeling: Boca Raton, 157; Fort Lauderdale, 126; Key Biscayne, 69; Miami, 81; North Miami Beach, 108-109; Palm Beach, 179-180; South Dade, 37-38
South Beach, map, 90
South Dade, 32-46; adventures, 33-40; camping, 43-45; festivals and events, 42; getting here, 33; map, 32; sightseeing, 40-41; where to eat, 45-46; where to stay, 43
Spanish Monastery, 109
Stuart: air sports, 219-220; diving, 217-219; Florida Oceanographic Society, 200-201; golf, 204; kayaking, 216-217; map, 198; sightseeing, 221-222; swimming, 207; tennis, 206; where to eat, 227-229; where to stay, 225, 226
Surfing, Sebastian Inlet, 233, 234
Surfside, map, 111
Swimming: Coral Gables, 51-52; Fort Lauderdale, 129; Key Biscayne, 70; Martin County, 206-207; Miami Beach, 95-96; St. Lu-

cie County, 206-208

Tennis: Boca Raton, 155-156; Coral Gables and Coconut Grove, 48; Deerfield Beach, 142; Fort Lauderdale, 125; Key Biscayne, 66-67; Martin County, 206; Miami, 78; Miami Beach, 92; North Miami Beach, 106; Palm Beach, 173; St. Lucie County, 206; South Dade, 34; Vero Beach, 232
Trap and skeet shooting, 184
Treasure Coast, 196-242; map, 196
Tree Tops Park, Davie, 121
Turtles, 15-16, 70, 171, 197, 201, 203

Vero Beach, 230-242; adventures, 231-238; boating, 234-235; diving, 237; fishing, 234; golf, 205, 232; kayaking, 236-237; map, 230; polo, 238; sightseeing, 238-239; where to eat, 240-241; where to stay, 239-240
Vizcaya, 56-57

Wall-climbing, 96-97
West Palm Beach: botanical garden, 167, 169; camping, 192; Centennial Fountain, 181; entertainment, 186-187; golf, 172; Lion Country Safari, 174-175, 192; map, 166; Okeeheelee Nature Center, 169; sculpture garden, 185; where to eat, 194-195; where to stay, 191; windsurfing, 181
Wetlands, 12
on Wheels, 20-21; Bike Miami Suitability Map, 79; Coral Gables and Coconut Grove, 50; Davie, 121; Hollywood, 116; Key Biscayne, 67-68; Miami, 78-79; Miami Beach, 92-94; North Miami Beach, 106-107; Palm Beach, 174-175; Pompano Beach, 142; South Dade, 34-35
Wildlife refuges: Hobe Sound, 200; Loxahatchee, 156
Windsurfing: Key Biscayne, 69-70; West Palm Beach, 181

Yachting, see Boating

Zoos: Miami, 41; Miami Seaquarium, 71-72; West Palm Beach, 184